O9-BUB-692

THE CREATIVE
IMPERATIVE

CHARLES M. JOHNSTON, M.D.

THE CREATIVE
IMPERATIVE

A Four-Dimensional Theory of Human

Growth & Planetary Evolution

CELESTIAL ARTS

BERKELEY, CALIFORNIA

© 1984/1986 by Charles M. Johnston, M.D.

Celestial Arts
P.O. Box 7327
Berkeley, CA 94707

All rights reserved. No part of this book may be reproduced or transmitted in any form or by any means without the written permission of the Publisher, except where permitted by law.

Cover photo by Jane English

Cover design by the author with Scott Freutel, Tom Schworer, and Dianna Slack.

Copyright permissions can be found on page 406.

Printed in the United States of America

Library of Congress Cataloging in Publication Data
    Johnston, Charles M., 1948-
        The Creative Imperative: A four-dimensional theory of human
            growth and planetary evolution
            Includes index
1. Psychology/Psychiatry. 2. Twenty-First Century. 3. Evolution. 4. Mind and Body 5. Myth. 6. Systems Theory. I. Title

ISBN 0-89087-479-4   86-71240

1 2 3 4 5 — 90 89 88 87 86

This book is dedicated to you,
who are drawn to read it.

WORDS OF THANKS

Through the lengthy course of bringing this book to form, a multitude of people have lent their ideas, skills and caring. I feel special gratitude to Dianna Slack for her generous help in the final stages of this book, to my editor Richard Brzustowicz, Jr., to Steve Herold for his work with final production, to Colleen Campbell for her editorial assistance, and to Scott Freutel for his consultation on design. Ronnie Bissett, Pamallah, Becci Parsons and Arturo Peal offered invaluable help in final proofreading and compilation. As well, I feel particular gratitude to Pamela Schick for her encouragement and her reading of preliminary drafts, to Regina Hugo for her help in editing early versions of this manuscript, and to Theresa Crater and Gina Rogers for their patience in typing ... and retyping.

The diagrams in the book are from the skilled hand of Dianna Slack. The drawings that introduce each chapter are by Gary Undercuffler, and those on pages 174-176 by Anne Gerdes. Cheryl Teague assisted in the early development of the diagrams.

I would also like to express gratitude to the people who have trained most closely with me through the Institute, for their support, for their friendship, and for their willingness to continually challenge my thinking. Besides Colleen, Pamela, and Ronnie, this includes: Patti Carter, Suzanne Edison, Dean Elias, Paul Finley, Peggy Hackney, Connie Hiatt, Mary Holscher, Larry Hobbs, Ron Hobbs, Jim Patterson, Lorriane Sandow, Jim Schmid, Fred Schwindt, Anne Shaw, Ken Smith, Charlie Thompson, Pam Weeks, Kris Wheeler, Gary Wieder, and Bill Womack.

Finally, I would like to thank my parents, who always encouraged me to see the world through creative eyes.

CONTENTS

Part III —A Larger Vision

BEFOREHAND:

THE CHALLENGE

CHAPTER ONE

ALIVENESS

"Perhaps the time is now ripe when the mystic can break the glass through which he sees all things darkly, and the rationalist can break the glass through which he sees all things clearly, and both together can enter the kingdom of psychological reality."   —Critic Norman O. Brown

"The great extension of our experience in recent years has brought to light the insufficiency of our simple mechanical conceptions."   —Physicist Niels Bohr

"We are at a very exciting point in history, perhaps a turning point."   —Nobel chemist Illya Prigogine

 We stand today at a critical threshhold in the evolution of the species. It is an exciting time, but also unsettling and fearsome. The future is demanding of us a wisdom and maturity beyond anything we have ever before known or needed.

To understand what we are confronting, and why, a good place to begin is a notion put forward in 1962 by historian of science Thomas Kuhn, a concept he called the "paradigm shift." His thesis was that historical change occurs not just incrementally, but as well through processes of qualitative reorganization. Some advances simply add more to what we know; others expand how we know, and the boundaries of what and how we *can* know.

The evidence is good that we are now in the midst of a paradigm shift of major proportion and significance. We are being

3

challenged from all around us to make profound leaps both in who we are and in how we understand. Trusted truths are not only failing to provide answers, they are often proving inadequate even for understanding the questions.

This book presents a new theory of personal and cultural reality, a theory that speaks from across the threshold of these changes. It is an attempt not just to understand our future, but to develop the larger kind of understanding we will need if we are to survive and prevail in that future.

Present ideas that speak in any complete way from across this threshold all lie in the physical sciences. The familiar first voice was that of Albert Einstein, his ideas challenging the mechanical certainty of the Newtonian Universe, and demonstrating the ultimate presence of a much more dynamic, powerful, and mysterious planetary order. Today, such thinking in physics has moved even beyond the ideas of Einstein, and parallel expansions of perspective have emerged throughout the scientific domains.

This book will touch on the hard sciences, but its scope is more inclusive, and its main focus elsewhere. Our primary concern will be with the human realm, equally the personal and the social. It is becoming increasingly recognized that qualitatively new kinds of models are needed in all realms of human understanding. In the same way that the simple cause-and-effect ideas of Newton are insufficient to explain what we now know about the universe, the ideas we are accustomed to using for understanding human questions are simply not large enough, and dynamic enough, to embrace today's dramatically more complex challenges. In all areas of understanding—psychology, economics, education, religion, politics, medicine, the arts—it is proving essential that we find more inclusive, vital and relativistic ways of comprehending our reality.

Up till now, attempts at developing new paradigm theories for the human sphere have met with limited success at best. They have pointed toward exciting possiblities, but we have yet to see anything like a comprehensive, practically workable, framework. My purpose in these pages is to put forward the basic contours of just such a framework. As my training and experience center in the psychological realm, it is there that I will develop these ideas most fully. But the basic principles, as I will show, are applicable to all realms of human concern.

THE CHALLENGE OF LIVING CONCEPTION

> *"I don't know what I may seem to the world. But as to myself, I seem to have been only like a boy playing on the seashore, and diverting myself now and then finding a smoother pebble or a prettier shell than ordinary, whilst the great ocean of truth lay all undiscovered before me."*
>
> —*Isaac Newton*

Why do we need new models such as the one I will be presenting? It is important that the reader have a solid sense of this, for while the ideas I will be offering are not fundamentally complicated, they demand a qualitative change in how we think: rather than simply adding to what we know, they place all that we know in a new and larger ordering context. One does not make such qualitative changes unless there are very good reasons for it.

Clearly something very basic in reality is changing. All around us our trusted maps and road signs are proving insufficient.

As recently as a generation ago, for example, we had a quite reliable formula for success in the realm of intimacy. Our culture offered specific guidelines for the appropriate behavior of each sex, and for what an appropriate relationship should look like. Anyone who did a good job of learning those roles could be relatively confident of finding someone who had learned the complementary behaviors and of having a fulfilling partnership. Today, this simple set of formulas is clearly inadequate. Meaningful love is suddenly demanding whole new ways of being, and much more personal and dynamic kinds of understanding.

Similarly, not very long ago everyone knew what progress was: new inventions and material growth. The answer in today's world is obviously not so simple. More and more we are inventing things that can do at least as much harm as good. And many current discoveries, while dramatic and exciting in concept, are simply too expensive in money and resources to be of actual value in a world of

5

increasingly pressing limitations. If future progress is to be real human progress, we will need very different kinds of frameworks for understanding and measuring it.

One final illustration: In our past, questions of national defense and safety were similarly clear cut. Our safety was proportional to the size of our stockpile of arms. Today, with each major nation having the capacity to destroy the world many times over, such a measure clearly has little meaning. Yet, there has never been a time when the ability to think about the safety of the planet has been more critical. Again, we clearly need whole new kinds of frameworks and whole new kinds of measures.

These are not isolated examples. With a little thought one could sketch parallel quandaries and challenges for each human sphere.

What is missing in our usual ways of thinking? What more do we need if our ideas are to serve us? To understand, we need to step back so that we can see with some historical perspective. To understand present change, we need to understand what we are changing from.

Our most recent stage in the evolution of culture began some four hundred years ago, with the first dawnings of the Age of Reason and Invention.* That period, like the present, was a time of dramatic change. People spoke of leaving the "Dark Ages" and entering a new "Age of Enlightenment."

In the Middle Ages, truth and order were based on the dictates of the crown and the moral laws of the church. With the Age of Reason, a radical new notion of order in reality developed, and with it, two radical new arbiters of truth: the individual mind and the objective laws of a rationally causal universe. Rene Descartes proclaimed a new basis for human identity, "Cogito ergo sum"—"I think, therefore I am." Isaac Newton described a universe control-

---

* The term "Age of Reason" is used variously by historians as a general term for the time from the end of the Middle Ages to the present, and more specifically for the period from the beginning of the seventeenth to the end of the eighteenth centuries. I will use it here in the broader sense.

led no longer by the whims of mysterious forces, but ordered by simple laws of mechanics.

This new reality had a profound new clarity and surity. Everything was seen as ultimately knowable and open to human influence. In the words of French mathematician Pierre LaPlace: "[for] an intellect which at a given instant knows all forces ... and the positions of all things ... nothing [is] uncertain." Man the obedient had become man the choice-maker, the logician, the determiner. Monumental advances were spawned from this new view of truth—democratic government, scientific medicine, our multitude of labor-saving inventions and technologies. From within this new reality, it appeared that the human journey had at last reached its destination. All that was left was detail.

But our present challenges suggest something very different. The journey is in fact far from over.

What is missing? There are many ways it could be put, but perhaps most simply, what is missing is *life*. In Newtonian/ Cartesian reality the universe and all within it are like a great clockworks, an immense and wondrous piece of machinery. A mechanical paradigm can offer us many amazing things. But no matter how great a machine's complexity, it can never be more than just that, a machine.

We get a first hint of the implications of this incompleteness with the recognition that in the Age of Reason this mechanical paradigm has been applied across the board—not just to the physical world, but to nature in general ... and to ourselves. It is inherent to fundamental paradigms that they are all-embracing. Thus while we may live dynamically, when we describe how we live, we most often turn to the mechanical language of gears and pulleys. We talk of history in terms of the causal interactions of governments; economics in terms of the stimulus-response interplay of supply and demand; education in terms of the additive accumulation of information and skills in a milieu of appropriate motivaters; religion in terms of the causal interplay of good deeds and divine will. Listening only to what people *say* the workings of a

7

person often sound little different from those of an automobile: genetics, parents and educators build it, doctors and theologians keep it running, economists and psychologists make observations about quality control, and historians keep production records.

When this way of thinking was most timely, its inability to address the living, I would suggest, was not a problem. Indeed, this inability was critical to its success. A mechanistic perspective was, at that time, just the lever needed to lift us out of the constraints of mysticism and moral dogma.

But this timeliness is of a past age. We have succeeded in emancipating individuality and choice. The key to meeting the challenges of our times lies now precisely in our ability to step beyond simple mechanical conceptions and understand life very specifically in living terms.

Looking at the current pivotal questions facing our species, we can see that what is most central to them all is that they are, at essence, questions of life. In the domain of intimacy, in asking how we might understand relationship beyond the causal materiality of roles, what we are searching for is a way to think about love that centers on what is uniquely "alive" between two people. In seeking to redefine progress, we are looking for ways of measuring value that make the bottom line our "quality of life." And in reform-ulating defense, we are seeking to find measures of safety based on the establishment of responsible, "living" relationships between peoples.

As I see it, in all domains we are being challenged to find per-spectives large enough to embrace the fact of our being *living* beings, and to place that fact at the center of the human equation. This is not just a matter of new liberal or humanistic ideas, a softening of the inevitable hard corners of the mechanistic. We are needing to find ways of thinking that are rigorous, detailed, and hardnosed— and which, *because* of that, take as fundamental the fact that we are alive.

THE MODEL

"Just as the organism pulls together random, formless stuff into the patterned systems of structure and function in the body, so the unconscious mind seems to select and arrange and correlate ... the concept is worth considering that the organizing power of life, manifest in mind as well as body— for the two are hardly separable—is the truly creative element. Creativity thus becomes the attribute of life."
—Biologist E.W. Sinnott
Matter, Mind and Man

The journey of developing these ideas began with an insight that came while I was playing with two very basic kinds of questions. From within our usual perspective, these questions seem quite different concerns, but in living reality they are intimately related.

First, I was thinking about how it is that living "things" change: what happens when something grows? It was clear to me that our usual explanations, while useful, were not addressing the core of what was happening. Second, I was wondering about what it is that links together the parts in living systems—within ourselves, in relationships, or between social bodies—*as systems.* Again, ideas within our usual paradigm addressed parts of this question, but were clearly not getting to the big picture.

Historically, I knew, there were two polar kinds of answers to these concerns—that of science, and that of religion. In the scientific view, parts are separate, analyzable entities, like balls on a billiard table; and change happens according to the laws of material cause-and-effect, like one ball bouncing off another. Conversely, from a more spiritual perspective, parts, rather than being isolated entities, are intrinsically connected—all is one. Here change—as fate, karma or divine will—follows directly from that oneness.*

---

* It is obviously a major oversimplification to equate all religious systems. Ahead, we will look more closely at spiritual perspectives on causality, and how they have evolved through the course of culture.

It was clear to me that neither of these polar perspectives was sufficient for the task of living conception. Each expresses a part of the picture, but each is in its own way deterministic, in its own way reactive and mechanical. In neither is there fully room for the vital respiration, the fundamental generative indeterminacy, that makes something living.

In sitting with this apparent impasse, it suddenly occurred to me that there was in fact a possible way of thinking which, rather than negating either of these earlier perspectives, could understand each as parts within a larger dynamic. It took everything I could muster to grasp it with any fullness, but I could sense the notion was significant. I saw that, ultimately, causality in living systems was neither just mechanical nor mystical, but *creative*.

What do I mean by this? At this stage the best I can do is offer an example, and then sketch out a few of the major contours of the model that came from that insight. The full meaning of this larger way of understanding causality will require the book as a whole to develop. But having this rough map in our pockets will help us keep track of the big picture as we explore the territory ahead.

What happens at the start of any new friendship makes a simple illustration of the fundamentally creative nature of living causality. While we may talk about relationship in deterministic terms, in fact what takes place is quite obviously neither just mechanical ("I do this to you; you do this to me") nor just fated ("It was meant to be"). If we look closely, we see that it is clearly a process. And it is quite specifically a *creative* process—a generative, evolving, and ultimately indeterminate process. When we meet, if that meeting is right and timely, something (we might call it an impulse to possibility) is born between us. If we honor it, it grows as a unique expression of who, together, we are creatively becoming. It is through taking the risk to give shape to, and be shaped by, this fundamental formative dynamic that our being together takes on the qualities we call relationship.

At the heart of the model lies the thesis that ultimately all of reality is creatively ordered. This notion, what I call the concept of *creative causality*, is the fulcrum around which the model reorganizes usual thought. Creative causality defines a new way of understanding what is fundamental in reality. In classical scientific thought, "fundamental" means the smallest atomistic bit—for example, a sub-atomic particle. Spiritual realities define the fundamental in an opposite way—as essence. The concept of creative causality bridges these earlier views: defines their living relationship. In this larger perspective, the fundamental is neither thing nor essence, but a particular kind of process, formative process— that is, the dynamic story of how it is that things come into being, mature, and transform. The creative can be thought of as quite specifically a description of the relationship between essence and the material: the mysterious, subjective, and undefinable is the reality of the source and soil of the creative impulse; the world of objective materiality that of the most manifest stages of creation.

I will argue that everything in and about us can be understood in terms of this single, time relative, "mechanism." I will show that we can see reality as a whole as a complexly interwoven interplay of large and small periodicities (wavelengths) of formative (creative) process; that, in the big picture, reality organizes as an infinitely multifacted, ever-evolving dance between form and not-form. And I will show how such a perspective offers a radically more living way to understand both ourselves and our world.

The concept of creative causality will be developed here in two integrally related ways. First, I will use it to define a post-material referent for truth, to address the question of what lies beyond the form-defined answers of our most recent age, beyond relationships as roles, beyond progress as material accumulation, beyond defense as domination. I will propose that ultimately what we want to measure is life itself—the degree to which something is living, vital. While we cannot define aliveness reductionistically, we can define it quite easily in terms of formative process: aliveness is the amount of creation, the amount of that fundamental formative dynamic present in a system at a particular point in time. I will argue that while measuring in terms of aliveness demands more than we are accustomed to bringing to measurement, there is no more critical task for our time than learning to do so.

What is it in this image that evokes an almost universal responsiveness? Clearly it is not something reducible simply to the objective, something definable purely by measurement of its physicality. But neither is it something merely subjective, something only personal. Such questions of the "aliveness" of things strike at the very core of what is most vitally human and significant, yet our usual ways of conceiving are of little help in addressing them. [Leonardo Da Vinci. Mona Lisa. 1503-1505.]

In addition, I will use the concept of creative causality as a tool for differentiating living reality. The issue of differentiation is crucial; this is what gives a model its practical usefulness. It is what lets us say, yes, this is how this relates to that, and then this is connected over here.

The question of differentiation has been the stumbling block in most attempts at post-material conception. We recognize that what is missing in atomistic models is the connectedness of things, and we define a unifying principle. But new notions of what connects have only rarely been significantly integral; they have more often been simply reformulations of essence, of oneness. Thus, when one tries to think differentially—to use the ideas in a practical way—one either discovers one has violated one's basic principle and ends up denouncing differentiation, or differentiates anyway and ends up back in the old mechanistic causalities.

In the model, differentiation is achieved through delineating the patterning processes that organize the dynamic of creation. Creation is not some vague essence, some invisible magic through which rabbit-out-of-hat things come into being, but a highly ordered progression of definition-producing realities. This fundamental sequencing repeats itself beneath the surface of each of the major rhythms of our existence: in the stages of an individual lifetime, in the feeling states that accompany the growth of a new relationship, in how we learn new tasks, in the truths that order the evolution of civilization. The reality of any particular moment can be seen as a function of all the interplaying rhythms of organization —personal to planetary—that converge at, and as, that particular nodal point in time.

The stages of creative process, along with the various rhythms of creative organization that relate to that moment, serve as the "parts" for differentiation in the model. These parts are not additive bits as in atomistic models, but instead time-relative statements of relationship. Because of this, we will be able to use the concept of creative causality to talk with a high degree of discrimination about living processes, and have our descriptions enhance rather than diminish our appreciation for the fact of their aliveness.

APPLICATIONS OF THE MODEL

*"The change in the concept of reality manifesting itself in
quantum theory is not simply a continuum of the past; it
seems to be a real break in the structure of modern science."*
—*Werner Heisenberg*

The model has extremely broad application. I think of three
primary ways that, in any sphere, it can be used to reframe our
thinking.

First, an understanding of creative dynamics makes it possible
to think four-dimensionally about any developmental process. This
chapter has offered just a peek at how one might reformulate historical thought. The model can be used equally well to look, in more
living terms at, for example, stages in individual development, at
how intimacy grows and matures, or at dynamics in learning.

Second, the concept of creative causality can provide a perspective for making the differentiations we need for thinking in
new, more living, ways. We can use it to reframe our categories of
thought in any sphere—roles in a family, tasks in an organization,
disciplines in education. Later in the book, I use the model in this
way to outline a way of thinking about psychological well-being
that lets us perceive from beyond the either/or of health and disease.

Finally, and perhaps most importantly, an understanding of
the dynamics of creative causality can give us tools for understanding our present place in the evolution of culture, and for planning
future policy. While we have never before experienced this cultural epoch, we have many times witnessed analogous "epochs"
within smaller creative periodicities—in creative projects, or in
the developmental stages of a lifetime. If it is true, as the model
asserts, that the same stages order the evolution of culture as order
other creative processes, then the ideas here should serve as very
precise tools for defining, and making, the critical choices ahead.

CHAPTER TWO

TOWARD A LANGUAGE OF LIVING CONCEPTION

"What is untouched is the question: Onto what sort of surface shall 'esthetics' and 'consciousness' be mapped?"
— *Gregory Bateson*

"The contradictions so puzzling to the ordinary way of thinking come from the fact that we have to use language to communicate our inner experience which in its very nature transcends linguistics."
— *D.T. Suzuki*

"The words or the language do not seem to play a role in my mechanisms of thought ... the elements are, in my case, of visual and some of muscular type. Conventional words (come in) a secondary stage."
— *Albert Einstein*

 Before we can begin the task of developing a "new paradigm, post-material, living, four-dimensional" model for human experience, we must confront a significant quandary. We must find a language adequate to this larger kind of conception.

Traditional theoretical speech alone will not be sufficient to the task. Logical thought is rigorously organized around the relationship between two parts of speech—the noun and the verb. The rules of that relationship are not essentially different from those described by Newton's Laws of Motion. Nouns are things, and verbs are the forces by which one noun affects another. A language constructed in terms of discrete objects and actions makes it hard to speak of anything but a commensurately atomistic and linearly causal reality.

The concept of creative causality points toward a fascinating solution to this predicament of language. It suggests that our task may be less to invent some new complex grammar, than simply to fill out what we already have. From a creative perspective, conventional language isn't inappropriate, but simply partial. It very effectively expresses truth within one part of the creative, the reality of the material, that slice of things concerned with fully manifest creation. The difficulty is simply that creation is much more than just finished forms. What we need are ways of thinking and speaking capable of addressing not just the manifest, but also all the more germinal realities that are parts of our natures as creation.

Rich evidence for this is all around us. While the livingness of things eludes our usual categorical thought, we often touch each other in deeply living ways. When we do, earlier configurations in our creatively developing natures usually have major roles. We play in the gestures of hands, eyes and trunk. We dance through the intonations of our voices and the colorings of metaphor. We put the needed flesh on language's stark bones by speaking through the rich complexity of our pre-logical natures.

In developing theories, we usually reject our more germinal sensibilities as lacking the precision necessary for conceptual thought. We lump our pre-logical modes of understanding together, posit them as opposite to the rational, and dismiss them as, at best, ornament. Creative causality suggests that, on the contrary, it is only with the inclusion of these sensibilities that we can mobilize the greater "precision" needed for living conception. Realizing this makes our job both easier, because the means for expression already exist, and more challenging, because we must bring a much more developed awareness to our existing use of the language.

There are several pieces to this. First, connecting with these more germinal sensibilities in a deep enough way to reorder understanding is not an easy task. In our present stage in culture, only their most surface layers are available to us. It is innate to us that we are amnesic to stages of reality that we have progressed beyond. Insects in their metamorphosis cast off old forms and take on new ones; we, in the stages of our own unfolding, cast off old realities, and are usually as unable to take them up again as an insect is to take up once again its outgrown body.

Much of the challenge of thinking from a new paradigm lies in what it takes to get beyond these amnesias. Adolescents find re-membering the reality of childhood almost impossible; adults find the behavior of adolescents positively baffling, though they them-selves may be only a few years removed from their own adolescence. In a precisely parallel way, it is very hard for us to feel our way in-to the realities of earlier stages in the evolution of culture. We see only "as through a glass darkly," and find ourselves immediately moving to denigrate or idealize the faint images we manage to per-ceive. In general, once past a stage, we lose our capacity to re-mem-ber its truth, to live from it, in any but the most superficial ways.

Such amnesia is quite understandable if we think of develop-ment in creative terms. In any creative progression there is a na-tural tension between the impulses to move forward and to regress. The amnesia serves to put distance between the present and the easily seductive safety of a known past.

A second piece in this challenge has to do with the fact that our task is much more than simply remembering and adding up what we find. Recollecting alone would only give us a confusing collection of disjointed, even contradictory, languages and exper-ienced realities. What we are wanting to do here is to find a way of thinking large enough to embrace the greater process that all these different modes of experience and speech are parts within. To do this, each language must be stretched well beyond its usual bounds. The challenge is not just to remember, to re-activate previous lan-guages as independent fragments, but to engage the larger living process that each of these languages is a co-generative element within.

What must we be able to include in our thinking to grasp this larger whole? As we shall see, at its simplest level we can think of formative process as moving through four kinds of "languages"— first the language of the body, then the language of symbol, then the language of emotion, then the language of thought.* The second

---

* As shall become clear, equating perceptual/conceptual modes and

half of formative process is marked by the finding of a larger integration for these previously distinct realities.

The language of the rational is familiar to us. The others—the body, the symbolic and the emotional—approached fully as languages, are less so. We might take a moment with each of these more germinal sensibilities, as they will each have an essential place in the model. They will be used not just as poetic garnishment, but as integral voices in the whole of understanding.

THE LANGUAGE OF THE BODY

"God grant me from those thoughts men think
From the mind alone,
He that sings a lasting song
Thinks in a marrow bone."

—William Butler Yeats

"Our most sacred convictions, the unchanging elements in
our supreme values, are judgments of the muscles."

—Friedrich Nietzsche

"The body is the soul."

—Theodore Roethke

The earliest knowing in any life process is bodily knowing. Developmental psychologist Jean Piaget speaks of the early intelligence of the child as "sensory motor" knowing. The infant's reality is organized kinesthetically, as interplaying patterns of movement and sensation. Similarly, bodily understanding organizes reality in the earliest stages of culture. To a tribal person, truth lies in one's bond with, and as, the creature world of nature. We live from this same place in the beginning moments of any process of creative manifestation. The first moments of new creative possibil-

---

creative stages in this way is a major oversimplification. In truth, each stage includes quite specific emotional, symbolic, bodily and intellectual dimensions. But it is also the case that each of these "languages" has one stage where it is most in its glory.

ity are felt as "inklings," kinesthetic sensings of life. In this first stage of creative reality, intelligence is "cellular."

Body in this most germinal stage in creation is very different from the body as we conceive of it through the isolated and isolating eye of the Age of Reason. It is much more than simply sensation; also much more than simply anatomy and physiology; and more than one side of an either/or: body versus mind, body versus spirit. In this first stage in formativeness the body is not something we have, but who we are. It is our intelligence. It is how we organize our experience of both ourselves and our world.

While we don't usually give it much status in formal thinking, the knowing of bodily reality has a central place in the living experience of our lives. For example, if you say you love someone and you are asked how you know, eventually you will begin to talk in the language of the body. You know you feel love because when you are with that person your "heart" opens, there is a warm expanding in the area of the chest. This experienced "heart" cannot be found by dissection, but it is undeniably not only very real, but close to what is most essential in us.

While we are often unconscious of this organically kinesthetic aspect of experience, it never escapes us totally. We give it colorful expression in our "figures" of speech. We speak of feeling "moved" or "touched," of being "beside ourselves" or feeling that something is "over our heads." If we take the time, a lot of this sort of experience is available consciously. As a simple example, if I attune to it, I am aware that I feel my bodily connection to different people at different times in quite different ways. With one person I may be most aware of a sense of solidity and fullness in my chest. With another, the vitality may be most prominent as a sense of animation in my eyes and face, or erotic arousal in my genitals. With some people, our meeting touches me very close to core; with others, the bodily experience of meeting may feel much more peripheral, more "superficial."

I will talk about the body as intelligence in two ways in the model. I'll speak about it as the language of creation's most germinal impulses. As well, I'll talk about it as one way to speak about a more integral understanding, a perspective from which to talk

about the whole of who we are. A notion we will explore in some detail is that with each stage in any creative cycle our experience of, and as, ourselves as bodies is markedly different. The body in this second sense is the body as the greater whole of these stage-specific bodily realities.

THE LANGUAGE OF SYMBOL

"Dreams are the true interpreter of our inclinations ..."
         —Montaigne

An essential voice in creatively-based thinking is the language of the body—here the body not simply as physicality, but as its aliveness. This is the body both in its simplest and most profound sense, the body as somebody.

ABOVE: *Martha Graham*. OPPOSITE: *Animal dance, Nothern Territory, Australia, mimicking the wing-outspread rush of the brolga, a native brush bird.*

21

"It would not be too much to say that myth is the secret open-
ing through which the inexhaustible energies of the cosmos
pour into human cultural manifestation. Religions, philoso-
phies, arts, the social forms of primitive and historic man,
prime discoveries in science and technology, the very dreams
that blister sleep boil up from the basic, magic ring of
myth."

—Joseph Cambell
Myths to Live By

Symbol—the vehicle of myth, dream, metaphor and much in artisic expression—also speaks from close to the beginnings of things. When a storyteller utters the words "Once upon a time..." it is more than simple convention. The words are a bidding to remember an ancient fecundity and magic.

The symbolic is, as I think of it, both the organizing truth and the major mode of expression in the second major stage of formative process. As myth, it serves as truth's most direct expression in the times of early high cultures: in ancient Egypt, early Greece, for the Incas and the Aztecs of Pre-Columbian Meso-America. As imagination, it defines the reality of childhood: the essential work of the child is its play, the trying out of wings of possibility on the stage of make believe and let's pretend. The symbolic is there in a similar way in the beginnings of any creative task. It organizes reality in the stage of inspiration, that critical time where bubblings from the dreamworld of the unconscious give us our first visible sense of what is asking to become.

The importance of the symbolic as part of any larger understanding is well illustrated by what happens when thinkers of the new physics set aside their mathematics and attempt to use conventional language. Niels Bohr expressed it this way in his *Atomic Theory and Human Knowledge*: "... when it comes to atoms, language can be used only as poetry. The poet too is not nearly so concerned with describing facts as with creating images and establishing mental connections.... Quantum theory ... provides us with a striking illustration of the fact that we can fully understand a connection though we can only speak of it in images and parables."

THE LANGUAGE OF EMOTION

*"There can be no transforming of darkness into light and of
apathy into movement without emotions."*

—*Carl Jung*

"The perception of beauty is a moral test."

—*Henry David Thoreau*

The next "language" in this developmental sequence is somewhat more familiar to us than the first two. It is one step closer to
the reality that today organizes our truth. It is the language of
emotions.

While more familiar, its use here will still necessarily stretch
our usual understanding. There are two parts in this. First, we will
use it here as an integral part of theory. In the past, we have specifically cleansed it from our theoretical thinking so our ideas would
have the rigor necessary for objective truth. Second, we will be
asked to understand the emotional in a deeper and more personal
sense than we are accustomed to. The emotional as we know it in
this stage of culture is only a faint vestige of the feeling dimension
at its full grandeur as a primary organizing reality.

The emotional orders truth in the third major stage of formativeness. When it is preeminent, life is imbued with a visceral immediacy, and strong ethical and moral responses. We can feel its
presense in the fervencies and allegiances of adolescence. It is there
in a similar way in the crusading ardency and codes of honor and
chivalry of the Middle Ages. And we see it in the courage to struggle, and the devoted committment, necessary to take any personal
experience of creative inspiration into manifest form.

In conventional thinking, we acknowledge just the most surface
layerings of this part of us. We treat the emotional as, at best, decoration, or as a pleasant diversion from the real stuff of understanding. That somehow we must be able to reengage this part of us
as integral in truth becomes obvious if we examine the issues that

When we attempt to express living experience with words, logical speech quickly becomes permeated with symbols and metaphors.

ABOVE: *Henri Rousseau.* The Sleeping Gypsy. *1897.*
OPPOSITE: *Eskimo Moon Mask.*

now confront us as a species. Solving the dilemmas of our future will require a keen sensitivity to the fact of human relationship and deep levels of personal integrity and ethical responsibility. It is our emotional selves that most appreciates and understands these concerns.

Since our pre-logical natures are an integral part of truth in the model, it will be important in these pages to keep ongoing connection with each of these parts of ourselves. Some of this connecting can happen through the medium of sequential words on a printed page, but that can only be a start. To take it further, throughout the text, I will include exercises designed to tap into these more germinal parts of ourselves and bring them more directly into the process of understanding.

SOME FINAL NOTES IN PREPARATION

*"... by yielding naturally to the business of subduing appear-
ances and upsetting the relationships of 'realities,' [we are]
hastening the general crisis of consciousness due in our
time."*   *—Max Ernst*

"It is the business of the future to be dangerous."
—Alfred North Whitehead

Several last thoughts seem important to share before we
plunge into the model. One has to do with the essential task of
crediting ideas and traditions, both ancient and modern, that are
either important antecedents to the ideas here, or that have significant parallels with them. I've felt very torn in preparing the

book as to the best way to handle this. Because of the breadth of the notions here, if I were to be in any way complete, this chronicling would itself take several volumes.

At the risk of seeming naive to, or ungrateful for, my heritage, I have chosen to keep such footnoting to a minimum. Besides the immensity of the task of giving credit with any academic thoroughness, two other factors move me in this direction. First, while there are a great many important antecedents to these ideas, there is nevertheless an important sense in which what we are working with here is a qualitatively new kind of perspective. It is not simply a next additive step in a tradition.

It is as well the case that the ideas have come less from any great depth of philosophical background on my part, than from the very immediate and practical frustrations of being a therapist and student of social change without models sufficient to my experience. Many of the most important historical antecedents I have discovered only after the fact. As a result, while I'm very fascinated with the roots of this sort of thinking in various fields, I feel my personal debt of gratitude really less to individual thinkers than to the whole of the evolution of culture to which these thinkers have creatively contributed. As I think of it, these sorts of ideas are simply an expression of how we are becoming able to think, and how we are finding ourselves forced to think, as a function of the particular point we occupy in culture as a creative process.

Yet there are names and traditions that I feel are very important to at least mention for their relationship to these ideas and their place in the growth of my thinking. I might start by giving some credit in my own domain of psychology and psychiatry as this realm will have such a central place in illustrating the model's ideas. Here, four areas of acknowledgement most stand out. The first is to thinkers of the existential-humanistic tradition in psychotherapy—people like Rollo May, Carl Rogers, and Abraham Maslow—for their commitment to keeping the humanity and generativity of the person central in their thinking. The second is to pioneers in work with the pre-logical: Sigmund Freud for his courage to challenge Victorian culture with the fact of an unconscious; Carl Jung and Roberto Assagioli for their explorations in the symbolic as a creative force; Wilhelm Reich, Alexander Lowen and Stanley Keleman for their work in bringing the body into the province of the psychological; and people like Fritz Perls and Jacob Moreno for the development of increasingly active and direct means for working with generative experience. The third area of gratitude is to the pioneers of developmental psychology, and here particularly Jean Piaget, for putting forth the first specifically process-oriented model of development. The fourth area of acknowledgement is to people whose focus has been on the relational aspects of psychological identity and change, on individuals as parts within larger systems: Harry Stack Sullivan for his interpersonal concepts in development, Alfred Adler for his emphasis on the social as well as the psychological, William James for his inquiries into the nature of spiritual interconnection, and the present generation of family systems therapists—Virginia Satir, Salvador Minuchin, and Carl Whitaker being those who have most influenced my thinking.

And the psychological is, of course, only one small piece of what these ideas are about, and one relatively small part in the history that has set stage for this kind of conception. Many important voices of our time have challenged the limitations of mechanistic perception, and with this been influences in my thinking: in philosophy, people like Alfred North Whitehead, Michael Polanyi, Martin Buber and the thinkers of existentialism; in literature, figures such as T.S. Eliot, Ralph Waldo Emerson, William Blake, Henry David Thoreau and Aldous Huxley; in education, John Dewey. Ludwig von Bertalanffy and the systems theorists that followed him developed ideas that are essential antecedents to the notions here. Certainly important to mention are the originators of post-mechanistic formulations in the hard sciences: Albert Einstein, the theorists of quantum mechanics, Illya Prigogine in thermodynamic chemistry, and the pioneers of modern ecological thought. Academically oriented explorers in the pre-logical, such as Joseph Campbell and Mircea Eliade, have had significant influence on my thinking. I feel a particularly deep debt of gratitude to Gregory Bateson for his work in detailing the importance of the kind of leap these ideas make and what might be required to make it. As well, people like Marilyn Ferguson and Fritjof Capra should be acknowledged for bringing the imperative of a shift in paradigm to the attention of an ever broadening audience.

A final note before we begin—a bit of a "warning label" for the book's contents. It has to do with what the reader will need to bring to the experience of understanding in these pages—and the kind of effects that understanding may have. With conventional theory, "getting it" is pretty much a function of being smart enough and persistent enough. With the ideas here, while intellect will have an important role, clearly other things will be equally important. In the end, the ideas will be graspable to the degree ways can be found to bring all parts of one's formative nature into the task of understanding.

Because of this, the ideas in the model will challenge most people not just conceptually, but in important ways personally. They will demand that we open in an integral way into parts of us that we are accustomed to keeping at arm's length and well segregated from one another. The particular coloration of this personal challenge will be quite different for different people. One of the really fascinating parts of teaching these ideas has been watching the very characteristic ways that different people respond to them —what parts come easily, which parts are more elusive or disturbing. As we shall see when we apply the model to the question of what makes different people different, we can understand different personality styles as simply reflections of our relative intimacy in ourselves with the various languages of formative process.

In playing with the ideas of the model, I encourage you to persist and learn from your relationship to them, even if at times they seem foreign or a bit uncomfortable. While many of the ideas are subtle, few are complicated. By the end, the reader should find the model a fascinating new friend—a tool for self expansion and a refreshingly simple and direct means for addressing all manner of otherwise seemingly elusive or impossibly complex questions.

THE MODEL : PART I
TRUTH IN A LIVING REALITY

CHAPTER THREE

CREATIVE CAUSALITY

"All my attempts to adapt the theoretical foundations of physics to this [new type of] knowledge failed completely. It was as if the ground had been pulled out from under [me], with no firm foundation to be seen anywhere, upon which one could have built."

—*Albert Einstein*

"Invention in the arts and in thought is part of the invention of life ... [it is] a single process."

—*Brewster Ghiselin*

 We must begin with a leap. We can't derive the kind of thinking we are looking for from conventional theory. Our situation is a bit like the old Nor'Easter's response to a tourist's request for directions: "Well, ya just can't get there from here."

Noting the parallel with the leap necessary at the beginning of modern physics can be helpful in getting started. Einstein saw that matter and energy were in fact not separate phenomena, but aspects of a more inclusive kind of dynamic. But no amount of tugging or stretching could fit his recognition into the tenets of classical physics. He did the only thing possible in such a situation: he formulated what he saw as specifically as he could, and let it prove its truth through its utility. Today the equation $E=mC^2$ is part of common parlance, and classical physics is understood as a subset of such more dynamic formulations.

We start here from a very similar place. The new concept is that by thinking of causation and interconnection as creative dynamics, we can understand living process in much more living terms. From this new perspective, the major dualities of the human sphere—polarities such as mind and body, art and science, sacred and secular, or us and them—like Einstein's matter and energy, appear no longer as opposites, but as complementary elements within larger dynamic processes.

And, as with the tenets of relativity, there is no way to extrapolate creative causality from conventional theory. We are outside of what can be described in purely material, mechanical terms. All that is possible is to present the concept in as clear a way as possible and then try it out, to see both whether it fits our experience, and whether it expands our understanding in useful ways.

Making the sort of leap these ideas require is challenging—not just because it asks us to venture into new territory, but also because it demands that we leave certain things behind. To engage a shift in paradigm is to take part in a kind of passage: it asks us to make sacrifice, to surrender certain things we have held close. And the surrenderings here are significant. For example, as I have suggested, if we want to move into creatively-based thinking, we must leave behind the security of determinism, both the determinism of gears and pulleys, and that of divine unity: a creative world is a world that includes uncertainty. Equally, from the other side of the coin, these notion challenge the institution of inviolable free will. Absolute free will requires an atomistic world, one where parts are fully separate and independent; parts in a creatively-ordered world are irrevocably interconnected. Related to each of these, and easily most unsettling, a creatively-based view of self and world demands that we accept a reality without final answers. Before, we have always had external, formalized truths—tribal taboos, codes of knightly honor, the laws of science. In a creative reality, form is never alone sufficient to define truth, and truth is never just external, but always in some sense participatory. Creative truth is four-dimensional—relative both to time and context.

While these are certainly most significant things to give up, things that have been central parts of our personal and cultural self definitions, we have really very little choice. While there will be many ways to frame the larger reality we are moving into—creative causality is certainly but one of many ways of understanding its dynamics—finding the courage to risk the transitions it asks of us will likely be imperative for our future well-being, and quite possibly our survival.

Let's turn now specifically to the model. The leap into creative/relativistic understanding is eased, at least conceptually, by thinking in terms of three related smaller steps. Each illuminates one aspect of what is needed for the full leap to take place:

The first step is the recognition that our customary notion of causation as a linear mechanism, one domino pushing over the next, is rarely sufficient when our concern is living systems. Effect is always a function of interwoven factors. The preeminent pioneer for this first step was German biologist Ludwig von Bertalanffy. His General Systems theory showed how causation in complex systems happens through interlinking networks of effect. Such "systems thinking" has spawned whole new disciplines: modern ecology, cybernetics, organizational development.

Systems thinking is a more satisfying approach to the intricacies of our natures, but importantly, it is not yet living conception. It still speaks the language of machines—wonderfully more complex machines without question, computers instead of adding machines, but still machines.*

To get beyond machine models, we need a second step. This is the pivotal recognition that the feedback processes that link parts in living systems are ultimately not just automatic, reflexive; they are generative. Living relationships, both between beings and between parts in a single being, are creative. Each "action" or "reaction" in a living system is part of growth, part of non-additive dynamics of change.

The most important work to date relating to this part of the leap is that for which Illya Prigogine received the 1977 Nobel Prize in Chemistry. Prigogine was struck by the obvious discrepancy between the accepted thermodynamic concept of entropy, the notion that in closed systems things run down, and the clearly generative

---

* More recent systems theorists, most specifically Erich Jantsch, have made important strides in taking systems thinking beyond the simply mechanistic.

story, atom to molecule to cell to civilization, told by our 4 1/2 billion years of planetary evolution. Prigogine demonstrated mathematically that open systems (what he calls dissipative structures) grow through generative leaps, reorganizing to more efficient and complex patterns as old ones become unstable and ineffective. While Prigogine's work is focussed on the inanimate, it is none the less quite relevant here. Indeed, it suggests the important recognition that creatively-ordered causality, "living" causality, orders not just systems that are living in the usual sense, but reality as a whole.

With these two steps we have moved effectively into the living, but we clearly need more if we are to address in any complete way the unique complexities of *human* experience. While it is interesting philosophically that creative organization is inherent to existence, and that systems tend toward more evolved states (and it can offer a welcome ray of hope when all seems chaos), we need to be able to think in much more detailed ways if we are to do anything at all practical with these ideas in addressing human questions. We need to be able to understand the unique roles that all the various elements of human experience, personal and social, play in this creative picture.

The third step gives this needed living differentiation to our thinking. This is the recognition that, in human systems, formative process is a very specific, intricately delineable dynamic. As we shall explore in detail, human creation moves through characteristic stages. As well, it takes on a very specific formative "architecture" by virtue of the human organism's unique stance in the world, an inner/outer patterning which serves as the ground-plan for all levels of structure in human experience.

CHANGE AND RELATIONSHIP IN A LIVING REALITY

"Science ... means unresting endeavor ... toward an aim which the poetic intuition may apprehend, but which the intellect can never fully grasp." —Max Plank

*"It is strange that you can change, you're always with
yourself."*   —Gwen Miller, age 7

*"[The natural] laws are not forces external to things, but
represent the harmony of movement immanent in them."*
                                    —I Ching

It will be in detailing these patterns of creative change and
interaction that the model will become most obviously significant,
and most easily grasped and utilized. But we would be getting
ahead of ourselves to start there. The right place to begin is with
creative causality at its simplest, as a concept "naked and
unadorned."

I should emphasize here that creative causality is for me very
much a concept in evolution. I am continually discovering new implications and new subtleties. It happens repeatedly that I will be
working theoretically with some historical concept, or in therapy
with a particularly intricate issue, and come to an impasse in my
understanding. Then I stand back and realize that the problem was
that I simply was not seeing the situation fully in creative terms.
Each time this happens the concept fills out in new ways.

As I have said, my first insights about creative causality grew
from playing with two different sorts of questions: how it is that
change happens in living systems, and how parts in living systems
are connected. I sensed these two essential concerns were in fact aspects of the same dynamic, but had no frameworks that could adequately address them as such.

It was in exploring these questions in the arena of human relationships that the idea that causality might ultimately be a creative dynamic first really solidified for me. The interpersonal is one
of the areas where our usual thinking is most obviously inadequate.
And to a therapist working with couples and families, this is much
more than just an inconvenience; it is a major obstacle. Our usual
cause and effect ways of thinking and talking about relationship
ultimately miss precisely what makes a relationship a relationship. It is by noting where relationships have become mechanical
that we know how they are *not* working (be this the reflexive

mechanicalness of "you do this, then I do that," or the enmeshment of oneness).

The "ah-ha" that relationships might, at their most elemental, be creative processes suddenly opened up whole new possibilities of thought. I found my ideas working in excitingly more dynamic ways. I saw that in approaching relationships from a creative perspective, for the first time, my thinking was coming close to being adequate to the wonder and subtlety of the phenomena I was addressing.

I saw that now I could think directly in terms of what makes relationship *relationship:* Ultimately the word relationship is a description of the fact that something living—something vital, creative in the largest sense—is happening between two people. In addition, I saw with satisfaction that when framed in creative terms, my thinking effectively bridged the phenomena of connectedness and change. From a creative perspective connectedness and change are intimately related concerns. The best measures we have for the health of the bond that defines a relationship is the capacity of that relationship for living change.

As I looked at other kinds of systems and the parts that comprised them, it became clear that this kind of perspective applied in equally exciting and useful ways to them all. It did not matter what kind of system I was examining. Being a therapist, it was internal sorts of relationships that first came to mind, things like the relationship between conscious and unconscious, mind and body, thoughts and feelings, or masculine and feminine. I remember playing through some of the common errors that therapists make in their thinking, and feeling excitement that this shift in perspective seemed to offer in each instance a straightforward way of thinking in larger terms. For example, therapists tend to set themselves up in warring camps over the primacy of mind or emotions. For one group it is insight that "causes" change, self understanding. For the other, the real causative agent is feelings, getting in touch with and releasing emotions. In fact, any good therapist knows intuitively that neither alone is the answer, yet within conventional causal thinking it is hard not to fall into the either/or. A creative perspective offers a simple integrative way of thinking. Here, mind and emotions are seen as complementary poles in a creative dynamic. From this vantage we can see that indeed sometimes insight can "cause" change. It will do this whenever the effect of insight is to make a creative bridging with a complementary body of feelings and experience. Similarly, expressing feelings will be "causal" if through it some new link is established between emotion and the person's being as a whole. The essential variable is the degree something living is happening at the creative interface; it is this that determines whether an idea is anything more than intellectualization, or expressing feelings more than just letting steam out of the teapot.

In time I saw how thinking in creative terms was relevant equally to more external concerns. (Indeed, I realized that one of the most important kinds of creative relationships was between those parts of our experience we call inner and outer—they are not the same, but neither are they fully distinct.) I recognized that "I do this to you, then you do that to me" was as partial a way to understand relationships between nations as between individual people. I also saw how reframing historical thinking in creative terms might provide new ways of understanding in another area where conventional thinking has always seemed to me disturbingly simplistic. Thinking of the development of civilization in causal, additive terms—as a sequence of new inventions and leaders— makes what is clearly as exciting a story as could be told ultimately dry and lifeless. But what would happen if we approached civilization itself as a creative process? How would that alter how we think about cultural change? And how would it change the way we see the relationships between parts within social reality—between countries, communities, or leaders; between leaders and their populaces, the left and the right, social classes or polarized ethnic or religious factions?

As this picture began to fill out, an important question came to me: If creatively-based thinking in truth more adequately explains things, why haven't we thought this way all along? It is not an inherently complicated way of conceiving. I found myself drawn to memories of different creative projects I have worked on, and I realized an important thing. I saw that in the early parts of projects, I would be so immersed that I really had no capacity for perspective. Then, at a very specific point in the process, I would begin to be able to have awareness about both the significance of what I was creating and what that process was for me. Thinking about it, I saw that a similar thing happens at about the midpoint in our individual lifetimes; we start to be able not just to create our lives, but to see that process of "self-creation" in some meaningful perspective. From this I began to play with the idea that we might be at some similar kind of "midlife transition" in culture as a creative dynamic. Perhaps we have just now moved far enough into culture as a creative process that we can begin to step back and realize how it in fact is, and has been, a process. The more I explored this, the more the parallels seemed overwhelming, and the more it became obvious that the ability to understand culture in creative systems terms might have powerful significance.

ALIVENESS

"The humblest fungus betrays a life akin to our own. It is a successful poem in its own kind."
—Henry David Thoreau

"I can't tell you what gives true intensity, but I know it when I find it."
—Catherine Anne Porter

"He who has a why to live, can bear most any what."
—Friedrich Nietzsche

What is creative causality at essence, at its simplest? If creative process is the "basic building block" of living reality, how might we best define it?

Unfortunately, as nice as it would be, having a simple definition is not in the cards. To define is to say: there is this, and then there is that. But with creative causality there is no "that;" there is nothing which is not an aspect of it.

38

A precisely parallel, though usually unacknowledged definitional pickle sits at the center of thought in the biological sciences. It makes a nice jumping off point for our explorings here.

Biology is the study of life. But ask a biologist what life is and you will get either a sheepish shrug or a tangle of tautology. Neither yardsticks nor fancy transducers are of any use in measuring it. Biologists find themselves in the curious position of asserting that all else must be understood in relation to life, but that life cannot be either defined or measured.

Is life then some rare and elusive creature? Obviously this is not the problem; life is everywhere we look. The problem is simply that our usual ways of addressing life are inappropriate to the task. In thinking of something as "having" life, we have created a causal separation between life and the thing which is alive. And just as the separation of matter and energy locks us into a mechanistic world, so when we demand an objective definition of life, we are left only with what life is not. In our brow-furrowed search for truth, this elusiveness might easily seem some perverse trick, but it is hardly that. We are simply witnessing nature's incorruptibility to the whole.

So if we want a full picture, we must do more than just define. We must as well explore—play off creative causality's different facets, immerse ourselves in it as experience. We will do this several ways here, then take the kernel of understanding that results and let it be challenged, expanded, and brought to maturity in the chapters ahead.

We can open one very helpful window into understanding reality as creative by taking some time with that critical question of just what we are going to call "truth" in times ahead. If isolated form-defined arbiters will no longer suffice—roles in relationships, education as facts and skills, the accumulation of goods as the measure of progress—what is it then that we are wanting to measure?

Our usual ways of thinking are not going to be able to help us. They are part and parcel of the same reality as our form-defined answers. Without a larger approach to understanding, the best we can do is stand by confused, and watch as what has worked before becomes more and more the problem rather than the solution.

From within a form-defined reality, it is hard to understand the loss of familiar truths as anything but chaos, a loss of order. A creative perspective offers a new way of understanding order, and with this a larger vantage from which to measure truth. From here, movement beyond truth as form reveals itself, in its timeliness, as the only way to have order. It does not reject form, but simply places it within a larger picture.

What are we wanting to measure? Put in creative terms, we are looking for a measure that concerns itself not just with the formed products of creation, but with those products in their living contexts. We are wanting to measure the degree to which something in fact makes existence, in whatever its sphere, more fully alive. We are wanting to measure the larger dynamic, the health and integrity of the creative process as a whole.

To do this we must leave behind the idea that truth is fact, an "objective" measure. Here truth becomes a much more dynamic and relativistic kind of quantity.

Actually, that living truth is larger than objectivity is not that hard to see; indeed, it is quite obvious if we examine our lives with honesty. While we usually have ideas about why we do things, they are rarely, in fact, sufficient to explain our actions. Pressed for the real bottom line, we are likely to end up, like the biologist trying to define life, in a maze of redundant verbiage. In the end, the best we can do is throw up our hands and say with a mixture of wonder and embarrassment: "Well, when you know, you know ... When something tastes good, it tastes good ...."

This need to step beyond objectivity as what defines truth is a central theme in emerging thought in the hard sciences. To quote physicist John Wheeler, there is nothing more important about recent observations than that "[they] destroy the concept of the world as 'sitting out there,' with the observer safely separated from it by a 20 centimeter slab of glass." In the words of Werner Heisenberg, "What we observe is not nature itself, but nature exposed to our method of questioning.... Natural science does not simply describe and explain nature, it is part of the interplay between nature and ourselves."

This is not to suggest that reality is in fact "just subjective." In saying that living truth is larger than objectivity, I am in no way taking sides in the battle of science and poetry. I am simply asserting that intelligence in action is ultimately a function of the whole of what we are. Truth in the big picture is an inherently participatory measure: it is a measure not just of things, but of relationships between things, and one of the key relationships is that between ourselves and what we are measuring.

While we can't define a larger referent in terms of other things, or measure it objectively, there is certainly nothing to keep us from giving it a name and defining it functionally. That we have a word, I call it simply *aliveness*. Defined in creative terms, it is the amount of creation, the amount of "living reality," embodied by a particular act or situation.

In talking with groups of people about using a referent like aliveness, I often start by having people take part in an exercise. There is an important sense in which it is easier to measure aliveness than to talk about it. I hesitate somewhat to use the exercise here as it is easily interpreted simplistically, but it can offer some very useful insights:

> Close your eyes and take some time to reflect over the events of, say, the last month in your life. As you do this, pick out seven or eight moments of different sorts from the month's goings on. Now, imagine before you a scale of from one to a hundred, a sort of "aliveness thermometer." As you remember each event, try it out on the scale: how alive was that moment for you, how full was it, how real. The numbers that come may surprise you; let that be okay. As you put the different events on the scale, notice what you can about the kinds of cues—thoughts, feelings, images, body sensations, whatever—you are using to place them.
>
> Once you have done this, reflect some on the significance of the different numbers you have put down. Do they say anything that might be valuable: about what is most important to you? about choices you are making or may want to make? Take time with your experience. Finally, ask yourself: if, in future similar situations you would like there to be somewhat more aliveness, what in each would you need to risk?

Doing exercises like this with different groups of people, a number of things characteristically stand out. First, people are surprised at how easy it is to arrive at measures that seem to have a high degree of precision. A common dialogue: "The notion doesn't make sense. I don't get anything." Me: "OK, let's play with it together. Pick a situation.... Now was what happened pretty real and significant for you, something we could pretty safely say was at least a 50, or not really very meaningful?" "Oh, it's over 50." Me: "Sixty, then?" "Well, even a bit more than that." Me: "How about if we just call it 75?" "Well, it's not really that much." Me: "72?" "Somewhere between 71 and 72, I'd say." *

Second, people quickly recognize that their measures, while significant, are not infallible. Lots of factors affect them. They reflect blindnesses as well as truths. (For example, for one person, experiences that are exciting and flashy get overly high ratings, for another, experiences awash in pathos, for another, acts that are serious and responsible, for another, things that involve struggle.) One quickly sees that part of the art of refining one's ability to measure aliveness is learning one's personal partialities in it. Aliveness includes all of who we are—equally the spiritual and the material, equally thoughts, images and feelings—and how we experience aliveness mirrors our relationship to these different parts of ourselves. The more that can be brought into play, the more reliable what we can sense becomes.

Third, people are struck by how different the experiences that feel alive can be. To the question of what might increase aliveness, there is always a startling variety of responses: risking to be more social, risking to be alone, risking to take it easy, risking to struggle, risking to say yes, risking to say no. Truth here is profoundly relative to both time and context. Aliveness includes all that we are. Depending on the situation, a part in the whole may be an answer, but it is never *the* answer.

An exercise like this is clearly only a first step in understanding what it means to think and measure in living, creative terms. For example, here we have talked as if aliveness exists

---

* The significance of particular numbers is, of course, purely personal.

42

along a single continuum. While for some kinds of questions this is a close enough approximation of reality, for others, aliveness is a meaningful referent only if we carefully distinguish its different kinds, qualities and domains. None the less, the exercise is significant. It helps point us toward a more inclusive and living way to think about intelligence in general. As well, it offers a start in addressing the question of what we must bring to our thinking in all domains if our measures are to be living ones.

Aliveness, just by what it is, confronts the key issues that now face us. At the personal level, the pivotal questions of our time concern purpose and identity: who are we—our roles, our beliefs, what we own, the images we get from media, parents and peers? Aliveness is a direct statement about, and measure of, purpose. We feel purpose and "are" someone precisely to the degree we risk living from, and in relation to, what makes us most alive. Culturally, what we are wanting to do in each sphere is find ways of thinking and measuring that are sensitive to the place of that sphere in the larger living whole. From here, there becomes no more important task than learning to ask together the relative aliveness that different social options offer us.

In one sense, making the creative our referent is a radically new kind of notion; in another the creative is what we have been measuring all along. Each of our previous arbiters—the voices of nature spirits, moral canons, the laws of science—were also measures of the edge of creation. The difference with a creatively-based perspective is simply that now, in measuring creation, we are being conscious of the fact that this indeed is what we are measuring. We have moved far enough into creation that we are able to be not just creators of culture, but beings conscious of, and in, this process of creation.

By making a notion such as aliveness our referent, our thinking, in whatever sphere we apply it, gains a radically new kind of precision. This is not because it is now more exact—in a creative reality truth is always partial, never fully objective and always in process—but because, in taking what makes something alive as basic, we are measuring what in fact we need to measure.

CREATIVE EXPRESSION

"Poetry is that which gets lost in the translation."

—*Robert Frost*

*"... something profoundly convulsive and disturbing
suddenly becomes visible and audible ..."*

—*Friedrich Nietzsche*

"To be real is to be surrounded by mystery."

—*James Joyce*

In order to understand creative causality with any depth, we must open ourselves to those layers in ourselves germinal to our usual understanding. It is these parts that have been forgotten, and which now must be reengaged if we are to expand our thinking into creation as whole. Here and in the next section we will take time with two of these more germinal voices.

The first comes from a realm we explicitly acknowledge as creative—the creative arts. Art can in fact only give us part of the picture—just half of the duality of art and science—but we can use it to help us connect into important aspects of what is missing.

One of the things that makes a concept like creative causality elusive to our usual thought is that it asks us to take seriously things that we cannot see. In a purely material paradigm, if something is not visible,* it does not exist. From that stance, the whole idea of a process being creative—that is, moving from the invisible into the visible—makes little sense.

To think creatively one must grasp the easily elusive fact that no-thing can be as much something as some-thing. The arts can offer us some useful windows into this larger understanding of things.

In thinking about the creative, my memory often turns to a jazz

---

* More precisely, if something is not objectively measurable it does not exist. Things like wind and electricity are valid material entities.

class that I took when I was about twelve years old. The concept of improvisation was new to me. I learned about it through the experience of "making mistakes." Looking back, I can see that the word "mistake" evolved through three successive meanings for me. First was the delightfully devious discovery that in jazz a mistake could be turned into a new riff and no one would be the wiser. Then came the unsettling recognition that the riffs I trickily chose to cover my "errors" were often the most exciting parts of what I played. The instructor encouraged me to "purposefully" make "mistakes." The mistakes became discovery spaces where I could let my creativity play in the music. The final realization—both enlightening and bewildering—was the clear fact that whenever the music really worked it was in an important sense "a mistake." I saw that whether what I was playing was overtly improvisational or written, it was my willingness to let the unexpected into each note that made it music.

Traditional art forms frequently include symbolic expression of this critical place of uncertainty. Traditional American quilts often have a "lucky square," one with a mistake, so the quilt can breathe and be alive. Navaho weaving similarly includes an "error," and ritual sand paintings a break in the circle through which the spirits can pass. The message is clear: images of perfection and completion alone cannot express life. In life, the invisible and inexplicable is an essential voice.

If we can appropriately extrapolate from the experience of the artist, the necessary conclusion is that living reality is in some way discontinuous. And there is a further conclusion implied, that the "holes" in reality are not just empty spaces, but intimately a part of what makes experience living: it is somehow by virtue of their presence that reality is generative.

How is reality different when we include this "nothing which is not nothing?" One of the most obvious things is that it comes to obey laws of organization quite different from our usual ideas about how things work.

In my late teens and early twenties, I became fascinated with doing sculpture, in large part I think because it gave such a direct

and tangible route to learning about these more mysterious layerings in things. I kept a journal as I worked. I include a few notes from
that journal, both to share some of my early grapplings with creative questions, and as a brief foray into the reality of the more germinal parts of our natures:

Notes —June to September 1968

"What is it I am doing here? In one way there could be
nothing more ordinary—just myself, solitude, a stone, some
chisels. And in it I am continually amazed. Sculpting for
me is a fundamental kind of unearthing. Things bubble
beneath this thin surface of ideas and words that I think I
am, and if I let them close enough, they take me and
challenge me in most frighteningly wonderful ways. To
sculpt feels huge and ancient ... and also very simple, just
me.

"What makes something true here is an endless source
of fascination. I explore a shaping and something in it
'works.' It may be a deep thrust of the chisel point. It may
be a gentle smoothing of a curve. It is never quite the same
twice ... What is this 'knowing?' None of the things I can
say about it are logical, yet it is anything but obscure. 'It is
what I am when I let the whole thing in.' 'It is the carv-
ingness itself.' Whatever I say comes out either mystical,
complicated or prissy. Yet, it seems to be what matters. If I
follow it, the work is alive; if I don't, it's dead. It seems
that simple.

"I don't think creation ever happens in a piece unless
it's happening in me at the same time. The stone changing
and leaving me safe isn't how it works. A question: Do I
change myself in order to create the image, or do I change
the image in order to create myself? Sometimes each seems
true.

"I've noticed as I work a curious relationship between
my sculpting and time. Rarely, it seems, do I have much
understanding of a piece while I am working with it. It is
usually several years before I can sense in any complete
way what a particular piece means to me, and often considerably longer before I can express this meaning with
any clarity to another person. Interestingly, I find the way

I approach a piece is intimately related to the length of the span between its execution, and this time of more conscious understanding. Pieces that I find known to me consciously in two to three years seem to meet me with the greatest immediacy and endurance of passion. Pieces where the duration will be three to five years I will often engage initially with great flashes of excitement, but then leave fallow for significant periods, often forgetting for a time what it was in them that had excited me in the first place. Where the duration will be less than two years, I often begin with great enthusiasm, then tire quickly, on some level seeming to recognize that the birthing in me that the piece represents is already well in progress, and not needing of my sculptural midwifery. I've written these words on the wall of my workroom: 'My art expresses not what I know, but what I am coming to be.'"

I think of something like a piece of art as a statement about our identities as both change and interconnection. It is a living cross-section through who we are as patterned transformation. As process it involves myriad levels of who we are, from the most germinal to ones much more conscious and manifest. Further, it is a function not just of one whole, but wholes within wholes. The work is not just that "piece" as creative process, but a statement of its creator's evolving aliveness, and ultimately the aliveness of each of its concentric contexts—community, culture, biosphere. We can think of a work of art as a statement about the "evolution" of intelligence. It touches us if it challenges and animates at the edge of who we are as creative entireties.

MYTHS OF CREATION

"Be patient with all that is unsolved in your heart. Try to love the questions themselves like locked rooms and like books that are written in a foreign tongue ... Live the questions raw." —Rainer Maria Rilke

*"What we call the beginning is often the end. And to make an
end is to make a beginning. The end is where we start from."*
—*T.S. Eliot*

*"You are not the oil, you are not the air—merely the point of
combustion, the flash-point, where the light is born."*
—*Dag Hammarskjold*

A second voice we might turn to in learning about more germinal
kinds of knowing is that of myth. We could make a good argument
that myth's function in the social whole is quite specifically to describe and evoke the germinal levels of our formative natures.

Actually, we can do better than to just look at myth, we can
listen to myth's own words about the fact of creation. Every mythic
system includes "stories of creation," tales that tell about the
beginnings of life: the Mayan Popul Vuh, the Babylonian Enuma
Elish, the Hebrew Genesis.

Let's play with a fascinating question about these tales. There
could be no more basic question, but within usual thought there is no
really satisfying answer. Quite simply, why do these stories exist?
Why through eons, and across cultures, has this curious creature
that we are persisted in telling strange and mysterious tales about
"how it came to be?"

The words of creation stories are universally poignant and
powerful:

> "In the beginning this was non-existent. It became exis-
> tent: it grew. It turned into an egg. The egg lay for the
> time of a year. The egg broke open. The two halves were
> one of silver, one of gold. The silver one became this
> earth, the golden one the sky, the thick membrane the
> mountains, the thin membrane the mist with the clouds,
> the small veins the rivers, the fluid the sea. And all
> things arose, and all things they desired."
> —From the *Chandogya Upanishad*

> "When time and waiting need split the ancient egg, out
> stepped Love the first born, fire in his eyes, wearing both
> sexes, glorious Eros."
> —Orphic Cosmogony

> "When Amma broke the Egg of the World and came out of it, a whirlwind arose. The *po* is the smallest created thing, invisible, at the center; the wind is Amma himself. It is the *po* that Amma produced first."
> —A Creation Myth of the Dogon Tribe of Mali
> (from Griaule, "Conversations with Ogotemmeli")

Even though their times and cultures may be remote, such images strike a vibrant chord within us. Among those living people who still use the mythic as a major conscious language, creation tales are told and retold, very often as if existence itself depended upon their retelling.

How is it that these stories hold such profound rapture for us? Is it perhaps just the human need to understand? The question of origin is indeed an eternal quandary, as elusive to the modern scientist as to tribal people of the stone age. When addressed rationally, creation seems to offer only two options: either reality has always been, or, rabbit-from-hat, it sprang from nothingness. Unfortunately, each of these logical choices is logically nonsensical. It is quite possible that we have "made up" these stories of origin simply so that in life's vast unknownness, we might have some answer to the question "why."

But this interpretation alone is really not sufficient. It does not address the incredible passion and poetry of these tales. And it says nothing about why these stories are so amazingly similar through eons and cultures.

A glimpse of fuller significance can be seen in some of the more elaborate tales. One native Hawaiian creation story, as recounted by David Maclagan in his book *Creation Myths*, begins with a list of special beings and their identities:

> "*Te Ahahge*—the swelling of an embryo in the body ... *Te Aponga*—appetite ... *Te Kune Iti*—inner conception ... *Te Kuna Rahi*—preparation ... *Te Kine Hagna*—the impulse to search ... *Te Ranga Hantanga*—ordering of the cells in the body ... and on."

Notice that while each of these "deities" presides over different domains of experience, their overall concerns are closely related.

*Myths of creation describe the beginnings of life. The explicit
reference is to an event far in the past, but their potency is
personal and immediate. They enliven by speaking to that
place in us where all things begin—a moment,
a relationship, a lifetime.*

They each speak of a first impulse into form and order.

The larger meaning hinted at in these descriptions seems much
more in keeping with the numinosity of these tales. Stories of creation are concerned not just with an event in the past, but with "be-
ginningness" in all its manifestations.

Creation is an ever present part of existence. To be alive is to be
engaged in acts of making first steps: from large ones—a first love, a
first job—to quite small—beginning a letter to a friend, a stretch on
a spring morning. Each is in its own way profound, risking a step
into something unknown and unknowable. It makes sense that we
might evolve such stories to serve as teachers and helpers for these
leaps.

ABOVE, LEFT: *Amma, creator of the universe in the beliefs of the Dogon people of Mali, and the* Po, *"the smallest thing at the center."* ABOVE, RIGHT: *Egyptian deity Ptah fashioning the "Egg of the World."* OPPOSITE: *Michelangelo Buonarroti.* The Creation of Adam. *1508-1512.*

This explanation is nicely supported in noting the occasions on which stories of creation are most characteristically retold. Their reenactments coincide with times, personal or cultural, of ritual turning: birth, naming, the new year, the coming of puberty, marriage, war, initiation, healing, the time of death. They seem to serve as midwives to the mystery of passage, hands that guide the magic by which something becomes more.

But, to be really complete, we must take this explanation one step further. If we speak of creation as any moment of beginning, where do we draw the line? If a stretch on a spring morning is a creative birth, how about each breath, or glance? Each moment, while a function of all that has been, is also something that has

51

never been before. While in one sense a moment is just a moment, in another it is the only thing that exists. The instant is that point at which all the infinite interweavings of creation that comprise our aliveness meet and are rekindled. Tales of creation are stories about what we must bring to each moment in order that this rekindling take place.

IT'S A MATTER OF TIME

"The fourth dimension is the relation to the center, to unity."
—*Rudolf Laban*

"The more one examines the concept of time, the more unanswered questions there are."
—*Richard Morris*
Time's Arrow

"How do I know the way of all things at the beginning? By what is within me."
—*Lao Tsu*

What is this voice of "mystery" that lives within and animates the creative? Ultimately it can't be defined. To understand it, we must journey toward it from as many of the many paths that connect from it as we can discover.

In physics, two concepts have particular pertinance to this unformed essence of things. The first is gravitation. Gravitation, in the thinking of General Relativity, is the ground of being, the fundamental invisible force.

The second related concept is time, time in its dimensional sense. Time and gravitation are kindred quantities. Gravitational fields alter the relative effect of space and time in reality. The closer one moves to a strong gravitational field, the greater the influence of time relative to the form-defining spacial coordinates.

What exactly is time as a dimension? It is a tricky notion, not the least because it demands that we leave so much we usually associate with time behind us. One could well argue that time as we usually think of it is not time at all, since its identity is a function of existence in a three-dimensional reality, a reality where time as a dimension is specifically excluded. Dimensional time is much more than our usual measure of linear duration; it is not a separate abstract measure, but something which acts to define the "stuff" of experience as fully as our more familiar material coordinates.

The ideas in the model are specifically time relative. Developmental processes are seen as going through not just distinct stages, but distinct realities. Truth here, rather than being invariant, is a direct function of an act's or idea's "timeliness," its place in, and as, time.

And dimensional time is here regarded as a specific ingredient in reality. It is most obviously present in the earliest parts of creative processes. The incubation stage in a creative project is a reality yet without form, and thus without defining spacial coordinates. Similarly what defines in the reality of earliest culture is previous to form: truth is regarded as an eternal turning; at this stage of things there is as yet no concept of material permanence, nor of time in our sense of linear progress. The reality of the infant is, in a similar way, an all-embracing, "timeless" present.

Relating time and gravitation in this way with creative mystery takes us beyond the most common thinking in physics. It is an important step, but easily a controversial one. Einstein saw time as "curving" reality, but explicitly *not* disturbing its material continuity; Einstein's ideas were expressly deterministic—in his own famous words: "God does not play dice with the universe." The thinkers of quantum mechanics challenged this, arguing that material reality has, in fact, marked discontinuities and uncertainties; in the words of Cal Tech physicist Stephen Hawking: "God not only plays dice, but sometimes throws them where they cannot be seen." Theirs has proven the more complete explanation. The ideas here make a next step in this progression of ideas. Here we add to the idea that reality is discontinuous the notion that the nothingness that defines these discontinuities is, in fact, a kind of "some-thing," and a something with profound significance.

LIFE AND NOT-LIFE

*"He whose vision cannot cover
History's thousands of years,
Must in outer darkness hover,
Live within the day's frontier."*

—Goethe

While our focus in these pages will be on the human sphere, it is important to note that the concept of creative causality is relevant as well to the reality of the inanimate and simply animate. It can be usefully used to frame a general theory of reality.

To think in this way, we take formative process at its most elemental—the basic pulse of form taking and release—and make it reality's fundamental building block. The different levels of existence—inanimate, animate, and human—appear then as expressions of specific leaps in organization within this simple basic dynamic. These leaps have been made possible through "inventions" that have functioned as "creative multipliers," innovations that have quantally increased the amount of creation that can take place per unit time within a system. Between the inanimate and the animate this invention was reproduction, bringing mutation and genetic recombination at regular intervals. Between the animate and human, the creative multiplier was conscious awareness, making possible creative leaps at a rate limited only by our capacity for new insight.

LIVING CAUSALITY AND THE
HEALING RELATIONSHIP

"Only that which is truly yourself can heal."

—Carl Jung

"It seems increasingly certain that healing and creativity are different parts of a single picture."

—Elmer Green

I will conclude each chapter in the body of the model with some reflections on the significance of the chapter's ideas for psychology and psychotherapy. My intent is less to be in any way complete in what I say—a thorough treatment would fill volumes—than simply to offer the reader an example of the model being applied within a particular domain.

The concept of creative causality offers a richly expanded perspective from which to view the psychological. It suggests both a more complete way to conceive of well-being and a larger "logic" with which to think about therapeutic process.

Modern psychology is unusual as a "science" in that it had its inception at just about the time of the first intimations of an expansion of paradigm. Its sensibilities reflect a fundamental ambivalence. One could argue equally well that psychology and psychiatry have been major first voices in the new understanding, or conversely that they have been desperate last attempts to solidify the old. Freud's concept of an unconscious, in suggesting that the self that is aware is not fully in charge of its destiny, was a radically post-material notion. Yet at once, such thinking opened entrance for the mechanical paradigm into the last refuges of our inner selves. Psychology is a curious odd-child, pulled one way by insights from beyond the doorway of passage, and equally the other by a mandate to keep understanding safely packaged within our familiar rules of order.

If we look at psychology's major systematic theories, we see that they are all fundamentally Newtonian, systems of intrapsychic and environmental parts in reactively causal interrelationship. In keeping with this, health within them is defined in terms of atomistic categories of pathology, discrete "bits" of disease.

Many people, acting in response to the mechanicalness of such ideas, assume a more humanistic or existential posture, choosing to think less in terms of disease entities and psychodynamics, and more in terms of the unique process of the individual person. But all too often this just leaves us erring from the other end of the teeter-totter. We make feelings the winner in the battle of mind and emotions, and end up throwing out one of healing's most potent tools, the power to discern. Clearly we need to be able to step beyond this either/or, to find ways to think discerningly, but in personal and living terms.

What kinds of changes would we expect to see with a new paradigm in psychological understanding? I will touch on a few of the major themes here and explore others in later chapters.

One critical change we should see is a significant expansion in the realms of experience that theories can adequately address. A curious and most frustrating thing about most of our major psychological frameworks is that they either ignore, or place well to the periphery, important aspects of human experience. The topics pushed aside, or treated simplistically, are frequently not at all peripheral in experience, indeed they are some of the most central concerns of our lives. We must look to the conceptual hinterlands of most theory if we wish to speak, for example, of wisdom, creativity, purpose, love, laughter, beauty or the sacred.

The simple fact is that the things that are most intimate in us do not conform to the rules of mechanical order. Restricted to the "forces and levers" rules of usual theory, there is not a lot we can say about them. Clearly a conceptual bridge is sorely needed. The crises of our times, whether we look personally or culturally, are ultimately crises of purpose, crises in our ability to connect into exactly those parts of us that lie beyond the reach of usual theory.

As we shall see, a creative perspective gives us a way to accomplish this bridging. It gives us a vantage from which we need neither to reject these parts of us as subjective, nor elevate them as separate and special. It gives us a way to understand them as integral elements in the whole of our functioning.

Another critical change we should see is in how we understand health. If one thinks about it, health clearly is what psychology is ultimately about. But interestingly, only rarely do we use it as the referent in our thinking. Rather than measure well-being, we measure dis-ease, symptoms, then discern progress in terms of how these symptoms change. We end up in the embarassingly simplistic posture of acting as if health is simply the absence of disease.

Why don't we measure wellness? A big part of it is simply that within our traditional paradigm it is not a very understandable notion. Wellness is a living quantity; behaviors alone are not sufficient for measuring it. Disease, on the other hand, can be defined quite well in terms of specific measurable quantities.

While we are not really measuring what needs to be measured, a good part of the time this doesn't really cause any great problem. But that is not always the case. If we let the symptom become the dragon to our white knight, we can significantly undermine our power to be effective. By focusing on symptoms we can forget the person. Or our vision can become narrowed so that we miss change processes in another part of the system. And we easily get into polar co-dependencies, one person playing the sick one, the other the savior, in the process cutting off effective creative connection, both with the client, and with ourselves.

But the biggest argument for being able to think in more living terms about what comprises health concerns our present changes in culture. Our usual notions of psychopathology are normative, defined in terms of accepted cultural standards for behavior. As we move beyond the timeliness of materially-defined truth, such notions will more and more frequently serve to confine and limit more than they help.

A creatively causal perspective gives us one way to conceive directly in terms of health. Framed creatively, our well-being is our aliveness. This is the quantity that defines everything else: Health is the total aliveness of a system; healing is anything that nourishes or challenges that system so that its total aliveness increases.

I endeavor as a therapist to keep aliveness always the central referent in my thinking. I am interested in a number of things: the amount of aliveness that a person, on the average, is able to embody; how that person customarily responds when the aliveness of a situation is more than they have the capacity to embody; and the "edges" for that person, the risks that, if made, would most increase their aliveness. With aliveness as the fulcrum for my thinking, the task of therapy is, at essence, conceptually quite simple: to help a person to be in touch with what most deeply enlivens them, and to risk to live from it.

Again, aliveness is not an objective measure. And the one "instrument" we have that can measure what is vital—ourselves—is notoriously fallible. But it is to the degree we can understand in these kinds of terms that our ideas and actions will most deeply honor the living processes that we wish to enhance.

We might take a moment with some of the basic discriminations I make when thinking in terms of aliveness. The first, the one that all others are made in relation to, concerns that fundamental question of a person's "degree" of well-being. I want to get a sense of what I call a person's *capacitance,* the amount of aliveness they are generally able to embody.

As we saw in measuring aliveness for ourselves, such questions of quantity are in one sense simple, in others very subtle. What I am interested in is the degree to which the person or group I am working with is able to creatively engage and manifest within the very real indeterminacy of living existence. There are good secondary indicators for this quantity: a person's ability to tolerate uncertainty, to feel and express love, to act effectively in their world. But looks can be deceiving. Exuberance may be as easily a way to bounce over the top of real issues as an expression of actual vitality, emotional complexity as easily elaborate diversion as real depth. It is important to be humble in the face of the inherent uncertainties in this way of thinking, and to be aware of one's personal blind spots.

This question of capacitance is an ongoing one. It is increase in capacitance, rather than simply the disappearance of symptoms, that for me ultimately defines the healing process.

A second aspect of aliveness I am interested in discerning is what a system most commonly does when it is challenged to embody an amount of aliveness greater than its capacitance. Presented with a creative challenge, we have a number of possible responses available. If it is within our capacity, we may simply engage it. If it is larger than our capacity, but not too much larger, we may respond to the creative challenge and grow. If it is significantly larger than we can handle, we may either choose not to take part, or we may do something to decrease the ability of the situation to affect us.

This last type of response defines for me the place and purpose of symptoms: symptoms are simply patterns of response that we mobilize when the aliveness demanded of us is greater than our available capacitance. Symptoms can function either internally or externally: internally, by blocking avenues of affect—depression and rigidity are examples—or externally, by diminishing the potency of the challenge—for example, combative or undermining actions. Symptoms can be parts of an ongoing way of relating to the bigness of our world, or a response to specific kinds and amounts of challenge.

Defined creatively, we can understand symptoms variously as: 1) ways we effectively protect ourselves, 2) diversions from what is in fact most important, or 3) indications for where new growth is possible. From this perspective, no symptom is simply pathology; it is a functioning mechanism in an evolutionary whole. By thinking this way, one can discern with great detail, while stepping beyond the causal polarity of health and disease.

Rather than thinking of categories of symptoms, I like, at least initially, to frame things more metaphorically. I ask myself, what, as an image, does this person do when they get hit with more reality than they can handle?

Do they put their aliveness in a box   ,

or dampen it under a wet rag   ?

Do they respond by elevating their aliveness above

the plane of daily experience so nothing can touch it   ,

or by putting it outside themselves so no one is really

home   ?

Or perhaps they just turn down the flame of aliveness so

there is less to be vulnerable   .

We each have specific styles unique to how we have formed our lives.

As an exercise, you might explore these concepts in relation to your own life:

First, compared to others, how would you rate your capacity for aliveness? How much reality can you let in before it is simply too much? Second, what are your "styles" when a situation seems to be asking for more than you know how to manage? What do you do with your aliveness? Try letting an image form. Do you confuse it? Rigidify it? Pull the plug on it? Jazz it? Is your style different in different kinds of situations?

A third kind of change we should see in times ahead is an important kind of reframing of the therapist's relationship to the healing process. Within a causal paradigm, there are two ways we can conceptualize our role in the healing relationship: we can think of ourselves as active agents, choosing and implementing interventions, or we can describe our posture in more "client centered" terms, in response to the client's cues. In fact, neither of these postures, as extremes, are very often effective, and neither helps us very much for understanding what is really going on when change occurs.

Thinking creatively can give us both a more dynamic image for defining therapeutic posture, and a better way to understand what in fact is happening when therapy works. From a creative perspective, it is not inconsistent that one can be at once very active and engaging in one's approach, and non-directive in the best sense. For me, this is the ideal. The key in this is that the client's experience of aliveness, and our shared felt aliveness in the space between us, serve as the referents. I challenge and question, but always in terms of these quantities. "What feels most true for you there?" "What do you think is the edge, what would you need to risk to have it be most alive?"

The creative power in this kind of posture becomes most evident when one is utilizing approaches that actively tap more germinal parts of our being. All therapists do some of this; asking about a dream, having a person free associate, even just asking a person what they are feeling, all tap less form-defined dimensions to some degree. In my practice, as well, I more actively engage the symbolic through things like waking imagery, and work with the body and the emotions with movement, active expression and kinesthetic awareness. To the degree that different creative levels are actively involved, reality inherently moves beyond the New-tonian. When germinal levels of experience are engaged in an integrated way, it is obvious that identity is not a static entity that changes only as the result of an applied force. The person knows themselves first-hand as self-generating and self-directing: creative in the deepest sense.

I see my task in therapy ultimately as that of a creative catalyst, someone knowledgeable and skilled in the art of invoking and facilitating formative process. While I am concerned with where the therapy goes and how behaviors change—the "pro-ducts" of creation—my primary task is to create a context where what is possible can actually happen. Not uncommonly, what in fact becomes significant takes both myself and the client by sur-prise. The power and wisdom that is available in us when we can connect deeply and courageously is an endless source of amazement.

One final way we should find our understanding expanding concerns how we approach the whys of health, questions of etiol-ogy. We have already made a start here—with the notion that there might be larger, more creative ways to think about symptoms. A second key piece concerns the importance of being able to think in terms of systems; and not just static systems, but systems in evolution.

Thinking of the causality of dis-ease in creative terms de-mands a number of shifts in our understanding. One we have al-ready seen: the need to break down the absolute boundary between health and illness. Two other boundaries that must soften are those between cause and effect, and between the system affected and its world. Health as a creative reality is no longer the isolated func-tion of a single system, but a statement about evolving qualities of relatedness between systems.

A simple place to see the importance of these shifts is in family dynamics. Not surprisingly, family therapy principles often include post-material ideas.

To explore how we might use a creatively-based systems per-spective in addressing an etiological question, let's imagine that we are working with a child who has been labeled as in some way emotionally disturbed. Talking to the child alone, we may reach the conclusion that the diagnosis is accurate and relatively complete—it seems to explain what is happening.

But then we enlarge our frame. We bring in the family. And suddenly the significance of the child's behavior looks very different. In this larger context, what appeared before as dysfunction now looks like quite novel coping. So we change our diagnosis: what we really have is a diseased family.

But, of course, there is no reason to stop here. After the family leaves, we reflect on the case and our focus broadens further. We realize that while this family is less evolved than some, considering its societal context, it is really not doing that badly. It is surviving, even growing, and against quite difficult odds. We muse, "Maybe the correct diagnosis is that it is the society that is sick."

But, while this last analysis may add something important to the picture, it, like each before, leaves something out. Here it is that critical dimension of time. Cultures, like individuals and families, are systems in evolution. We miss the point if we judge ourselves as an end product, something that must either be perfect, or be condemned.

Clearly each of these levels of "diagnosis" has something to contribute. And each is obviously partial. To be maximally helpful as a healer—to that child, and in relation to these larger systems—we need to be able to move from an understanding large enough to embrace all of these analyses and to see their creative interrelationships. Only with this kind of vantage is it possible to effectively determine which sorts of etiologic factors are in fact most pertinent, and where the most creatively potent use of our energies really lie.

Creatively-based thinking, then, opens a number of key doors in psychological thought. It lets us conceive in ways that more fully embrace all the parts of who we are, not just those that are form-defined—behaviors and physical abnormalities—but as well those parts of experience more intimate within us. In addition, it lets us step past conceptual either/ors that conventionally fracture our thinking, polarities such as health and disease, healer and healed, and cause and effect. And it offers ways to think about psychological dynamics that have the capacity to embrace the myriad layers of complexity that are a part of any moment of truly living experience.

More living perspectives such as this will be critical for psychology's future. They are essential if our thinking is to continue to honor the evolving edge of our reality.

CHAPTER FOUR

THE LIFE-PULSE:
CREATIVE RHYTHM AND THE
REAL-IZATION OF ALIVENESS

*"There is an instinct for rhythmic relations which embraces
our entire world of forms."* —*Friedrich Nietzsche*

*"In being's floods, in action's storm,
I walk and work, above, beneath,
Work and weave in endless motion,
Birth and Death
An infinite ocean;
A seizing and giving
The fire of living:
'Tis thus at the roaring loom of time I ply..."*

—*Goethe*, Faust
("Speech of the Earth Spirit")

"It don't mean a thing, if it ain't got that swing."
—*Duke Ellington*

 Now we take formative process and begin to look at its parts. How do we best differentiate the living whole?

As I suggested earlier, it is the issue of differentiation that has thwarted or sidetracked most previous efforts at four-dimensional thinking in the human sphere. The first step in a larger conception—the recognition that what we have forgotten is the fact of interconnection—is an increasingly accepted notion. We recognize that we need to be able to think in terms of

65

wholes as well as parts: the human organism as a whole, ecosystems as wholes, our planet as a whole. The difficulty has come when we have once again turned to the question of parts. Parts are key; they are what make a model a model, something of practical usefulness. At this stage, we have tended to do one of two things. We've either dismissed the whole issue of form and difference in creation, ending up with theories which are ultimately just fancy ways of saying "all is one." Or we've connected wholes and parts with mechanistically causal systems, in the end bringing ourselves no closer to the life of things.

Differentiation in this model is based on the recognition that creation is a specific sort of four-dimensional patterning. It is not just essence or thing, but a recognizable sequence of organizational dynamics. The stages in this sequencing will serve as our parts for differentiation.

This again takes a leap. We must leave behind our customary way of thinking about parts. "Parts" in this model are not atomistic bits, but time-relative statements of relationship, organizing realities, slices through the living whole of creation. Recognizing this, we step beyond the either/or of wholes and parts. We become able to think in highly detailed terms and yet honor the essential fact of our livingness.

CYCLES WITHIN CYCLES

"The nervous system is ... a river of a million sparkling synapses—like a golden loom perpetually weaving and reweaving." —Neurologist Sir John Eccles

About fifteen years ago I taught a course called "Beach Creatures" at the University of Washington Experimental College. We would journey to beaches in Puget Sound, on the Strait of Juan de Fuca, out on the ocean coast, experiencing the miraculous microworld of tidepool, mud flat, wave-beaten shore and estuary. During the first class, I would often guide the group in a fantasy experi-

ence, asking them to see themselves as some kind of mind's eye creature in the intertidal—tunneled in the sand, hidden in the kelp,
attached to the underside of a rock. As images came to them, I
would present the predicaments that form intertidal life—gathering food, protecting one's self from being eaten, buffering the waves'
force, coping with daily rhythmic changes (from submersion in the
ocean's salty water to baking in the sun's rays), reproducing. The
students would then describe, often in shared hilarity, the phan-
tasmagorical adaptations they devised in order to ensure their
survival. As they did, I would describe real creatures that ingen-
iously met their rhythmic needs in similar ways. It was a good way
to begin: to become witnesses/participants in nature's reality of
profound improvisation.

At some point, a student would always describe the wonderful
protection provided by being attached to a rock—the life reality of
such creatures as barnacles, limpets, and mussels. All would go well
until the last question. If one is firmly part of a rock, how does one
reproduce? Nature's answer to this question never failed to bring
silence and amazement to the group. These creatures, minutely sensitive to the seasons' influence on the temperature of their fluid
world, have evolved so that all release their gametes at a single
time, sometimes synchronized even to a single tide. For a few short
hours, the primal sea is a teeming bacchanalia of new beginning.

A sense of awe would hush the group as I described this process.
Noticing this, I would often ask the group what was it about that
image that touched so deeply? Usually someone would respond that
it had something to do with cycle and rhythm, that somehow the
perfectness of rhythm in that image reached into an ancient and
powerful place.

Life is rhythmic. It is through rhythm that we recognize the
fact of aliveness: the slither of a salamander, the millisecond beat
of a hummingbird's wing, the tiny ocean waves in the fur of a many-
legged caterpillar as she ambles along. We ourselves acknowledge
and celebrate life with the gift of spontaneous rhythm. In delight,
we jump into the air; or, in careful silence, we crouch low, and with
eyes and mouths open wide and bodies breathing, we utter "oh,
ahh, come look, see," those timeless chants of wonder.

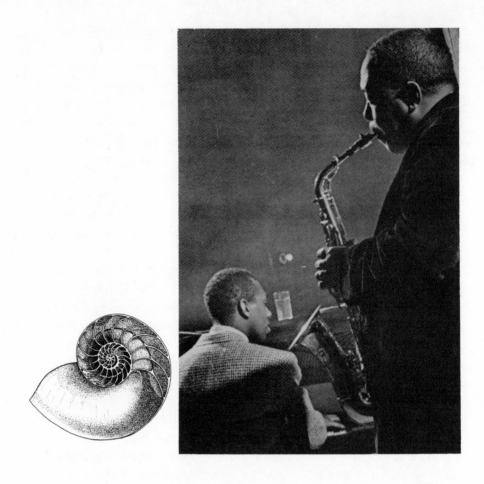

Creation speaks in the language of rhythm.

ABOVE, LEFT: *A nautilus shell.* ABOVE, RIGHT: *Music touches at multiple rhythmic levels, from sound frequency, to pulse and meter, to one's time in the rhythms of culture as a creative process. Charlie "Bird" Parker.* OPPOSITE: *What is it about a swing that gives such joy?*

CREATIVE RHYTHM

"... Rising and sinking without fixed law,
Firm and yielding transform each other.
They cannot be confined within a rule.
It is only change that is at work here."

—I Ching

The pivotal awareness for differentiation in the model is that creation organizes as a very specific sort of four-dimensional cycling. The coloration and "size" of a particular moment are an intricate function of each of the interplaying rhythms of creation that intersect at, and as, that particular point in time.

Within the model, our primary focus will be with one particular piece in the whole of nature's cycles: the rhythms of human creation. We might take a minute to look at the place of this particular kind of turning in nature's larger story.

Two layers of distinction are important. The first is between rhythms that are creative in a primary sense and those that are either secondary functions of those primary transformations or else are essentially mechanical oscillations. An example of the first of these is the rhythmic creation story of the universe as a whole. Here, four dimensions of thought are essential for any depth of understanding: a mechanical model cannot explain something coming from nothing. An example of the second might be the planet's rhythms of glaciation and volcanic activity. We can usefully think of these as parts of the ongoing process of inanimate creation, but they are far enough into the form-defined stages of that process that for most purposes three dimensions of understanding are quite adequate. Examples of the third are the cycles of day and night or summer and winter. While we symbolically associate the darknesses of night and winter with the dimension of mystery in our own turnings, each is quite fully explained by the geometry of planetary motion. In these pages, our main interest is with rhythm in its primary creative sense.

The second distinction is between levels in primary creative cycles. As I have mentioned, creation can be thought of as having

70

quantally related layers of organization. Each can be understood in rhythmic terms. For the inanimate, the first layer, this rhythm takes expression as a timeless dance between existence and non-existence. In the dance of the animate, the second layer, one partner is life, the other is not-life. Human existence is the third layer. We are different in that we are aware, conscious of our goings on. And we create—objects, beliefs, civilizations. Through the great and small rhythms of consciousness—through cycles as small as the moment or as large as civilization itself—we step forward, not just as parts in creation, but as creators in creation. This last layer of rhythm is our concern here.

One of the best ways to understand rhythm as a creative dynamic is to contrast it with common mechanical images. In thinking about four-dimensional rhythm, we can use three-dimensional images to help us—a piston, a turning wheel—but we must go beyond them so the dimension of time is fully embraced.

I think of four essential differences between creative rhythm and simple mechanical oscillation. First, while the movement of a piston is always visible as form, creative rhythm exists equally as something visible and invisible. It is creatively discontinuous, a dialogue between form and formlessness. Second, a piston's cycle endlessly repeats, returning again and again to its place of origin, while a creative cycle at once repeats and continually progresses. The disappearance of form in creative rhythm is more than a return to nothingness; it is integration, the creation of source and context for a next larger cycle of form taking. Third, while a piston's movements can be thought of as complete in themselves, this is never so for creative rhythm. Living reality is cycles within cycles of creation—wheels within wheels. Creative rhythm is vital by virtue of its existence as relationship. And finally, while our piston's movements can be objectively and repeatedly measured, creative rhythm is never fully accessible to this arm's length kind of understanding. In the big picture we are always, at least to some small degree, a part of any rhythm we might wish to study.

The idea of trying to think in terms of interweavings of a pattern that can't really be visualized may at first seem a bit overwhelming. Indeed, if we use just our intellects, our thoughts quickly become contorted pretzels. The art here is to think with all of ourselves. Attunement between rhythms is the foundation of all intelligence, be it of earthworms, earwigs, or academicians. If we can perceive from the whole of our own rhythmic natures, we should find these ideas, rather than distancing us by their complexity, enchanting us with their organic simplicity.

THE STRUCTURE OF HUMAN CREATION

"The painter passes through states of fullness and of emptiness. That is the whole secret of art."   —Pablo Picasso

How might we best think about and depict the "structure" of human creation? What are the parts in creation that includes consciousness? Sensitive understanding is essential here if one wants to use the model with real effectiveness. In this chapter and the next, I will set out the language and images that I find useful in talking about the unique structure of human creation.

Let's begin by looking at creative rhythm in its entirety. I depict it visually with a simple sine curve, like the arc etched in graphing the movement of a pendulum—but with one important modification. The bracket at the right and the horizontal continuity of the line at the peak of the curve indicate that the process, while returning to its point of origin, is also doing more than this. The origin for the next rhythm will combine the heritage of the old and the contribution of this added cycle. A purely additive phenomenon graphed like this would be: and a simple repetitive one:

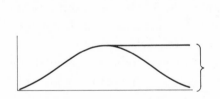

FIG. 4-1. Creative Rhythm Represented as an Amended Sine Curve

This "hybrid" image represents not merely the average of these two, but a transformational whole that includes them as parts. This image will be developed from many angles in the model, but the basic transformational architecture will remain the same.

For the length of a particular rhythm, I will use the word *periodicity*. Within this model, I will give special attention to five specific periodicities from among the infinite possibilities. These five are not unique as cycles, but they are each of special significance for us as human creatures. The first we could claim is not a rhythm at all, or we could see it as an expression of all rhythm. It is the improvisational moment: each instant to the degree it is creatively alive. The second kind of periodicity I call simply a creative event—an innovative task, a new learning, a job. The third is the course of a relationship. What these rhythms have in common is that they are short enough to be placed within the perimeter of the fourth rhythm, a human lifetime. In the model, the story of individual development—our progression from infancy, to childhood, to adolescence, to adulthood and elderhood—will be treated as simply one expression of this fundamental cyclic patterning. The fifth rhythm is the story of human history.

Let's now begin to look at parts, starting with the simplest discriminations, then moving toward more detail. Looking at the biggest picture, we can see the creative cycle as having two halves involving two quite different kinds of processes. In the first half of the cycle, the new thing created buds off from its context, gradually matures and takes its unique form. I diagram this process of creative differentiation thusly:

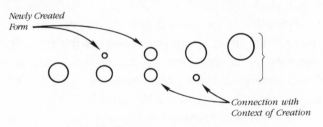

FIG. 4-2. Creative Differentiation

The entity creatively formed can be anything. In the four specific periodicities we will be looking at, the emergent entities are the newly created object, individual identity, the shared interface of relationship, and culture as form.

In the second half of the cycle, the thing created begins to integrate back into its creative context to create a new larger whole:

Differentiation Phase   Integration Phase

FIG. 4-3. Differentiation and New Integration

When I am learning a new skill, at first it is something separate and distinct. With time, it will begin to become "second nature:" I come to experience it as simply one part of a new expanded me. When a new idea arises in a culture, at first it creates excitement and controversy. Then with time it begins to become an accepted part of the culture. Neither the culture nor the new idea remain the same in this process—the idea tempers and matures; the culture creatively expands to accommodate it. We can usefully think of the first half of the cycle as the rhythm of knowledge, the second as the rhythm of wisdom: it is in the second half of the cycle that we become capable of seeing the larger picture of what we are, and have been, up to.

The dynamics of the second half of the cycle are significantly more difficult for us to grasp than those of the first. There are a couple of reasons for this. First, while the initial half of formative rhythm is creative—inclusive of generativity and mystery as well as form—its direction is toward the world of light and form. Its dynamics are for most purposes adequately thought of in terms of goals and structures, things that are concrete and visualizable. The second half of creative rhythm, in reintroducing mystery, takes us more and more beyond what can be articulated in form-defined terms.

The second reason has to do with our particular point in culture as a creative process. In the Age of Reason, mystery ceased to exist as anything "substantive." Darkness became seen as simply ignorance. The key ingredient for understanding the changes in rhythm's second half is thus, for us, at best a faint memory. We have no problem with the concept of knowledge; wisdom is a much harder thing for us to grasp—or really even to take seriously.

TWO JOURNEYS

"The individual is a path. Man only matters who takes the path."   —Antoine de Saint-Exupery

"Writing, like life itself, is a voyage of discovery ..."
                  —Henry Miller

Because the relationship of the two parts of the cycle is subtle and critical, we will take some further time with it. The mythic offers us a beautiful window into the more germinal levels of this relationship.

The mythic theme that speaks most directly about our formative nature is the motif of the journey. The stories of creation tell us about beginnings; the stories of the journey tell about how living creations grow, mature and, with time, die. Joseph Campbell, one of our most sensitive modern interpreters of myth, calls the tale of the journeyer the "fundamental monomyth." All other mythic motifs can be thought of as subthemes within it.

Told in the many-hued language of heroes, dragons and magical deeds, stories of the journey are like treasure maps: they show what we must face if we wish to live with the courage of real aliveness. Like myths of creation, they are much more than descriptions of particular events. They are templates which trace the experience of any moment that is at all imbued with the timely-timeless savor of living discovery.

All cultures contain these symbolic "developmental psychologies" in their legends and lore. Often they take the form of major epic tales. The journey of Odysseus, the Arthurian legends, and the life of Christ are those most familiar in Western European tradition. In cultures where the mythic is a living language, these tales are revered as divine records of the social soul.

The journey is also a common theme in stories written for that time in our personal lives when the symbolic is most fluent. We all have our favorite stories from the fables of childhood: the adventures of Alice in topsy-turvy Wonderland, Dorothy's trek on the yellow brick road, Hansel and Gretel's travels in seeking the home they had been denied.

To grasp the journey's deeper relevance to change, we need to examine the journey as a whole. The mythic journey is really two journeys, or perhaps two half journeys. Each viewed alone can tell only part of the tale, but juxtaposed and interwoven, they reveal the magic of the whole. There are many ways to speak about these parts. The journey is ultimately always a cycle—a going out and a return—so the two themes can be thought of as the journey's first and second parts. We could also differentiate the themes in terms of the age groups they attract: one theme seems central to young people's stories, the other seems most evocative to adults. In any case, the two themes express the juxtaposed faces inherent in any full process of creation.

In the first type of tale, the journey has a specific destination; the challenge is to reach it. The stories involve heroic conquest, good against evil, or finding a happiness "forever after"—a fair prince or princess, a pot of gold at the end of the rainbow, a wise person who knows all, a charm that grants lifelong safety. In this mode, the quest has a goal that can be visualized, and success is quite appropriately understood as simply its achievement.

In the second type of tale, the rules change. Here the destination is anything but explicit; indeed, an initial theme is often disenchantment. The protagonist pursues something only to find it empty. In stories in the first mode, we often see at least some intimation of this second kind of truth. Dorothy's wizard, for example, is a fraud, a lovable fraud, but also clearly not the keeper of the great solution.

This second type of tale is especially pertinent to our task here. It addresses that point in formative process where what can be visualized and measured will no longer suffice as referent. It speaks of the necessity of the leap, the surrender of truth as form.

The Western tale which most eloquently addresses this second reality is the venerable legend of the Holy Grail. It relates how King Arthur inspired his greatest knights, Lancelot, Gawain, Percival and others, to quest for the sacred vessel of life. When Gawain, one of the most illustrious knights, finally glimpsed the Grail, these were its shattering words to him: "You are attached to the glory of battle, and thus you cannot understand me, for I am the battle itself." To Lancelot, it said: "Your deeds, though great, have been done not for themselves, but that they could be seen by Guenevere. Thus you have missed that which all along has been in your deeds." King Arthur's message was similar: "Your acts have been great and of high ideals, but your ideals have kept you from truly knowing your acts." The true task, to which only Percival proved sufficient, was both the most simple and the most difficult: to respond spontaneously and honestly. Percival, upon meeting the suffering king who was the Grail's gateway, was so struck by his pain that he forgot the Grail. He asked of the king only what pained him so. And the Grail, with radiant countenance, revealed itself before him.

These two modes of the myth of discovery tell us several key things about living change. First, they assert the fundamental fact that ultimately one can distinguish, but not in any way divide, identity and change. The story of existence is a journey; if we are not journeying, we in essence have ceased to exist. The journey is all there is; the only question is the degree to which we are risking it.

The journey reminds us as well of the essential truth that living change is creative: it always takes us beyond certainty. Whether the journey has a concrete task—slaying a giant, reaching the top of a mountain—or whether one's destination demands the surrender of intent, there is no guarantee of success or even safety.

And finally, journey tales suggest that to understand change in its entirety, we must explore two very different kinds of dynamics. There are two kinds of stories; on the surface they have quite opposite messages, yet each is necessary if we are to tell the whole tale. To understand living change, we must know both, and see how they are parts of a single telling.

THE SECOND HALF OF CYCLE

"Well now, would you like to hear of a race course that most people fancy they can get to the end of in two or three steps, while it really consists of an infinite number of distances, each one longer than the previous one?"

—*Lewis Carroll*
"What the Tortoise
Said to Achilles"

As the second half of cycle, and most specifically the point of transition into it, has special significance in the thinking of the model, we should look at it more closely.

Truth in the second half of the journey makes a radical shift. At this point we must let go of truth as something that can be explicitly defined. The path is now paradox: there is no goal and the "goal" is all that matters. The goal at this point becomes the integrity of the creative dynamic as a whole.

This shift can be seen at the midpoint of any formative process: a creative act, a relationship, a lifetime, and, of particular pertinence here, in the creative forming of culture. To understand the full implication of this in our times, let's look first at this passage as it happens in a lifetime—the midlife transition.

The pivotal message at that time is this: if life is to continue as something creative, we must risk releasing the images we have held as absolutes. Such notions include the personal ideal we must achieve, the perfect mate, all-loving (or all-malevolent) parents, the ever-faithful friend. If we can surrender these images, the possibility opens for much deeper and more personal kinds of relationships to self, mate, parents and friends. If we cannot, our later years become more and more empty and arid. The tasks of life's second half—from this critical confrontation with one's ideals and ambitions to one's eventual meeting with death—increasingly demand a truth large enough to embrace life's ultimately mysterious nature.

A central tenet of the model is that we are just now reaching this same transition point in the creative process we call civilization. We are being challenged as a species to become mature adults.

The self-confrontation that in the past has defined movement into the second half of the lifetime rhythm, while significant, has always before been a limited confrontation. We might have needed to accept a tempering of our personal ideals, but beyond the personal sphere there were always cultural definitions of truth and appropriate life tasks. While we needed to confront the myth of the perfect other, there were always well defined roles for relating to mate, parents and friends that we could fall back on.

Today, this is clearly changing. In all domains of culturally defined behavior and belief—work roles, sexual identification, family structure, religion, notions of personal success—we see dramatic flux and re-evaluation. And it seems clear that the task is not simply to define some new formula. As I see it, we are being challenged by our own formative process to leave behind the simple answers of the cycle's first half, and to accept responsibility in the much more dynamic and creative reality of the second.

THE CREATIVE "MECHANISM"

"Out of chaos the imagination frames a thing of beauty."
—John Livingston Lowes

"After experiencing a desire to invent a particular thing, I may go on for months or years with the idea in the back of my head. Whenever I feel like it I roam around in my imagination and think about the problem without any deliberate concentration ... then follows a period of direct effort."
—Nikola Tesla

In differentiating along the length of a rhythm's periodicity, two kinds of language will be used. This duplication may cause some initial confusion, but in the long run it will allow us to capture some phenomena that otherwise might elude us. The first of these differentiates the period of rhythm according to shifts in what I call the *primary organizing affinity*. I will explain this in a moment. The second makes divisions as a simple additive sequence along a rhythm's length.

The organizing affinity is the principal esthetic that orders any part of a rhythm. The question is: which are strongest, the forces of form or those of formlessness? I think in terms of three modes, which I call simply *first, second and third space*. Implicit in the esthetic of form is another principle—that of separation: creation starts as a unity, splits into polarities and then rejoins as a larger whole. Thus, first space is the mode in which the esthetic is oneness; second space the mode in which it is duality; and third space, that in which the esthetic is defined by a new, expanded integration.

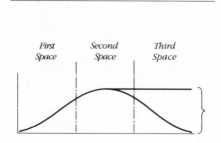

FIG. 4-4. The Creative Cycle Differentiated According to Primary Organizing Affinity

In the small rhythm of childhood, first space is the period during which the maternal bond is far stronger than the will to self assertion; the time before standing, exploring, and no-saying begin to express the child's individuality.* In the larger rhythm of a lifetime, first space is childhood as a whole, when primary identification resides with the family and the shift to wider social engagement is yet to come. In cultural evolution, it is the stage in which the individual identifies primarily with the circle of the tribe or village, and separate identity has yet to become a significant reality. In a creative event, it holds the last part of the mystery of incubation,

---

*As we shall see, each stage in a creative progression itself goes through the stages of the creative cycle.

and the first glimmerings of inspiration. It is that period when the intangible magic of germination predominates over solidity of form.

The shift into second space is defined by the transfer of emphasis to form, to identity as what can be physically defined. In human life this extends from adolescence through middle adulthood. In a creative project it is that period in which the major part of attention is with the created object. In second space, duality predominates. For an individual struggling with issues of sanctioned behavior, duality might manifest in such polarities as the tensions between moral and immoral actions, or pleasure and responsibility. For the struggling artist, duality might manifest as the gap between what can be imagined and what can be realized, or between personal satisfaction and cultural acceptance.

As we move past the midpoint of a rhythm, we feel the first resolutions of separation; as we move into third space, these resolutions become the primary reality. The integration that typifies third space is not just an addition of one plus one—for that would be a regression to origin—but a meeting of old with new that transforms both of them. On entering mature adulthood, the individual begins to see past career or family goals as ends in themselves (a separation of self and destination), and begins to experience identity in a newly enlarged and personal kind of way. Finishing a piece, the artist's focus begins to widen: the piece transforms from isolated object into something integral in its personal and social context. The piece as central object of attention in a way disappears. What is forefront now is an artist and culture each a bit more alive than before, each transformed from their relationship in this creative process.

The second way I differentiate the creative whole is to divide it at the common points of quantal reorganization. (See next page)

The four stages in the first half of the cycle I call *pre-axis, early-axis, middle-axis,* and *late-axis.* (The significance of the term "axis" will become apparent in the next chapter. It refers to the fact that each stage-specific reality is reflected in specific patterns of organization along and around the bodily axis).

In practice, these are the only stages we can speak of in generalizations. The dynamics of the second half of a rhythm are always

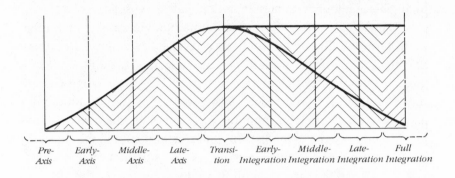

Pre-	Early-	Middle-	Late-	Transi-	Early-	Middle-	Late-	Full
Axis	Axis	Axis	Axis	tion	Integration	Integration	Integration	Integration

FIG. 4-5. The Creative Cycle Divided
According to Organizational Stages

relative to the first. The point of transition is not a single spot; it may occur at any point along a rhythm's length.

Transition may occur short of full material form for a variety of reasons. Sometimes, it is simply what is appropriate to that task. We may brainstorm some ideas for a project together, then decide it is really not worth carrying out. In rhythmic terms, we can say we took the process of creation barely into the inspirational phase—early-axis—then called it done and let it integrate back into the greater whole of our work.

Early-   Early-   Middle-
Axis   Axis   Axis

FIG. 4-6. Integration Occuring From
Early- and Middle-axis Respectively

As well, this happens as a function of the limiting realities of larger rhythms. The potential progression of any rhythm is defined by the cycles of larger periodicity that encircle it. Thus, when a people are at middle-axis in their cultural evolution, the creative projects they undertake will seem complete when they reach middle-axis dynamics (or if the project is at the leading edge, a slight bit beyond). Similarly, a young child's paintings may be ready to hang on the wall when the realities they depict are those of the most germinal stages of adult creativity. The shorter rhythms that define them have reached the edge of truth possible at that moment in the child's lifetime rhythm, and thus they appropriately then make their turn and find completion.

The basic rhythmic curve is thus more accurately depicted like this:

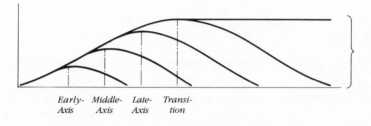

Early-   Middle-   Late-   Transi-
Axis   Axis   Axis   tion

FIG. 4-7. The Creative Cycle Depicting
Multiple Potential Points of Transition

We can speak of stages in integration, but for each axial point of transition they are different.

We can take this concept of creative stages and depict it more specifically and dynamically by including our earlier recognition of the evolving relationship of form and context in creation. This

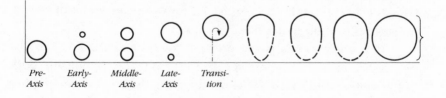

Pre-   Early-   Middle-   Late-   Transi-
Axis   Axis   Axis   Axis   tion

FIG. 4-8. Stages in the Creative Cycle

representation allows us to begin to appreciate how creative rhythm organizes as polarities. As we shall see, each stage in our formative process manifests itself as a specific sort of dialectic. Creative rhythm is the patterning dynamic through which the human whole expresses itself in the poetry of parts.

STAGES IN CREATIVE RHYTHM

> *"What animal walks on four feet in the morning,*
> *two feet at noon, and three feet in the evening,*
> *yet has only one voice? "*
> > —*The Riddle of the Sphinx*

> *"The Human being."*   —*Oedipus' Solution*

Briefly, let's go through the stages in human creation as I think of them:

The reality of the first stage is a womb world, before the appearance of creation as form. It is defined by darkness and the unbroken whole. The essential process is germination. The new impulse to form lies within, finding its first embryonic shapings, waiting for the right

Pre-axis

moment to break through the circle of the known. Here, reality is organized according to our most elemental kind of knowing, the organismic, kinesthetic language of the body.

For a simple creative act, like my working on a piece of sculpture, this is the incubation stage. I may have an inkling that something is preparing to happen, but there is as yet nothing visible. If I am sensitive, I can feel some of the primordial formings in my tissues—an attraction to a certain kind of movement, a feeling of contained shape, a gentle expanding. Isadora Duncan spoke of this as the stage of "complete suspense."

In a lifetime, this is the prenatal period and the first months of life. The unbroken whole speaks in the infant's relationship both to the mother and to itself. Even after birth, the bond to the mother is primary. The light of conscious volition, that evidence of first distinction of both self from self and self from other, is yet just preparing to awaken. The reality of the infant is an unselfconscious creature world. To feel is to act; separation is absent. Intelligence is immanent, organized as patterns of movement and sensation, Piaget's "sensory-motor" knowing.

In a new relationship, this is the time before there is anything really visible as relationship. I may have a sense in my body of being ripe for a new connecting. I may have even met the person and felt good in his or her presence. But it is not yet time for the spark of conscious attraction to ignite.

In the story of civilization, this is the stone age. For the most part, this is a reality of our distant past, though there are still a few places on our planet—in the New Guinea highlands, the upper Amazon basin, some places in the Australian outback—where bits of this primordial reality prevail. The unbroken whole is multi-layered, at once the tribe, nature and time. In primordial tribal realities, while in one sense there is individual existence and identity, in another critically important sense it is really more accurate to see the primary organism as the "body" of the tribe. If someone breaks a taboo of sufficient importance to get them expelled from the tribe, it is not uncommon for a person to simply go off and die. To be excluded from the womb of the tribal whole is tantamount to nonexistence.

In this first cultural reality, truth and nature are a single thing. Tribal deities are simply the faces of animate nature: the wind, the mountain, bear, eagle, coyote. Health represents one's degree of harmony with this living nature. Knowing is one's connection in, and as, it.

Time, as we think of it, is just coming into existence during this cultural period. The dance of reality is regarded as taking place in an eternally cycling present; each generation and each turning of the seasons are seen as reenacting a timeless story.

Early-axis

It is in the next stage that we tend to feel most directly the magic and numinosity of the creative. This second stage begins with the new creation stepping forth from mystery into light. With this dramatic transmutation comes an important change in how we perceive and conceive our reality. Truth shifts its primary mode of expression from the kinesthetic to the symbolic: it speaks most eloquently in myth and metaphor.

In my working with chisel and stone, this is the stage of first inspiration. What was before only a faint quickening is now born as visible possibility. This is the time for playing with images, for feeling where in those images the deepest power lies, for trusting that power and risking giving it first form.

In a lifetime, it is here that we enter the magical world of childhood. The curtain opens with the first luminations of individual consciousness. The opening scenes tell the story of a dramatic sequence of first acts of distinction from nature, source, mystery, mother: the making of first words, standing, the beginning of mastery of bowel and bladder. This new reality is organized according to the laws of imagination. The critical work of the child is its play, exploring what might be in images of "let's pretend."

In intimacy, this part of the story begins with the first blush of real attraction. It is a magical time, filled with tentative first touchings and fantasies of the possible. Still largely strangers, we connect more as numinous symbols than as simple mortals ... a fair princess, a handsome prince.

In the story of culture, we are now in the time of the early civilizations: the sacred splendor of ancient Egypt; the golden grandeur of pre-Columbian Meso-America—the Incas, Aztecs, Mayans; the epic drama of early Olympian Greece. In more recent times, powerful examples of this mythic stage of culture can be found in places like Tibet (prior to the Chinese invasion) and Bali or Java (prior to the tourist invasion). This is the time of culture's amazing first flowerings, elaborated in a symbolism that establishes for itself a flawless authority.

Something more than just nature—spirit, essence, magic, beauty: no single word quite does it—emerges as the new referent for truth. It takes its most direct expression mythically, speaking through epic tales and complex pantheons of major and minor gods. This is a time of rich artistic potency. Art is much more than decoration at this stage; it is the most immediate language for depicting the workings of reality.

Middle-axis

At the beginning of the third major stage, there is easily a feeling that something is being lost. The stage before was magical and numinous. Now the predominant feelings are as often as not struggle and conflict. But this stage is in no way a decline or disaster. The moment of first inspiration is indeed wondrous, but it is only the first small step along the road toward fully realized creation. After inspiration comes necessary perspiration.

In this stage, truth shifts from the mythic to the domain of the moral and emotional. The work progresses by virtue of guts and heart. We face the very real facts of limitation and human differences, and we face too the temptation to retreat from them by hiding in the child's world of golden fantasies or by forgetting that we ever had dreams.

Struggle here is twofold: at once a struggle against limits in the world of form, and a struggle to establish limits so that the newly created form will not fall back into formlessness. By the middle of this stage, the power of the newly created and the power of the context of creation are experienced as equivalent. Reality exists as an isometric polarity between at once opposite and co-conspiring forces.

As a sculptor, it is here that I first have to grapple with the fact that there are limitations both in what a piece of stone can be made to do and what my talents will allow me to do with it. I easily rage against these limitations; and in the struggle that ensues, two things happen. What I am capable of grows. And the original vision matures, reflecting both the fact of limitation, and the esthetics and values of the new reality that my participation has demanded I enter. The new shapings are less ideal, less magical, but they are more solid, and more expressive of the journey as a human story. Katherine Mansfield has spoken of this as the time of "terrific hard gardening."

In a relationship, this is the stage at which we begin to deal with the fact that we are separate people—that we have real, everyday needs, real imperfections, and real human differences. The glow of the honeymoon period, the other as dream image, necesarily fades somewhat. It is easily a very emotional time, in which feelings vacillate with remarkable rapidity between love and antipathy. This is when we begin to grapple with issues of control and territory—when we face the question of who takes out the garbage.

In a lifetime, this is adolescence: heroic, but also awkward and often troubled. The innocence of childhood must be left behind in the need to challenge external limits and establish inner ones. Emotions are strong. The adolescent's reality is morally ordered, composed of extremes of black and white. As with any such isometric polarity, the extremes are at once in mortal combat and in total collusion. Adolescent reality is one logical contradiction after another. Independence is a major issue; yet, while assumptions of dependence can provoke fierce self-assertion, acts that on the surface express independence always at once function to guarantee parental response and involvement. While non-conformity is highly prized, it takes its most common expression in the rigid conformity of cliques and fads. The prize for taking on the struggle with these paradoxes is the experience of identity, of self as created form.

In the cultural history of the West, this stage spans the period from the Roman Empire through the Middle Ages. Again in this period, it easily seems that something critical has been lost. We often speak of the middle years of this period as the "Dark Ages." If we wish to find cultures with significant amounts of this dynamic in present times, we need only look to the places on the globe where struggle seems ever-present: Southeast Asia, the Middle East, Central and South America.

But again, while there is loss, it is not regression. These are times of struggle, but also ones of significant advances. In Europe we saw politically a new solidification and complexity of organization under kingly rule. In religion we saw the church step forward as an organized power and the new establishment of formal moral codes. Economically we saw the linking of territories by roads and the establishment of formal structures of commerce.

As with this stage in the other periodicities, reality speaks in polar isometrics. Social structure is feudal: landed lords and conquerors above, serfs and the conquered below. Thought is similarly split. With the ascendance of monotheism, truth becomes based upon one pivotal question: whether an act belongs to the sunlit domain of the good, or the opposed realm of murky evil.

Late-axis

The last stage in creative rhythm's first half takes us into the reality of finished forms. The new creation moves ever more fully into the light. We have made the major choices; what remains is to perfect, to put in final order. Truth in this phase of the whole is material, defined in terms of things that can be seen and measured.

In my work with that piece of stone, this is the stage of finishing and polishing. I have risked engaging with what wants to take form through the work, and risked grappling with the major practical tasks involved in the realization of that form. The work now sits before me as a "piece." My concerns here are with its surface layers—with detail, with finished appearance.

In love, this is the stage of increasingly established relationship. The major conflicts of being together have been sorted out. We have reached general agreement on the roles and boundaries of the relationship—who does what, how and when we are together. For the most part, we've stopped asking what our relationship will be, because it now is. Our attention shifts from big issues to details, and away from the relationship to concerns in the outer world. We assume that things in the future will be minor variations of what we have finally achieved.

In a lifetime, this is young adulthood. The major tasks of establishing identity as individual existence here find completion. Our twenties and early thirties are the one time in our lives when in any good conscience we can say we know who we are. Identity is that which we've become as form. "I'm a psychiatrist. I live in Seattle. These are my friends. These are the things I like to do." We tend in this stage to regard the major developmental aspects of life's forming as largely finished, to see the future as simply an additive extrapolation from this known form. "I'll ascend the ladder of success in my profession. I'll raise my kids. I'll reap the rewards of my labors."

In the evolution of culture this is our most recent age, the technological age, the age of reason and invention. Here we see morally defined truth increasingly giving way to a new atomistically and causally defined reality, a physical reality of individual actions and their concomitant reactions, a human reality of individuality, intellect and achievement. The Age of Reason offered the image of a profoundly new kind of assurance: All could be elucidated and resolved through the light of objective understanding. The form was set; what remained was simply to finish and polish, and culture and knowledge would be complete.

Point of Transition

As we move through this stage, we begin to approach the point of transition into the creative rhythm's second half. While the journey may have seemed complete with this last, most form-defined of stages, in truth we were barely approaching its mid-point. The new object of creation (the piece of sculpture, individual identity, relationship as thing, culture as structure and invention) has reached realization, but it has yet to be tested. The second half of the rhythm is marked by the reconnecting of what has been newly created with the personal and social source and context of that creation. The previously necessary amnesias begin to fade, and we become increasingly able to see the new creation within the larger process of which it is, and has always been, a part. This is not a process of addition or averaging, but of integration. In creative integration, the two parts with each stage become more; each changes and grows through their meeting.

Integration

I finish that piece of sculpture, and am confronted by the easily disturbing realization that the journey of its creation is in truth far from over. The piece has yet to be placed in the world. What will happen to it? Will it do good, harm, be ignored, be destroyed? Too, it has yet really to be placed in me. I begin to recognize that this process, which I have looked upon as the creation of a thing, is at the same time a process of creating myself—and that there is much yet to happen in that process. In the first half of creation, the conscious object of creation was the stone; in the second, increasingly, it is me as my aliveness.

In love, we easily regard the finding of workable roles as an endpoint in the establishment of relationship. But in fact, we find if we hold to this reality of relationship as form, what was before exciting more and more loses its juice. Interaction becomes habitual, mechanical. We start to feel like objects to one another.

Actually, what at first seemed the endpoint in the journey of love, is just a beginning. The new challenge is to see beyond the material reality of roles, to meet each other as fully living beings, to move past a reality of two halves that make a whole, to find ourselves and each other as dynamic whole beings. Commitment defined by form gives way increasingly to a shared commitment to what is mutually most true and alive.

In the story of a lifetime, transition is the point of passage into mature adulthood. The primary themes for the first half of this story have been knowledge, skill and self-definition. At the midpoint, we begin to see that what we have become able to say about truth and identity is only a small part of the picture. Big new questions present themselves, ones that can't be answered in the old ways, questions of purpose, of life. "Yes, I'm a therapist. But to what degree is my being a therapist really a statement of me?" "To what degree does it reflect what I most deeply believe?" "More than this, even if it succeeds in expressing what is most intimate in me, what about its effect in the world? Does it really have much?" "If I were really courageous, if I were really committed to what I know as truth in myself, would I somehow do my life differently?" The central themes in life's second half are meaning and interrelationship. Truth shifts from establishing identity as form, and from the either/or of self versus world, to a third referent: the living relationship of self with self, and self with world.

The parallels between our present time in cultural history and this point in these smaller turnings are striking. If we look at the new questions being raised in our time, we see that they too are questions of context and meaning, questions of life in a complexly interconnected and ever-evolving world.

On the following page, I've briefly summarized the dynamics of these creative stages.

THE CREATIVE CYCLE

CREATIVE STAGES:

Pre-Axis	Early-Axis	Middle-Axis	Late-Axis	Transition	Integrative Stages
○	○	○	○	○	(nested ovals)

MAJOR PERIODICITIES:

A Creative Event -

Incubation	Inspiration	Perspiration	Finishing & Polishing	Presentation	Becoming "Second Nature" (Integration of the Newly Created Form into Self and Culture)

A Lifetime -

Prenatal Period & Infancy	Childhood	Adolescence	Early Adulthood	Mid-life Transition	Mature Adulthood (From Knowledge to Wisdom ~ Integration of Self as Formed Identity with the Ground of Being)

A Relationship -

Pre-Relationship	Falling in Love	Time of Struggle	Established Relationship	Time of Questioning	Mature Intimacy (Relationship as Two Whole People ~ Marriage of the "Loved" and the "Lover" within Each Person)

The History of Culture -

Pre-History	Golden Ages	Middle Ages	Age of Reason	Transitional Culture	Integral Culture (Larger Meeting of the Form and Context of Culture)

PAST AND PRESENT

"Bowed down then preserved;
Bent then straight;
Hollow then full;
Worn then new;
A little then benefitted;
A lot then perplexed.
Therefore the sage embraces the one
and is a model for the empire."
—Tao Te Ching
(trans. D.C. Lau)

It is popular today to equate ideas at the edge of emergent thought with the thinking of Eastern philosophy and certain aspects of Western mysticism. There are important parallels—but also critical differences. A moment with these similarites and differences can help put the model's concepts in sharper focus.

The parallels are indeed fascinating and significant. We see strong kinship with the concept of aliveness in such notions as the Tao in Chinese thought, or the "suchness" of Zen Buddhism. The image of the Alchemical "marriage" is a powerful metaphor for the creative relationship of opposites. And references to the cycles of things are timeless parts of what William James called "the perennial philosophy." The ancient *Heart Sutra* of Mahayana Buddhism beautifully expresses the paradox of the moment as rhythm with the simple phrase "form is emptiness and emptiness is form." God, for Meister Eckhart, was that which "becomes and disbecomes." The *Baghavad Gita,* holy book of the Hindus, offers this description of life as rhythmic pattern: "Through my nature I bring forth all creation and this rolls around in the circles of time." And perhaps most succinctly, from the tongue of Po-Chang, an early Chinese Zen master, comes this simple formula: "When hungry eat, when tired sleep—that is enlightenment."

Why these similarities, and what are the critical differences? I see two reasons for the similarities. First, these notions come from relatively early stages in the evolution of culture, or in the case of Western mysticism, times somewhat later, but from people who gave primary homage to the power of the unformed. Thus they embrace major parts of what we have forgotten, and need to remember, if we are to think in more integral ways. Second, these notions come from times when the second half of the creative journey was not only acknowledged, but treated as a highly respected part of reality. In a material reality, it is very hard to understand movement beyond form as anything but degeneration; on the other hand, in early cultural times, because mystery is recognized and valued, the integration phase in creative cycle is given great importance. A simple place to see this difference is in how we regard old age. In early cultural stages elders are venerated, and the second half of life is treasured as a time when attention can be gradually turned from daily concerns to things more of spirit and wisdom. For us, old age is often seen as little more than being "over the hill." So these early notions also have parallels with new paradigm thought because they come from times where the common truth is that reality is cyclic (and these being early-axis rather than pre-axial times, cyclic in a generative, rather than simply repetitive, sense).

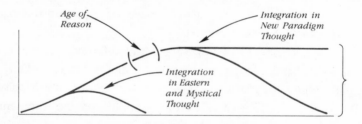

FIG. 4-9. The Creative Relationship of Eastern Thought and Western Mysticism to Fully New Paradigm Thought

But these early notions are different from those needed for fully four dimensional thought, and the differences are marked and critical. Their source is simply the flip side of what makes these early notions such rich teachers. While these notions are extremely articulate within the realities of the early parts of creation, they cannot deal at all adequately with the critical dynamics of creation's later, more form-defined stages. Because of this, while they can help us explore certain aspects of the essence of things,* when it comes to questions that have their base in the very real complexities of our modern world, they are necessarily very limited. People who miss this essential difference are embarrassingly prone to making naive assertions in the name of enlightened thought.

This fundamental difference can be seen mirrored in a number of different ways. One is simply how, in these more ancient notions, the emphasis is always ultimately on the esthetic of unity. The one and the two are both parts of reality—and indeed from within the isolated realities of these times, these parts seem equally balanced—but, from a larger vantage it is clear that interconnection ultimately has the last word. Put in the framework of the model, while distinction and unity are both present and in creative relationship, this relationship is happening within the ultimately unity-biased esthetic of first space.**

Another place these differences are mirrored is in how outer reality is perceived. In Eastern and mystical traditions it is given at best secondary significance, not uncommonly viewed as a temptation to be avoided, or even as something with no real existance of its own, something projected from within. Fully new paradigm thinking no longer posits material reality as a separate, objective "out there," but neither does it return to this earlier mode

---

* One could argue that such notions are limited as well for understanding essence, for essence from a four dimensional perspective is not something abstracted from form, but a function of the entirety of the creative reality that manifests as a particular form.

** A common error among people who equate Eastern and new paradigm thinking is to confuse an essentially unitary paradigm with integral understanding. The use of words like "holistic" or "transformational" always has me check to be sure such an error is not being made. The essential recognition is that while unity may appear to resolve polarity, in fact it does not. Since the fundamental either/or in reality is between unity and duality, a bias toward unity is quite specifically choosing one pole over the other. An essential part of understanding in the model is recognizing that unity and integration are qualitatively different concepts.

in which physical reality borders on being simply illusion. In the ideas developed here, the material is an integral and explicit part of reality as a creative process.*

One further way to note this difference is in the emphasis in Eastern and mystical writings on the repetitive rather than the generative aspects of rhythmic phenomena. Reality "becomes and disbecomes," is "bent then straight." To the degree a perspective has a first space esthetic, the foreground idea in describing creative rhythms will be how each cycle follows a timeless course. (In pre-axial reality, creative rhythms are closed circles: the tribes attunement to turning seasons, the baby rocked in mother's arms. In contrast, by the peak of transition, there is almost no repetitive element: progress in modern, technological times is thought of as essentially a linear vector.) In the thinking of the model, the repetitive and the uncharted aspects of reality are equal parts in the creative patterning of change.

A simple way to frame the difference between new paradigm and mystical thought is in terms of the relative balance within each between the dimensions of space and time. The thinking of earliest reality perceives from a paradigm of essentially no space and all time; it is the timeless, reality cleansed of form and linear time, that is "real." In contrast, in isolatedly form-defined thought, the dimension of time is essentially absent. Eastern and mystical traditions are useful because they embrace the dimension of time; their definite partiality comes from the fact that they are able

---

* Modern spiritual philosophies and psychologies that are in effect recreations of these earlier perspectives in contemporary clothes deal with the relationship between essence and form in a number of ways. They may simply focus on inner reality and pay little attention to other things. Or they may actively denigrate more form-defined aspects of experience, depicting such things as technology, institutions, and traditional leadership, as in and of themselves problems (carried to its extreme, the rise of civilization itself becomes a mistake). Or in contrast, they may give the material great importance, but see essence as existing in causal relationship to it, and the key to controlling it—"We create our own reality"—the word create here less a recognition of the generativity of experience, than a reversion to, and elevation of, magical causality.

to address the dynamics of the more spacially-defined in only the most rudimentary ways. Our challenge is to think in fully four-dimensional terms.

CREATIVE RHYTHM AND THE HEALING RELATIONSHIP

"A poet's rhythmical energy is, I should say, the index of his psychic energy."
　　　　　　　　　　　　　　　　　　　—Theodore Roethke

"The crucial question of communication's mechanisms at work within human systems seems to lead to the recognition of resonance as perhaps the most important basic principle involved."
　　　　　　　　　　　　　　　　　　　—Erich Jantsch

"Interest in the changing seasons is a much happier state of mind than being hopelessly in love with spring."
　　　　　　　　　　　　　　　　　　　—George Santayana

I have spoken of health as the capacity for aliveness, of symptoms as what happens when more aliveness is demanded of us than we know how to embody, and of healing as any connection which increases living capacity. The idea that aliveness is just another name for the moment as cycle within cycle of creative rhythm allows us to understand each of these concepts more dynamically and in more detail. We can begin by simply substituting the word "rhythm" for "aliveness." Health then can be expressed as the total available rhythmicity of a system, symptoms as what happens when a situation demands more creative rhythm than is available, and healing as any connection out of which the capacity for creative rhythm increases.

The concept of creative rhythm richly enlivens phenomena that easily seem cut and dried when thought of in causal terms. For example, the link between the aliveness of client and therapist that lies at the root of the healing relationship becomes much more vital when we recognize that it is not just a static thread, but a dynamic play of rhythmic processes. Our colloquial speech hints at the pulsatile nature of human connection. We speak of two people who are in agreement as being "in accord," or of getting "attuned." The implication is that real connection is a phenomenon of resonance.

Connecting with the experience of a client is not unlike listening to the sound of a musical instrument. At the simplest level, we attune to the notes that are played and sense how they move us as other resonant instruments. Our commitment is to sharing our experience of these notes and what might allow them to be most rich and "vibrant." This connecting is simple, and yet infinitely complex and multi-layered. A single tone in music is not just one frequency, but a profound interplay of changing harmonic relationships.

The periodicities of rhythm involved in a healing relationship range from the most gross to the most subtle. The degree to which we really hear a person—beyond mere listening—is a function of the degree to which we engage each periodicity not just mechanically, but as something living. Life's longer rhythms—age, occupation, marital status, interests—become poignantly vital meetings along the slow curves of life's unfolding when they are personally engaged. And within these, we encounter life's shorter rhythms—a particular friendship, a period of schooling, an illness, a day's event—all the way to the complex micro-rhythms of momentary feelings, images and sensations. Our connectedness lies at the dynamic intersection of all these rhythms.

When this connecting is effective and new growth occurs, we see expanded freedom and potency in our rhythms. We often use rhythmic words when speaking of our aliveness. We say something "rings true," referring to its sense of rightness. We say that an experience is "stirring" or "scintillating," or that a person who seems especially vital looks "vibrant."

We are healthy when we are in touch with our rhythms and risking to live them. At an everyday level this means knowing the what and when of our needs—sleep, companionship, adventure, solitude, whatever—and forming our lives so these things can be honored. In the musical metaphor, the therapeutic alliance is a shared commitment to honoring these notes and how they wish to be patterned.

We can now approach in somewhat more depth the essential question of differentiating health, of understanding the various ways that we feel and behave. The recognition that formative process is patterned, that is, has stages, is what will let us use the model to think with real detail about health.

In the last chapter, we began exploring how we might use a creatively causal perspective to think diagnostically, first by addressing the question of capacitance, and then by using simple metaphors to depict what happens in a particular system when aliveness over-challenges capacitance. The concept of creative rhythm lets us fill out these observations. With this next step, three new variables become important.

The first variable is how far a person (or group) has moved developmentally in each of its major rhythms? For an individual, this includes the creative stage of the person's culture, their stage of growth within the rhythm of a lifetime, and where they are in other relevant periodicities (career, a particular relationship, a particular creative project).

Each stage brings with it both a new reality and an expanded capacity for aliveness. An adult who is fully alive has more potential rhythmicity available than does an equally healthy child. And a person fully alive in modern times is similarly able to deal with greater challenge and uncertainty than would someone living during the Middle Ages.

The second variable is the "how big" of rhythm. Two people can be at similar developmental stages, but with significant differences in how much creation each stage can embody. Two children might be the same age and at the same place developmentally, and one might simply be more competent and more able to deal with challenges than the other.

The third variable is the "shape" of rhythm. The myriad of rhythmic events that make up our being combine to create a specific patterning that people recognize as us. I call this rhythmic "signature" a person's *primary energetic*. While we each move through similar developmental stages, our experiences in these stages can be very different. As a result, the stages can, for different people, be colored with distinctly different hues. And there can be significant differences between people in the relative "size" of different stages. Two people may be developmentally at the same point and have similar overall capacities for aliveness, but be quite different in what stages carry the major part of that capacity. The wheel of life is never quite round. It may have quite marked "lumps" and "flat spots."

It is this last variable that differentiates personality style in the model. Basic patterns of difference are seen as expressions of the parts of the formative whole that each person preferentially embodies.*

Variables in the primary energetic include both the stage or stages where that person tends most to "live," and the relative balance between the polarities that define that stage.

I will develop these notions in detail in later chapters, but a few quick illustrations might be of value at this point. Profession can serve us as a crude shorthand, since people with particular personality styles tend to be drawn to certain kinds of endeavors.

For example, artists, particularly visual artists, commonly have personalities with strong amounts of the upper (more manifest) pole of early-axis (magically-ordered causality). Working with children is a classic kind of activity for a person who lives a lot in the lower pole of early-axis (the generative context for inspiration as form). People like generals, labor bosses and school principals—people concerned with questions of control and right and wrong, commonly carry the major part of their aliveness in the upper pole of middle-axis (morally-ordered causality). People who would identify themselves as part of the "working class" are likely to live more in the complementary lower pole of middle-axis. People whose endeavors are concerned with the abstract and

---

* The particular qualities derived from these stages are relative to the stage of cultural evolution. For example, a middle-axis personality style, as we will speak of it here, is biased toward middle-axis, but within the context of a fundamentally late-axis reality. What we would see here is very different from that of middle-axis in culture. The music of a country western singer and a medieval bard both have strong concerns with right and wrong, but those of the country singer speak from a decidedly more material and appearance ordered reality.

material—with ideas and money—generally carry a lot of their aliveness in the upper pole of late-axis. The people in culture who are most visibly, "on stage"—actors, media people—will commonly carry a major part of their aliveness in the lower pole of late-axis.

When a system's capacitance is insufficient to an impending challenge, what we will see is intimately related to the system's primary energetic. In times of crisis we tend to shift to those parts of the whole where we have the greatest capacity. If the challenge is too great, we then use ways of reducing the challenge characteristic to that stage. "Symptoms" are simply exaggerrations of normal polar dynamics.

For example, a person who carries a major part of their aliveness in the upper pole of early-axis might respond by ascending further within this reality and "space out." Someone who inhabits most strongly the lower pole of middle-axis might drop further and become passively controlling or oppositional. A person who lives most in an upper pole, late-axis mode might start to intellectualize.

Symptoms work by lifting us above, or by dropping us below, the plane of experience—or, as we shall see, moving us outside of or within the primary layer of experience. The natural polarities become separated in an exaggerated way, and there comes to be isolated identification with a single pole in the dynamic. This cuts off the creative connection both between the primary parts of self and between self and world. The vital uncertainty of life as creative interface becomes replaced by the safety of predictable and familiar absolutes.

The symbols that emerge for people in doing dream and image work often speak quite directly of the rhythmic nature of creative existence. Frequently they do this by talking in the language of the mythic journey. Sometimes such images depict concerns of the journey's first half—inspiration, struggle, achievement. Other times they are more specifically integrative, concerned with issues of maturity and perspective.

Following is an exercise that uses the motif of the journey as a mirror for reflecting on one's life as a creative progression:

Find a relaxed place and close your eyes. Begin by letting an image come that somehow speaks of the "terrain" of your life right now. Is it like a mountain meadow, a desert, a busy streetcorner, a deep woods? Then notice your path in that terrain. It might be a broad roadway, or a trail that is barely visible, a tunnel under the earth, a trajectory through space. Take the time to notice the quality of your movements along that path. Are they spritely, hesitant, seductive, aggressive? Let yourself step into the image and become these movements. Take time with the experience, letting both the image and the movement fill out. What seems most important to this experience?

When you have had enough time to take this in, turn around in your image and note where it is you have come from. How was the terrain and your presence in it different earlier in the journey? What does it bring up in you to notice this?

Then turn around and look toward the future in your journey. What seems to lie ahead? What do you sense you will need to bring to this next part in the journey for it to be most deeply alive for you?

In examining these images, ask yourself how they relate to these concepts of rhythm. What do they say about the stages you presently occupy in the major periodicities? How do they reflect your primary energetic—the parts of the cycle that for you are most "home?" What do they say about your "edge" as a formative being—the parts of the creative cycle you are risking to more fully become?

CHAPTER FIVE

THE POSTURE OF HUMAN CREATION: RHYTHM AND ERECT BEING

*"Poetry indeed seems to me more physical than intellectual
... I could no more define poetry than a terrier can define a rat
... we both recognize the object by the symptoms it evokes in
us."*
                                                    —A.E. Housman

*"The bodily appearance of man speaks to us of... a particular
relation to heaven and earth. Man cannot fly nor need he
crawl. He is neither bird nor worm. He stands and moves
upright, based on the earth but pointing towards heaven."*
                                    —Karlfried von Dürckheim

"The body does not lie."

                                                    —Martha Graham

 Up to now, we have been addressing formative process abstractly. But we can't really speak about the rhythms of human creation without also speaking of the unique shape given to human creation as these rhythms incarnate as human form. We need to go beyond thinking about creation in a general sense to asking what it means to be creation from, and as, the unique posture and perspective of embodied flesh-and-blood sentience.

What is the relationship of the physical body to human rhythm? Very simplistically, we could say the body is the container in which these rhythms occur. The container is important to consider because its shape and size influence the sorts of rhythms that will be available to us. But, to be at all complete, more than this three-dimensional sort of explanation is needed. The dynamics of creative rhythm do not just happen within the shape of the body; they are intimate parts of the process through which the body takes its shape. In a four-dimensional reality, psyche and soma are not separate causal entities. They are integral elements in the mechanism of self-creation.

Our task in this chapter is to begin exploring the unique shape of human creation: who we are as bodies in the largest living sense.

Where are we to this point? The themes thus far examined describe an organism something like an amoeba with awareness. We have a picture of a vital creature, a growing creature, a creature that is capable of innovation within the periodicity of its lifetime. But it lives in a world with just one basic kind of rhythm. For this creature, in and out, left and right, up and down are all pretty much the same thing. Its reality is spherically symmetrical.

What are we as living form that goes beyond the reality of bacterium or amoeba, or beyond that of ourselves at the moment egg and sperm first meet? Besides the ingredient of consciousness, three factors seem most immediate.

First, and most obvious, we are not made up of a single cell, but of many. Just as our outer lives are complex, so are our inner bodily lives made up of complex relationships of boundary and rhythm. Second, our cells are not arranged simply in a large mass, but in a specific shape. We are elongate, and the cells at different points along the "tube" of the body are differentiated for interrelated, but unique, functions. Third, and of special importance here, this "tube" is usually oriented in a specific relationship to gravity. One end makes a connection to the earth's surface; the other reaches perpendicularly away from it.

Since it is within, and as, this shape that human rhythm organizes as human reality, we can learn a lot by examining the four dimensional architecture of human posture and just how the major rhythms of human experience relate within it.

A CREATION STORY

*"From the roots the sap rises up into the artist, flows through
him and his eyes. He is the trunk of the tree. Seized and
moved by the force of the current, he directs his vision into
his work. Visible on all sides, the crown of the tree unfolds in
space and time. And so with the work."*

—Paul Klee

*"We are but a noble meeting of spirit and nature in their
yearning way to each other."*

—Thomas Mann

The story of erect being is a powerful chapter in biology's epic of creation and journeying, and well deserves a moment of our attention.

This tale begins millennia ago in the tides and currents of the sea, our first home being the rich, salty embryonic fluid of the ocean's ebb and flow. Our structures were simple. We took our nourishment as breath from the medium we lived in. Our course was determined by the ocean's pulse.

Then, in a major step of differentiation and form-taking, we became two cells instead of one, then four and eight. With time our movements changed from a passive drifting with the sea, to active movement within her. These movements took us not only to the far reaches of the oceans, but to their ample borders.

The next chapter began with a simple yet momentous movement. We slithered up onto the ocean's banks, venturing from our watery womb onto solid soil. Our relationship to our source became quite different. In the fluid world of the sea, our source was our entire surround. But on the solid earth, we were *upon* it, our bellies pressed against moist soil, backs open to a totally different world— a world of sun, of wind, and of creatures which, by virtue of what before was simply size, now took on an added dimension, height.

105

With much time, and after many changes of form, came a further, most heroic, change: Sitting back on our haunches, balancing on the ends of our spines, we lifted our forelegs from the ground. We *stood*. For the first time in our relationship to nature, the axis of our being was placed not against the earth's body, but perpendicular to it.

The implications of this last act were immense. From our new loftier altitude, we could see far out over the horizon. Feet earthward, heads looming toward the heavens, to grow was now to grow up. Our forelimbs, once simple means of locomotion and support, were now free to develop as subtle implements of action and expression in our world. And our soft underbellies, before safely juxtaposed to the earth, were now at the forefront, statements of a dramatic new potential for shared creation in social interaction and for truly personal intimacy.

The act of standing is both phylogenetically and ontogenetically a critical achievement for the human organism. It is a bipolar movement, both a lifting up of form and awareness, and a pressing

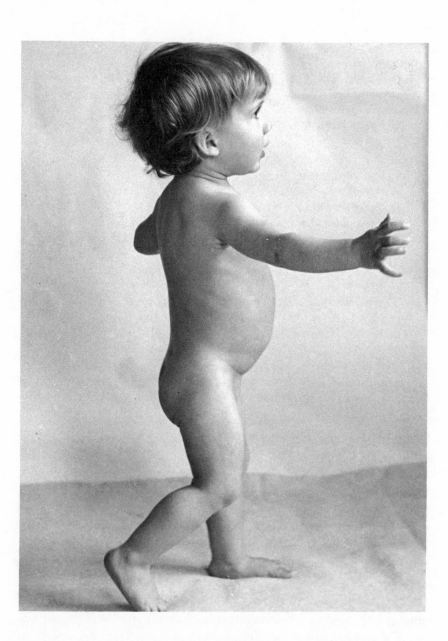

*downward of ground and nature. Organization becomes
increasingly differentiated as movement from and toward an
elongate axis. [A fourteen-month-old child learning to walk.]*

THE SYMBOLOGY OF ERECT BEING

*"The 'this' is also 'that.' The 'that' is also 'this'… that the
'that' and the 'this' cease to be opposites is the very essence of
Tao. Only this essence, an axis as it were, is the center of the
circle responding to the endless changes."*

—*Chuang Tsu*

*"I remember the giants born at the dawn of time,
 And those who first gave birth to me.
 I know of nine worlds, nine spheres covered by
 the tree of the world,
 That tree set up in wisdom which grows down to
 the bosom of the earth."*
—The Voluspa *A part of the Scandinavian* Eddas

*"And behold a ladder set upon the earth, and the top of it
reached to heaven, and behold the angels of God ascending
and descending on it."*
—Genesis 28:12

It is easy to see how erect posture affects the physical acts of
our lives: how we move, what we can accomplish. More subtle is the
pivotal place of erect being in other aspects of experience: the psychological, the emotional, the spiritual.

The language of myth offers a useful glimpse into some of this
more inclusive importance. Elongate vertical symbolism is ubiquitous in myth, and is commonly responded to as if it lies at the very
fulcrum of truth. It manifests in the vertical aspect of the Christian
cross and in the uplifted architecture of cathedrals. We see it in the
erect ritual stones of pagan Europe. (It is said that in early Ireland
the high chief was chosen by the stone at Tara, which roared to
announce its decision.) Many of the richest examples of such symbolism use the motif of the tree: plants such as flowers and trees are
among the few other living forms that differentiate principally
along a vertical axis of symmetry. We might use this ancient motif
of the tree of life to help us begin to connect with the generative
significance of our unique posture.

One especially rich image comes from ancient Scandinavia, and the Eddas, cosmogonic tales first put into writing in the tenth century. Standing central in the stories of the Eddas is the great tree Yggdrasil. Yggdrasil resides as a living passage between three planes of reality. Its trunk is said to lie in Midgaard—the middle realm, the domain of mortals. Its branches rise into what is called Asgaard. This is the domain of the heavenly gods. In the farthest reaches of Asgaard resides an eagle and the god Odin, his throne set in the topmost branches so that he may survey the realms below. The base of the tree divides into three great roots. These roots descend into a tripartite underworld. In this underworld we find Aesir, the realm of the subterranean gods; Hel, the realm in which the dead reside; and a third domain for the giants who inhabited the world before time's inception.

Over 4,000 miles and 1,000 years away, among the Arunta, an aboriginal tribe of central Australia, their creation story tells of how their creator, Numbakula, fashioned a pole from a gum tree. After completing the world, he climbed this pole up into the sky, where he then came to reside. A nomadic people, each Arunta clan carries a gum pole like the one in the story on all their journeys. They determine the direction for their travels by holding the pole, and following the way it points. Several years ago, one Arunta clan lost hold of their pole while walking along a cliff. It fell and was broken. After drifting about aimlessly, the entire clan stopped, lay down near the pole, and died. Their connection to source and knowing had been lost, the axis of their life severed.

In *Black Elk Speaks*, John Neihardt's richly poetic description of an Oglala Sioux medicine man's life, the life tree is a key symbol in Black Elk's initiation into shamanhood. The initiation follows a severe fever in which Black Elk has dreams and visions that disturb and excite him. The old medicine man asks that Black Elk tell them to him, and sits with the young boy as he recounts what he has seen. He was carried off to the center of the world, and met the powers there. They appeared as old men, and as horses from the four quarters. The medicine man tells Black Elk that he must enact this dream for the tribe, and that it is a calling. Black Elk does this, sharing in story and song the primal image of four great

Axial images have a central place in the language of the symbolic.

ABOVE: *Arunta tribesman climbing the sacred pole.* BELOW: Tree of Death and Life. *Miniature by Berthold Furtmeyer. 1481.* OPPOSITE, TOP LEFT: *The* kekayon, *a tree of life image from the Javanese shadow theater.* OPPOSITE, TOP RIGHT: *Snakes symbolizing cosmic energy coiled around an invisible lingham. India. c. 1700.* OPPOSITE, BELOW: Black Elk at the Center of the Earth. *Drawing by Standing Bear from* Black Elk Speaks *by John Neihardt.*

horses, bringing from each of the cardinal directions the powers he would need: first, a bow, the power to destroy; second, an herb (the day break star), the power of understanding; third, the pipe of peace; fourth, a branch from the tree of life which sprouts leaves and singing birds. A grandfather says of the tree: "Place it at the center of the hoop of nations, and by your powers you shall make it blossom." Black Elk was to be holy man for his people through times of war in which his powers for balance and meaning would be deeply tested.

Such images are endless. In the Javanese shadow theater (epic ritual enactments of the Ramayana central to Javanese spiritual life) the first image is that of the *kekayon*, a life tree with a doorway in its trunk. In the mind's eye, participants enter the *kekayon*, and travel through it to the various levels on which the mythic drama unfolds. On the other side of the world, there are the glyphic vertical poles—displaying ritual figures like eagle, bear, salmon, and frog—carved by natives of the Northwest American coast. Hindu myth has the banyan tree; in Islam, the tuba tree sits atop the holy mountain, Qaf. The tree of knowledge of the Old Testament grew the fruit whose eating expelled the primal pair from the womb world of the Garden of Eden, setting them on the journey of embodied existence. The Mayan tree of life was Yaxche, and the Mayan universe was imaged as the circle of earth on which Yaxche stood. In modern western culture, the Christmas tree and the Maypole are the most obvious holdover from more overtly mythic times.

Clearly these symbols touch something of immense significance, for a people to find something so powerful in a plain wooden pole that they would mistake it for life itself and assume its ending was their own; or for a small tree (like that in Black Elk's vision) to be taken not only as a message from one person's soul, but from the soul of an entire race. But what is it these images represent? I see them as mythic monuments to the core of human creation, resonant expressions of the innermost layerings of our unique rhythmic natures. They are expressions, from myth's germinal position in creative reality, of the critical place of our unique posture in defining and creating human truth.

THE ARCHITECTURE OF HUMAN RHYTHMICITY:

*"The so-called core of solid fact which forms the point of depar-
ture as well as repose, is deeply embedded in me: I could not
possibly lose it, alter it, disguise it, try as I may. And yet it is
altered just as the face of the world is altered, with each moment that we breathe."*

—*Henry Miller*

In the last chapter I presented a way of diagramming the patterning of the creative cycle:

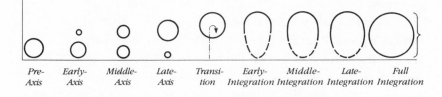

| Pre-
Axis | Early-
Axis | Middle-
Axis | Late-
Axis | Transi-
tion | Early-
Integration | Middle-
Integration | Late-
Integration | Full
Integration |

FIG. 5-1. Basic Structure of the Creative Cycle

Here we will begin to look at how this simple progression organizes
in, and as, our bodies.

To do this we need to differentiate between two kinds of
movement in creative rhythm. The amoeba extends and recollects
from a single point of organization. We have rhythms that extend
and recollect in a similar way from the axis of our being. And we
also have rhythms that organize along that axis. These two kinds
of creatively cyclic organization are intimately related, but their
forms and functions are very different. And in these differences lies
a major part of our uniqueness as human organisms.

I will speak of rhythmic movement toward and away from our
core as our *horizontality*, and will use the term *verticality* to talk
about rhythmic organization along the length of the body.

The horizontal defines our identity when we risk reaching out
to express and give form to our worlds. It is also who we are when
we open and receive, risking to let ourselves be moved. Related to

113

both of these is the way we create our boundaries, and the way we structure our interactions across these boundaries. The horizontal spans everything from the self as marrow and heartwood to the farthest point that, with flesh, voice, vision or idea, we can reach. Stated most simply, our horizontality is who we are as a dialogue with, and as, our worlds.

Our ascending and descending rhythms are equally simple and familiar. We can see in each day's journey a reenactment of the vertical poetry of our biologic creation story. In morning we emerge from the dark, oceanic world of sleep; we meet the dawn, and stand. We enter the world of light to observe, discern, and with the unique higher capabilities of humankind, affect our surroundings with hands, voices, and ideas. In the evening we return in sleep to the dark primordial womb, and swim in the timeless images of our origins. Every time we risk taking a stand, or let something excite or inspire us, every time we engage the challenge of a new pinnacle, we feel the rhythm of ascent. Every time we risk questioning, losing control, or releasing into our depths, we enact a small death and descend. Our verticality is who we are in dialogue with ourselves and the cosmos.

These movements are more than just causal vectors. Expression is more than just push and pull; surrender is more than just giving up. Real rhythmic movement is transformational, creative. With each real ascent or descent, what arises or returns is more than it was before. Similarly, in each real act of expressing or receiving, the figure who emerges from the engagement is always in some sense a new being.

For depicting horizontal rhythm, our simple polar diagram is sufficient. All we need do is to turn it on its side so that the body axis becomes the point of departure and return, and to remember that the content of rhythm is different depending on what part of the axis it relates to.

For depicting vertical rhythm it must be modified somewhat. For all but the most creature-level dynamics, vertical rhythm is bipolar. For example, if we look closely at the act of standing, we see that it is really a bidirectional act of extension. With feet, legs and pelvis, we press downward, pushing into and off the earth's surface. With those parts above our bodily center of balance—chest, neck, head—we lift upward into our erect stance. Our vertical rhythms are elongate from a central point of organization.

The following diagram depicts this elongate bipolarity:

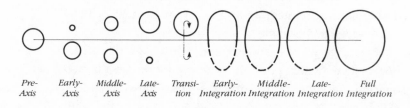

Pre- Axis	Early- Axis	Middle- Axis	Late- Axis	Transi- tion	Early- Integration	Middle- Integration	Late- Integration	Full Integration

FIG. 5-2. Creative Cycle in the Vertical

Some rhythms organize principally in one area of the body. But the rhythms we will be most concerned with—major creative tasks, lifetimes, the evolution of culture—are large enough that the whole body clearly takes part in their turnings. In them the vertical and horizontal aspects of rhythm organize for all intents and purposes as a single pulse. We can derive the basic contours of this pulse by putting our depictions for vertical and horizontal rhythm together. For now, simplifying the body diagrammatically to a crude ellipse, we get something like this:

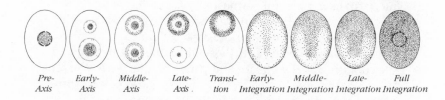

Pre- Axis	Early- Axis	Middle- Axis	Late- Axis .	Transi- tion	Early- Integration	Middle- Integration	Late- Integration	Full Integration

FIG. 5-3. Vertical and Horizontal Rhythms
Together as a Single Cyclic Progression

---

* The outer line represents the surface of the body—but a very specific body: the adult body in our present stage of cultural evolution. We are playing with cycles within cycles of integrally related rhythm, and thus what comprises the primary "surface" is always relative. For example, in a

As illustrated in this diagram, in step with the stages of creation, the patternings of aliveness evolve through a specific bodily sequence. In the first half of rhythm, the edge of aliveness extends vertically and moves outward from core to periphery; above separates from below, within from without. In the second half of rhythm these polarities reintegrate and a new increment of potential aliveness is added to the whole.

Later, we will examine in some detail the fine structure of this progression. At this point, however, a more general and more personal approach will do to clarify it. Try the following:

> Play for a moment with the experience of being a young infant suckling at mother's breast. How do you feel the bodily reality of this? (We tend to experience pre-axial reality in two ways, as a connecting into a place deep in the center of us, or if we immerse ourselves deeply in that experience, as a fluidly undifferentiated creatureness that infuses both our own tissues and our experience of the world around us.)
>
> Now try being a five or six year old child. When you recapture the living sense of that age, where does your aliveness focus from? (In the magical, child-reality of early-axis, aliveness organizes most as a dance along the core of one's being. There is some separation now, a sparkling curiosity in the eyes set in relation to a deeper connecting from the belly, but distinction is still as yet diffuse. Interfaces have a playful permeability.)
>
> Then imagine being an adolescent; see how your bodily reality changes. [With middle-axis dynamics, our aliveness organizes one layer further out, in the soft tissues and musculature, in the "heart and guts" of things. A clearer differentiation of "Above" from "Below" also takes form: we feel the upper pole of middle-axis reality most in the facial musculature, in the chest, and in the shoulders ("shouldering a burden"), and the lower pole in the intestines and abdominal musculature ("having guts").]
>
> Then try walking around the room as a young adult, and see how both your body, and the room and its contents,

---

child, early-axis dynamics may infuse nearly the whole body, not just the more inner realms. The situation is similar for people in early cultural stages.

change. (In late-axis, aliveness organizes even closer to the surface. In addition, the center of balance in the body shifts upward. This is the finishing and polishing stage: appearance becomes ever more important. And truth becomes more and more our ideas about things and the fact of physical objects around us.)

If it is part of your experience, you might also explore the body experience of mature adulthood and elderdom. (While from the isolated perspective of late-axis culture we often find it hard to think of these parts of one's life bodily in terms other than loss, in fact, if we live them vitally they are times of rich bodily connection. Here we begin to make room for all these layerings of bodily experience. One aspect of the acceptance that increasingly permeates later years is this process of bodily reintegration.)

BODILY REALITIES:

"I wish you to consider, finally that all the functions which I attribute to this machine, such as... waking and sleeping; the reception of light, sounds, odors... , the impression of ideas in the memory; the inferior movements of the appetites and passions... ; I desire, I say, that you consider that these functions occur naturally in this machine solely by the disposition of its organs, not less than the movements of a clock."

—*Rene Descartes* Discourse on Method

"... the soul is not more than the body... and the body is not more than the soul."
                                              —*Walt Whitman*

At the most basic level, we can think of the bodily aspect of the stages of creative rhythm as simply a progression through a series of psychophysical locales. But this is just a first step in understanding. If you were sensitive in doing the preceeding exercise, you will have noticed that each stage involved not just different locations of bodily organization, but very different feeling qualities in the body and different senses really of what a body is.

Each stage in creative rhythm defines a specific experience of self and world. One part of that experience is who we are as bodies.

117

At different points in the creative cycle we experience who we are bodily in markedly different ways. As I see it, the body in its largest sense, the four dimensional living body, is the greater whole of these more time-specific bodily realities.

How different these "bodies" are can at first be hard to fathom. When we are alive in a particular layer of our bodily selves, that layer defines our experience of our bodies as a whole. Thus, living within the late-axis/transitional body of present cultural times, we think of all of the body, not just the surface layers, in the language of anatomy and physiology. Even though we pass briefly through the other realities in any creative cycle, it is hard for us to think about them. The cultural body imposes a necessary amnesia.

I first began to grapple with these differences when, as a psychiatric resident, I invited a Chinese acupuncturist to come and speak to our resident group. Traditional Chinese medicine is fascinating in that what the healer "sees" is so different from what we Western doctors are trained to observe. To conventional anatomy and physiology, acupuncture meridians make no sense; there is nothing there to dissect, and no obvious relationship to the structure of the nervous system. The only "physical" evidence we can come up with is small conductance changes at the skin surface. Yet acupuncture has very specific effects, and not just in the context of Chinese culture.

At one point in our talking, the Chinese doctor turned to one of the residents—who by now had several large needles stuck in different parts of his body—and commented that the resident had a severe imbalance in his liver. We asked questions about this and a significant thing became apparent. The Chinese doctor was not talking about the liver as we knew it—this largish organ that we evaluate by palpation and liver function tests. The resident's liver function values were perfectly normal. But the doctor was clearly concerned about something in the same general locale, and the comments he made about symptoms made sense to the resident. Interestingly, when we talked about the liver in anatomical terms, it seemed as puzzling to this Oriental doctor as his energy notions did to us. It was not just that we had different concepts: in an important sense we were looking at different bodies.

Understanding the early bodily stages with any completeness requires a significant transcendence of our cultural amnesia, but at this point in-depth understanding is less important than a general appreciation for the overall fact of sequence in bodily evolution. Here then let me outline briefly the bodily realities of the creative stages as I understand them, and as words can describe them.

The body of pre-axial reality we could call variously the creature body, the body as nature, the body as mystery, the body as oneness. This is the body of the child in the womb, or the infant held close in its mother's arms. It is the body of the tribesperson—hunting, gathering roots, ritually dancing to images of creature deities. The feelings are ancient, diffuse, animistic, instinctual.

The body of early-axis reality we could again call by a number of names: the body as essence, the spirit body, the meditative body, the magical body. In culture, this is the energy body of the acupuncturist or that of the yogi with his prana and chakras. It is the subtle body of the mystic. In the cycle of a lifetime it is the dreambody experience of the child's world of symbol and make-believe.

The middle-axis body is the emotional body or visceral/muscular body, what I have referred to as the body of "heart and guts." Here we are outside the body as essence; this reality is much more personal, impassioned. But it is clearly not yet the body of anatomy. Neither "heart" nor "guts" can be found by dissection. This is the body of medieval medicine. Health then was defined by the movement of visceral humors—black bile, blood, phlegm—each with a specific emotional coloring. Words like "phlegmatic" and "choleric" are remnants from that time in the cultural body. This is as well the body of adolescence, torn in its passions and emotional allegiances.

The body of late-axis is that with which we are most familiar. It is the body of the assurance of young adulthood. It is the body as a thing: something we try to keep from getting old, that we feed, clothe and exercise. It is the body of "looking good." From a more upper pole perspective it becomes the body of medical textbooks, Descartes' body as machine.

And we can speak of a further kind of bodily reality, the integral body. At the midpoint of any cycle we begin to embrace the larger whole of these bodily realities. At midlife, if we have the courage to leave behind the dream of perpetual youth, we find that we begin to "listen" to our bodies in new ways. Often at first it is just a grudging resignation to the fact that we are getting older: if we don't listen to what our bodies say we hurt ourselves. But, if we move very far into rhythm's second half, this listening becomes much richer. We begin to notice that when we listen, what we hear is much more than just physicality. More and more it speaks of the whole of us: increasingly, the body is also the soul; we discover that wisdom is simply the ability to hear the body in its full sense, to recognize when responsiveness embraces all the parts of who we are.

In theory, in this era we should be seeing the beginnings of a similarly more integral understanding of the body in the cultural sphere. And this is clearly happening. In this century we have seen the rigid morality of Victorian times give way to a much less stern posture toward bodily pleasure. More recently we have seen a growing movement in health care toward people being more knowledgeable about their bodies and responsible in their well-being. We have seen growing curiosity about approaching the body in other than just physical ways: interest in Eastern body disciplines, in psychotherapy that acknowledges the body, in the psychology of illness. And we find growing interest in physical activities such as athletics and dance, with an increasing awareness of the richness to be found in approaching them not just as achievement—using the body—but as renewal and communion—things done in, and as, the living body.

ERECT BEING AND THE HEALING RELATIONSHIP

"Yes, Yes
that's what
I always wanted,
to return
to the body
where I was born."
—*Allan Ginsberg*

"It seems to me that I have found what I wanted. When I try to put all into a phrase I say, 'Man can embody the truth but he cannot know it.'"

—W.B. Yeats

"When my creative energy flowed most fully, my muscular activity was always greatest."

—Friederich Nietzsche

Thus far I have defined health—at its most fundamental—as our capacity for aliveness, and aliveness as the creative turnings of formative process. Here we have simply added the fact that human creation creates from, and as, a specific sort of organic patterning.

The connection which heals, whether it is within a person or in a healing relationship with another, is a connection through our living bodies. When fully grasped, this can be a most powerful kind of understanding.

Health is a statement about how we as bodies pattern the rhythms of experience. Much of this is reflected in direct physical clues. For example, we can notice how we pattern our breath: is it full and easy, or do we in some way distort it, use only part of the whole—hold it up, hold it in, force it out, force it down? Another good indicator is the "quality" of our tissues and how that quality is different at different bodily locales. For example, the skin over areas that we are embodying most deeply tends to be warm and vital, neither chronically flushed nor clammy. Similarly, where muscle tissue is most alive, we find it neither chronically tensed nor flaccid, but in that state of vital potential we call "tone."

Earlier we explored the concept of the "shape" of a person's fundamental energetic as a useful tool in differentiating health. While helpful enough in the abstract, the value of this concept becomes much more striking when we are able to understand it as a statement about the living body. A person's energetic "signature" manifests both vertically and horizontally with each propagation of living formativeness, with each new creative development. In asking how people pattern their aliveness, vertically I am asking at what levels—head, belly, heart, pelvis—that aliveness seems most easily manifested. Horizontally, I am asking: Is this a person who connects easily with surface concerns, but is not as in touch with things close to core? Or perhaps it is the opposite, perhaps this individual can bridge easily from essence to essence, but has trouble dealing with the more mundane details of daily life.

Symbols that speak metaphorically of psychophysical organization are common in dream and image work. Often they speak very graphically of where in the living whole attention is needed: an image of a church with a broken spire; a tower with a crumbling foundation; a tree with a sick old man living among its roots.

In the following clinical example, we see an issue of vertical rhythm explored simultaneously with image, movement and idea. The theme is a common one: the resolution of a split between two different qualities of being.

> Several years ago I worked with a woman in her mid-forties, I'll call her Jean, around issues of trust and the simple ability to feel pleasure in her daily life. The effect of early sessions could be seen in some relaxation of a posture that had before been held hyper-erect and a softening of her need to keep control over herself and her surroundings.
>
> During one important session, Jean described a recent period when she had felt depressed. The image that came to her—one of deflation and lack of direction—was of a large jellyfish. I asked her how she escaped from that posture when she needed to. She shared the painful, but to her necessary, image of her spine as a tall metal coat rack. While she seemed distressed by the rigidity of the image, her words were clear and moving: "What I know is that I would rather be a coat rack than a jellyfish."
>
> I asked her to get in touch with her body and to sense what kind of movement would be most fulfilling to her at that moment. "I'm tired of holding myself up; I want to lie down," she said. She did this, and for quite a time just lay motionless, letting her body release. As this happened, she began to be aware of subtle feelings reflecting a new quality of movement. "You know," she said "my spine is beginning to feel less like a coat rack and more like a snake. I like that. I'd certainly rather be a snake than a coat rack."

After some time, I invited her to explore the experience of standing from this image. I asked her to go only as far as she could while maintaining the quality of the snake in her spine, returning to the ground whenever she lost it. The feelings, images and memories that arose in this process were the opening for her of a rich vein of transforming experience.

As she worked with these experiences in her daily life, Jean gradually began to learn bodily and emotionally how she had more options than just rigidity or collapse. She began to find in herself a place from which it was possible to feel soft but also strong, a place from which she could give up her rigid control yet not be out of control. From this more living place she could see how pleasure and identity could co-exist, indeed that they were necessary for each other's existence.

Similar kinds of images speak within all of us. The following exercise invites you to use some of the more germinal parts of your creative nature to begin exploring patterns in our own psychophysical organization. Further on, we will return to the feelings, images, and sensings that you have accessed here in examining in more detail various aspects of psychophysical development.

Begin by standing in a posture that is comfortable for you, and close your eyes. Turn on your mind's eye, and imagine before you a very large old mirror. This mirror is not your usual mirror, but a magic mirror. In it, you can see yourself reflected as anything you might ask: if you wished to see your mood mirrored as a kind of weather, it might show you, and you would see a clear day by the ocean, a storm—whatever would be an appropriate metaphor. If you wanted to have your feelings toward someone mirrored in the form of a creature, that too would be possible. Here what you will ask is to see yourself reflected as a kind of plant, bush or tree. Give the mirror very specific instructions: you don't want to see an idealized image, but a reflection of precisely who you are at this moment.When it feels right, allow an image to come ...

Notice all you can about the image. Does it have branches? Leaves? Flowers? What are they like? How would you describe its midregion? What is the quality of the soil around this plant—moist and boggy, dry, rocky, dark and fertile? What kind of pattern do the roots make in the soil? Are there other plants or animals in the vicinity?

What qualities in your plant are you most conscious of: its height, fullness, color, or needs (for things like water, sunshine or protection)? What parts of the plant seem most distinct? What parts are less fully delineated?

Looking at the plant, what feelings are you aware of in yourself? What happens in your body, to your breath, to how you are holding yourself? Take time to draw your plant. As you do so, jot down observations of bodily sensations, emotions, and memories that come up as you represent the different parts of your image.

What does the image seem to be saying to you? About your relationship to yourself? About how you live in your body? About your relationship to your world?

As a therapist, I am interested in my own ongoing bodily dynamics at least as much as I am those of the client. I keep sensitive to how I am connected in different parts of myself, what is happening with my breath, my overall quality of aliveness. The connection that heals, whether it is within a person or in a healing relationship with another, is a connecting through our living bodies. While I may have many ideas about what is going on therapeutically, I know that ultimately it is my body as a whole that is the sensing instrument. And while my interventions may often take the form of words, I know that those words can have the power to catalyze real change just to the degree that they are statements from the whole of me.

To this point, our inquiries into the nature of health have been weighted strongly toward the psychological. But if our interest is in understanding the human organism as a living whole, then we should clearly address not just soma's role in psyche, but also the relationship of mind and body in physical health.

Within usual thinking, there are only two options in thinking about the relationship of mind and body: either they are separate and causally related, or they are one and the same. These are reflected in our two rather polarized perspectives on the nature and significance of the mind/body relationship in physical well-being.

124

In the traditional medical model, psyche and soma are separate. In both ancient practices and modern "alternative" or "new age" perspectives, with their emphasis on the unitary, the physical and psychological are assimilated to one another. In early systems of medicine, the same causative situations—disharmonies (with nature, with or between spirits, with or within the social network) are seen working in dis-ease within each; in contemporary spiritual models, just as we create our own realities, we create our own illnesses.

The model suggests that the fuller truth is larger than either of these kinds of views. From a more integral perspective, psyche and soma are neither distinct nor analogous: they are creatively connected dynamics existing in an ongoing, evolving relationship.

The capacity to step beyond the late-axis absolute separation of mind and body is one of the critical frontiers of modern medicine. The trick is to do this without simply falling back into old causalities. We will need to learn to address the body within all its realities, and to make subtle discriminations about when the perspectives of different realities have the most to offer: when the greatest good can be done by putting on a cast or giving a medication, when what is most important is to delve into environmental factors, when the richest rewards are to be found in engaging the person at more emotional or spiritual levels.

The fact that mind and body are never fully separate is readily apparent if we are at all sensitive. Clearly, every psychological process is also physical: some "body" is doing all that thinking and feeling. We can measure all sorts of physical events: neurotransmitter levels, brain waves, breathing patterns, skin conductivity .... And clearly, too, the opposite is true: every physical process is psychological. When we get ill, a plethora of related feelings arise. Some are general, coming simply from the experience of incapacitation; others are specifically related to illness dynamics. If we look deeply, we can almost always find that there is something an illness process seems to be trying to "say," some sense in which it is a kind of bodily language.

And it is just as clear that psyche and soma are not the same. While bodily changes are always a part of psychological change, changing just our beliefs requires minimal bodily interaction; and even when there is major growth, the bodily changes that occur are generally subtle. Similarly, while bringing the psyche more into the picture in physical medicine offers exciting new possibilities, it is also the case that much of illness can be treated adequately quite oblivious to it.

At this point, the most immediate challenge in working with the relationship of mind and body in physical health is to be humble to how little we actually know. The amnesias that have led us to see mind and body as wholly separate are just beginning to fade. We wait in suspense as the curtain begins to rise on the drama of our discoveries.

THE MODEL: PART II
A PLAY OF POLARITIES

This first section has given us an overview of the model's core themes: First, that human reality is creatively ordered. Second, that it differentiates in a predictable sequence of creatively related polar dynamics. And third, that this sequence organizes in a particular shape by virtue of our unique stance in the world.

The remainder of the book takes this basic creative architecture and examines it at a next level of detail. The section that follows focuses on the subtleties and interplays of creative differentiation; the final section on the dynamics and issues of integration.

In looking more closely at the first half of the creative cycle, we will engage it from several different perspectives. We will take one chapter to examine it from the viewpoint of each of the polar directions it organizes in relationship to: vertically, from the "Below" and the "Above;" horizontally, from the "Within" and the "Without."

CHAPTER SIX

THE GROUND OF BEING: NATURE, SOURCE, AND MYSTERY

"All matter is created out of some imperceptible
substratum ... nothingness, unimaginable and
undetectable. But it is a particular form of nothingness
out of which all matter is created."

—*Paul Dirac*

"The spirit of the valley never dies.
This is called the mysterious female.
The gateway of the mysterious female
 is called the root of heaven and earth.
Dimly visible, it seems as if it were
 scarcely there,
Yet use will never drain it."

—*Lao Tsu*

"The most beautiful thing we can experience is the
mysterious."

—*Albert Einstein*

 We start our detailed exploration in the vertical, and within this, with the more unformed half of experience. In the earliest parts of creation, the unformed, the "nothing" that is at once something, is reality's predominant force. As creative cycle progresses, it manifests in the vertical in evolving permutations as the lower pole of our experience.

It is our time-relative relationship with, and as, the unformed in creation that defines the "ground" of our being. Through this relationship we experience the fact of our generativity, and the "foundation" of our existence. When this relationship is in timely balance, it imbues life with such essential qualities as belonging, playfulness, passion, and compassion.

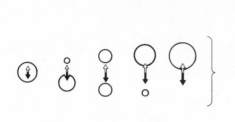

FIG. 6-1. Ground as Creative Relationship in the Vertical

This part of our exploring will require particular subtlety, for several reasons. First, what lies at essence in our concerns here is inherently invisible. Rather than pointing directly, often the best that will be possible will be to say: "Go look over there behind that tree, behind that rock; it's there if you can be open to it." What can be seen and described in usual terms will necessarily be the smaller part of what is significant. Second, this is precisely that part of us from which our present culture is most distant; its manifestations are at best discounted, often given no acknowledgement at all. In a form-defined reality, truth is form; nothing is ... well, nothing. And third, as with each polar tendency, how we experience the ground of our being is not a single thing, but an evolving dynamic that takes us through a sequence of markedly different experiential realities.

THE FEROCIOUS BEAUTY OF MYSTERY

"We work in the dark—we do what we can—we give what we have. Our doubt is our passion and our passion is our task."
                                                        —Henry James

As it is in the earliest stages of creation that the unformed speaks with greatest fullness, this seems the appropriate place to begin. To our minds in present times, the themes that manifest from this part of things easily seem a most strange and disconnected array of topics. Indeed many seem decidedly contradictory: emptiness and fullness, wildness and silence, mystery and clarity, the ancient and the instant, the child and the elder, death and birth, freedom and belonging. But the contradictions are a function of our point of view. From within the reality of these times in creation, we know these themes as parts in a single kind of telling.

Let's turn briefly to languages and times where this part of us is held more closely:

"As a poet I hold the most archaic values on earth. They go back to the late Paleolithic; the fertility of the soil, the magic of animals, the power-vision in solitude, the terrifying initiation and rebirth; the love and ecstasy of the dance, the common work of the tribe."

—Gary Snyder

The magic doorway into this part of us is the courage to surrender known form ...

"And we say, 'Our god is an erotic wind and shatters all bodies that he may drive on' and if we remember that Eros always works through blood and tears, destroying every individual without mercy—then we shall approach this dread face a little closer."

—Nikos Kazantzakis

In this surrender there is a wildness, easily even terror ...

"I became aware that I was losing contact with myself. At each step of the descent a new person was disclosed within me of whose name I was no longer sure and who no longer obeyed me. And when I had to stop my exploration because the path faded beneath my steps, I found a bottomless abyss at my feet, and out of it comes—arising I know not from where—the current which I dare to call my life."

—Tielhard de Chardin

At once, if that surrender is risked, there is a peace. There is knowing too—but a very different kind of knowing from the knowing of objects ...

"When energy, form and matter are present, but not yet separate, we call this chaos ... if one looks there is nothing to see, if one listens there is nothing to hear ..."

I Ching
"Chien"

There is a feeling here of being in some mysterious sense very near the source, the everything and nothing ...

"from spiralling ecstatically this
proud nowhere of earth's most prodigious night
blossoms a new born babe.
... not one heartbeat of this child; nor shall
ever prevail a million questionings
against the silence of her mother's smile
—whose only secret all creation sings."

—e.e. cummings

There is something here that nurtures ...

"Now, in this waning of light,
I rock with the motion of morning;
In the cradle of all that is
I'm lulled into half-sleep
By the lapping of water ..."

—Theodore Roethke

Something that heals ...

"Nature will have clefts where I may hide, and sweet
valleys in whose silence I may weep undisturbed ... she
will cleanse me in great waters and make me whole."

—Oscar Wilde

Something eternal ...

"The land is a mother who never dies.

—Maori saying

And something that challenges us to new beginning, to risk the birth of the possible ...

"The way is empty, yet use will not drain it.
Deep, it is like the ancestor of the myriad creature."

—Lao Tsu

The unformed is the secret shared by the very old and the very young. It is the place into which we die and from which we are born. It is from here that we know the eternal magic of things. In ancient Celtic myth it was the Tir-nan-og, the land that existed before the beginning of time. Winter rituals often pay homage to its irrational latencies. In medieval Scotland, the week of winter observances was marked by the banishment of the abbot, his duties assumed by one chosen from among one of the town's beggars and idiots, appropriately dubbed the "Monk of Unreason."

SEPARATION

"The word for universe is Au-Ki. It means heaven and earth. The naming of man cannot take place until the two have separated."
—From a Sumerian creation myth

"In the mother's body, man knows the universe, in life he forgets it." —Jewish Saying

"The egg that just sits there is nothing, it is destroyed by the sperm to release new form."
—Jean Huston

Right relationship to, and as, the unformed contains an essential irony: while it is the source of life, to live we must leave it behind.

In the rhythm of a lifetime, we hear the voice of this essential severance in the child's first utterances of the primal "No." A child's "no" is a statement made with the whole of its being. It is made as if life depended on it; and ultimately, life does. Life is creation: it stays life only to the degree that we find the courage to let it manifest.

The child's "no" is an all-embracing statement. It is much more than just an utterance to parents. It is a statement to ground, to origin, in all its manifestations: to nature, to the unconscious, to biology. It says, "I—as form, as something of the light, as something distinct—exist."

This spoken "no" is but the latest in an essential series of such statements of separation. At the moment of conception, the unbroken whole of the egg is shattered into life. At birth, the infant leaves its womb world behind and takes first breath. In standing, the toddler places itself in juxtaposition to mother nature and defies the essence of nature as absorbing mystery—gravity. In learning mastery over bowel and bladder, it makes a similar statement of separation from the primitive creature self of instinctive biology.

This no-saying is, importantly, not just one-way. If the parental bond with the child is a healthy one, separation is equally important to all involved. Separation is not just causal, but a creatively causal dynamic. Healthy parents may be nostalgic over the loss of their child's infancy, but they also ultimately are excited by these changes, and facilitate them. Similarly, the child as an organism becomes more by virtue of being "mastered" by the budding powers of consciousness. Indeed, nature demands that this happen. We see both sides portrayed in myth. The hero takes the initiative in slaying the dragon. But Adam and Eve must be expelled from the garden.

The symbology of primitive ritual often powerfully depicts the critical importance of severance. At early moments in the human story, the gravitational inertia of origin is so strong that passage beyond the child world can take place only through the most intricate preparation and the ritual participation of everyone in the tribe.

A male puberty rite practiced until recently by a tribe in New Guinea illustrates the immense ritual potency necessary for this severance. It began with the creation of a special ritual dwelling and the choice of the one young woman from among those approaching puberty who was most beautiful and ideal. Both the young woman and the initiates would go through weeks of special preparation: fasting, learning ritual stories, isolation.

On the day of passage, the tribe would gather early around the ritual dwelling for chanting and dancing. After several hours, the boys would arrive, their bodies specially painted, and stand in a line beside the open dwelling. The young woman then came forward, and after a special ceremony, lay down at the dwelling's sacred center.

One by one, to the sound of chant and drum beat, the boys would step within the dwelling. At the ritual instruction of the shaman, each would sexually enter the young woman, then withdraw. The last boy-man to do so was the youth revered as the most strong. With the "divine couple" in ritual embrace and the tribal circle in slow dance around them, the shaman would step back. Before the frightened eyes of all the initiates, he would push aside the log that was the dwelling's principle support. The heavy timbers would fall, crushing the holy pair at the moment of consummation.

The critical message of separation was now a part of the initiates' tissues: "You must step forward; there is no return. The passageway to childhood has closed."*

This dynamic of separation is critical in every creative process, and it is essential not just at the first appearance of distinction, but as an evolving voice throughout the stages of creative transformation. The distinctive qualities of the different formative stages can be thought of as simply expressions of different creative balances between the oneness of origin and the twoness of separation.

Our bodies reflect this progression during any formative activity. In first space we experience as a bodily whole. In second space, there is always a sense in which we make our tissues "other," place the organismic aspects of our bodily selves at arm's length. Then, as we move into third space, our bodily experience becomes again more integral, but now expanded to include the aliveness of our new capacity.

The sequence comes beautifully alive for me in the process of learning a new piece of music. On first hearing a piece that really moves me, my whole body resonates and dances with it. Together we are a first space. It is a beautiful feeling, but I know that if I wish to learn the piece, I must give up this particular sort of

---

* The importance of the dynamics of severance are most obvious in male psychology. Gender distinction from the mother has a central and early role in the establishment of identity. But ultimately, in healthy development, the role of severance is as critical for girls as it is for boys.

beauty. In time I will find it in a new way, but if the piece at all challenges me, learning it will demand that this initial bodily wholeness be left behind.

Each substage in this learning is a different bodily relationship. Early on, my body has a magical sensibility. My fingers may be fumbling, but my ears are hearing what is possible. Later, with brow creased and belly tight, I struggle, even rage ... How do I get my misbehaving fingers to play what my ears can so easily hear? Now the body is a very different sort of experience. It becomes a thing, even an adversary. Eventually, if I am sufficiently persistent, vulnerable and patient, the piece and I begin to find our third space. My body again becomes a single gesture—my breath full, my sensibilities open and alert, each part of me offering its particular shapings and colorings to the pulsing flow of notes and meter within this now expanded capability.

Separation is critical to growth; paradoxically, it is also necessary for the experience of oneness. Separation, whether through cultural ritual, individual instinct, or individual choice, is like the click of a cog on the wheel of life. It is an acknowledgement that the wheel turns only one way and the wheel must not cease in its turning: any state of ripeness, no matter how beautiful, held past its moment, becomes decay.

GROUND AND SEVERANCE IN THE EVOLUTION OF HUMAN REALITY

"We know that the whiteman does not understand our ways. One portion of the land is the same to him as the next ... He takes from the land whatever he needs. The earth is not his brother but his enemy, and when he has conquered it, he moves on. He leaves his fathers' graves and his children's birthright is forgotten."
—Chief Sealth of the Duwamish

With each stage in the first half of cycle, we see two related things: an ever greater distancing from the full, primal potency of the germinal unformed, and a new appearance and reality for the lower pole in creation. Ground is not just the Below, it is our experience of what lies below as an expression of a specific relationship between Above and Below.

There are two places where these evolving dynamics can be seen with particular acuity. The first is in how we experience our bodies—our bodies being quite literally the "underworld" of our experience. The second is how we depict the feminine, in part in relationship to women, but, more specifically in relationship to the archetypically feminine, the feminine half in each of us. The unitary, less form-defined pole in experience is commonly depicted mythically in feminine symbolism. As we go through the stages, I will give special attention to these two themes.

Pre-axis

In pre-axial reality the unformed is the primary definer of experience. Truth here is original wholeness: in stone age culture, wholeness with nature;* in individual development, wholeness within the maternal bond; in a creative task, wholeness within the bounds of the known (the new is percolating within but yet to make appearance).

The qualities of ground that predominate at this stage are feelings like peace, security, and connectedness. While faint rumblings of new possibility can be felt, we must wait a bit for more chthonic themes like wildness and passion to reach forefront. These require at least some degree of separation. Here truth is mystery, and the beauty of the unbroken whole that is the container for that mystery. This reality is expressed wonderfully in the following quote from Colin Turnbull in his study of the Pygmies of the Congo:

> "The complete faith of the Pygmies in the goodness
> of their forest world is perhaps best of all expressed in
> one of their great Molimo songs, one of the songs that is
> sung fully only when someone has died. At no time do

---

* In comparing this stage to other points in culture, I will often treat it as if it occurs right at the rhythm's origin. In truth, just by virtue of being *homo sapiens*, original unity has already been left behind. Such capacities as language and the making of tools are not possible without significant separation. Bear with the simplification, as it greatly aids conceptual clarity in the big picture.

their songs ask for this or that to be done, for the hunt to be made better or for someone's illness to be cured; it is not necessary. All that is needed is to awaken the forest and everything will come right. But suppose it does not, supposing that someone dies, then what? Then the men sit around their evening fire ... and they sing songs of devotion, songs of praise, to wake up the forest and rejoice it, to make it happy again. Of the disaster that has befallen them they sing, in this one great song, 'There is darkness all around us; but if darkness is, and the darkness is of the forest, then the darkness must be good.'"

A fascinating question about earliest culture concerns the paucity of remains from these times. There are a few cave paintings and remnants of burial sites, but beyond this not much. Were it not for the survival of a few Stone Age peoples into modern times—in places like New Guinea, parts of Africa, Australia, the Amazon headwaters—there would be very little we could say about them.

Why this lack? Our modern chauvinism easily ascribes it to "primitivism." But my hunch is the reason is much more interesting. If we look to the next major cultural stage, for example, to ancient Egypt or the high native cultures of Mesoamerica, we find suddenly a grand flowering of monumental pagentry. Is this the result of some dramatic increase in intellect or a great invention that somehow made it all possible? I think not.

I think what we are seeing is the simple fact that in this earliest stage, the formless is preeminent. This is literally "prehistory." There is as yet no concern with the future and little interest in the material. There would be no reason to create monuments for posterity or accumulate objects as symbols of power and worth. The primordial mother is simply not interested in these things. Her concerns are intense and constant, but they are not concerns of form and future.

In culture at this stage, there is as yet no notion of progress as we think of it. Each season and each generation are seen as reenacting the same timeless story, like the ancient uroboric serpent whose mouth and tail merge. In *The Sacred and the Profane,* Mircea Eliade describes it this way: "In a certain sense, it is even possible to say that nothing new happens in [this] world ... this repetition constantly maintains the world in the same auroral instant of beginnings."

At this stage, the relation to the feminine is total. Historically, we see that all cultures in their origins are, mythologically speaking, matriarchies. The ordering truth is the primordially feminine. Deific symbols take one of two main forms: images that personify human experience in the "mother" language of nature (deer, bear or raven; the breath of the wind; the spirit of the forest), or representations of the great goddess, abundant of hip and breast. The primal goddess speaks of the values most basic in us—sustenance, fertility, belonging, survival.

The relationship to our bodies is total in a similar way. In this first stage of things, in a very important sense we are our bodies. As infants our world is one of creature responsiveness. Our learning is patterned movement, rather than ideation. And there is still no separation in time: when we're curious, we explore; when we hurt, we cry. The reality of pre-history is similarly immersed in nature and tissue. In the movements of an aboriginal hunter, distinction is at best embryonic: self, nature, and cell express themselves a single gesture. Here we are our movements, and the mysterious forces of body-nature are our linkage with the larger world.

Early-axis

As we move into early-axis reality, we enter into a new relationship to our origin. Before, it was everything—we were it and immersed in it. Now there is it—and something else. In the vertical, mystery now has a specific direction: it bubbles as the underworld of experience. It is something which, when we are identifying with the conscious upper pole of experience, we specifically stand upon and exist in relationship to.

Our attention in this stage is often with the magic and numinosity of the newly ascending form, but the power of source and mystery is still unquestionably primary. Culturally, while we may have ascendant pantheons, the primary esthetic is still unitary. We are in a reality of soothsayers and oracles, a reality in which mystery is decidedly present and most often prevails. Similarly, while the magical child may say no and take center stage to the oo's and ah's of doting parents, it is yet far from any capacity for independent life. When it hurts, it knows where to go ... to "Mommy."

Two interesting sorts of changes can be seen in our experience of our ground as we move into this stage. Let's take them one at a time. First, it begins to take on passional, and easily even frightening qualities that before were at most peripheral parts in it. Now that there is form, death and birth become central motifs—there is something discrete to "become and disbecome." Related to this, with reality now overtly polar, the "chaos" of the unformed begins to present in ways that can be felt only when there is some tension of contrast: as wildness, as primal passion.

A fascinating place to see this is in the ways the mythic feminine finds depiction. Pre-axially, the primary manifestation was the primordial mother, the mother as source. Here we begin to get additional forms whose chthonic potency evokes very different feelings. One example is the "death mother" or "terrible mother." In early-axis culture, rituals that focus on death have an essential place; sacrifice, not uncommonly human sacrifice, is a central theme. It is through such ritual that connection is maintained with the primal source. The ferocious form of the "death mother" is a common visage.

She is only a faint memory in contemporary consciousness. We see her in the face of Lilith in the Old Testament, and Hecate in Greek myth. She can be heard in Shakespeare's reminder that "Nature's bequest gives nothing but doth lend." In tribal ritual and much Eastern mythology, we find a different story. Here she resides with a visible audacity that is unsettling to most Western temperaments. In the rituals of Bali, Rangda, the ferocious and all powerful, battles illusion, bringing what is not timely to its demise. In Mexico, the death mother, her body clothed in snakes, is called Coatlicue. In India, she is Kali. Say the Vedas, "All this, whatever exists, is made to share in sacrifice." Skulls around her neck, corpses beneath her feet, Kali is fire, dancing that life can be renewed.

We meet the death mother in those fearsome/embracing moments when life confronts us and leaves us shaken, demanding that some part of who we are be released to the test of the phoe-

nix's eternal flame. When we feel the ferociousness of creature passion, she is close.

The second major change as we move through early-axis concerns our proximity with the primordial. At the same time that the
images of the below are more overt in their expressions of potency,
we are gradually moving away from that potency. We can see this
change nicely in classical Greek culture.

I think of classical Greek civilization as beginning just at the
end of what I have called pre-history and extending through the
dynamics of early-axis. As we have seen, in pre-history the ritual
world was our entire surround, and its primary inhabitants were
creaturely or feminine. Over the span of classical Greek culture, two
critical changes took place in this: first, the gods became increasingly ascendent, and second, they more and more became human,
and male. During earliest times, the primary deity appears to
have been the earth goddess Gaia. The pantheon of gods had not
yet taken up residence atop Olympus. Homer speaks of Gaia as the
"universal mother, firmly founded, the oldest of divinities."

The changes took place in two steps. First, during the middle
years of Greek flowering, the pantheon settled in its familiar lofty
abode. With that ascent, male figures increasingly assumed positions of greatest influence, though the realms below generally
maintained female representation. In the second step, the female
mythic keepers of the underworld were replaced by male over-
lords—Poseidon for the sea, Hades for the earthly underworld,
Dionysus for the wisdom of the body and intuition. (There is evidence of some tension in these "assignments;" stories suggest that
Hades and Poseidon were not always comfortable with them.)

By the late years of Greece's eminence, this transposition had
become virtually complete. Zeus resided as supreme patriarch, his
ascendency only slightly tempered by the persuasions of his wife,
Hera, the most powerful remaining feminine figure on Olympus.

While there is now clear separation from the unforming
potency of the Below, even by the end of early-axis reality the
underworld of experience is still seen in predominantly positive
terms. For example, the Greek Hades, like the Celtic Tir-nan-og
and Scandinavian Hel, was dark and unfathomable, but it was

The germinal pole of creation is represented symbolically in a great multiplicity of motifs: the earth, water, death and birth, descent, nature, fertility, the untamed, community, ancestory. The most ubiquitous motif is the archetype of the "mother."

ABOVE: *Pablo Picasso.* Mother and Child. *1921. An image of the "nurturant mother."* OPPOSITE, TOP LEFT: *The "Venus of Willendorf." c. 30,000-25,000 B.C. An image of the "primal mother."* OPPOSITE, TOP RIGHT: *A Northwest Coast Indian totem pole, symbolizing the generativity of the unformed.* OPPOSITE, BELOW: *From Tibet. Shrinmo, a manifestation of the "death mother," holding the "Wheel of Life." Late 18th century.*

thought of as a domain inhabited by largely generative forces.

What is our relationship to our bodies during this stage? While there is definitely now distinction—it is possible to separate the concept of self and body—the relationship is an overtly co-generative one.

To the child, the body is an endless fascination—to explore, and to explore with. In early-axis culture, we are never far from the poetry of the body, whether in ritual warfare or the ever-present sacrificial voice in religion. Spiritual disciplines—the asanas of Hatha Yoga, sweat baths and fasting, the practices of tantric sexuality—not infrequently engage the body directly, defining magic and enlightenment as a right relationship with its potency. Where the cultural dynamic is highly ascendent, these may take the form of ascetic practices; but, where the lower pole is acknowledged we often see quite the opposite: central in Greek culture was the cult of Dionysus, with its rituals of abundant drink and unbridled sexuality. The lower pole of early-axis is the "pagan" underworld.

Middle-axis

As we move into middle-axis dynamics, our relationship to, and as, the lower pole of our being changes in marked ways. Here the issue of distinction between the poles becomes defined in terms of what are now experienced as unquestionably opposite realities. The poles have become of equal strength; the forces of the creative tug this way, then that, in a battle of control.

Culturally, this stage begins about the time of the emergence of monotheism. In a way not seen before, the world below begins to be regarded as specifically evil. Truth is no longer magic and mystery, but a struggle between two great forces: an all-loving god of light above, and the black forces of damnation below. Darkness and the unformed are more and more equated with sin, wickedness, and deprivation.

Actually, there is a subtle but very important distinction to make here. It is only part of reality's lower pole that is seen negatively. Certain aspects have important, if not always acknowledged, "positive" roles.

A cultural example is feudal society, in which the peasant is regarded by the overlord as inferior, but, as long as he remembers

his place, valuable. The culture marches on the back of the peasant's labors. (Similarly, while the peasant may resent the overlord's power, as long as the overlord's use of authority is kept within certain bounds, he is ultimately respected. The peasant depends
on him for protection and leadership.)

Feminine symbology also nicely delineates this distinction.
The faces of the great mother that we have looked at to this point
—the mother as ancient source, the chthonic mothers of death and
passion—in middle-axis reality are relegated increasingly to the
demonic, and their representatives in the outer world denigrated:
witches burned, pagans "converted" or killed.

But one face of the great mother remains, and her role is central. We could call her the nurturant mother, the good mother, the
hearth mother. She is the mother that cradles, the part of us that
is supportive and unconditionally caring. She is embodied in the
image of the peasant farm woman, children all about, loaves of
bread just warm from the oven. When someone says, "Now that's a
kid only a mother could love," this mother is the part of us that can
see the child as nothing but beautiful.

The value of these positive aspects is often not acknowledged
by the upper pole, but this dismissal is more a reflection of concern
that the lower may gain too much power than of actual disdain.
The lower pole is seen as demonic only when it steps outside these
appropriate bounds of control, when it partakes too deeply in the
great unformed.

These same dynamics of creative struggle are mirrored in our
relationship to self as body in this stage of things.

In a creative task, the relationship to the body is ambivalent.
We struggle with the limitations of what our bodies can do, but
have to acknowledge that in the end, it is the body that will do
them. It is a subtle balance. If we push too hard, the work loses its
"juice;" if we don't push hard enough, the body as the unformed
steps outside its bounds and engulfs the task in laziness or loss of
focus.

The adolescent's relationship to, and as, the body is similarly
ambivalent: the body has become a whole new sort of "other," at
once emerging identity and adversary. The dramas lived out across

the moat of separation are not unlike medieval tales of conquest and courtship. On one side stands our newly personal capacity for emotion; opposite it, our equally new and amazing powers of will. Allegiances between the two sides can go through rapid flip-flops (with concomitant shifts in how the body is perceived). Who will win out: the forces of impulsiveness or those of responsibility? The battle is wonderfully ironic. It is essential that we engage it as a life and death struggle, yet there can never be victory, since that would forever break just the thread of life for which both "sides" fight.

In culture, the body is now viewed distinctly as other: the body is a creature; our task is to tame it. When it is obedient, its power is respected; when it is not, it is the very face of evil. Where middle-axis religious practices recognize the body, it is almost always in terms of ascetic denial: isolation, self-flagellation, abstinence.

Late-axis

As we move into late-axis reality, this polar tension fades considerably. This is due less to resolution than to the simple fact that the lower pole is now small compared with the power of the formed. Its contributions can be more overtly acknowledged because there is little to fear from them. Form is largely established. What remains below is markedly diminished in potency; in it there are but faint memories of the unformed's primordial power.

Culturally we see this new relationship in the emerging mythology of reason: consciousness has prevailed, and it is only a matter of time before we vanquish darkness—"ignorance"—once and for all. And at the same time, images such as the killing of dragons, or the murder of heathens—symbols most evocative in the stage previous—become regarded as antiquated, even barbaric. Separation is sufficiently complete that fears of re-engulfment need no longer be major preoccupations. The aspects of the primordial feminine that remain are relegated to specifically separate realms: feelings to the subjective, intuition to the arts. These things are valued—sometimes even elevated—but they are also clearly secondary, regarded as decoration rather than substance.

In the story of a lifetime, the primary focus has turned in a similar way to questions of role and achievement: to form defined concerns. The lower pole manifests in sensitivity to such things as personality and appearance—things to which we may give considerable attention, but which are none the less, in the big picture, regarded as secondary.

In creative endeavors, the primary tasks of shaping and forming are largely complete at this stage. The part of us that speaks from the lower pole manifests here in the esthetic sensibilities we bring to the final treatment of surfaces.

The same combination of reacknowledgement and relegation to a secondary status is reflected in our relationship to, and as, our bodies. By the Age of Reason, our distance from the body as instinct is sufficient that we can turn and regard it with a certain "objective" curiousity. We simultaneously let it closer, and experience it less. On one hand there is somewhat more room for bodily gratification; on the other, we regard our bodies in more and more isolatedly physical terms: something to feed, clothe, exercise and occasionally pleasure. Notions like soul or spirit, if present at all, are distinct, at best dropped like chocolate chips into our anatomical cookie.

The bodily dynamics of early adulthood are similar. There is commonly a new body appreciation. We are at the height of our vigor; we have discovered our sexuality and begun to find a place for it in our lives. Yet, we are more and more regarding both our bodies and those of others as objects. To "pay attention" to our bodies means to cultivate its surface attractiveness and to keep it "like a well oiled machine."

Moving into the final substages of late-axis reality, approaching the transitional point in the cycle, the lower pole increasingly simply ceases to exist. The direction of movement here is well illustrated by changes culturally in the first half of this century. We saw "woman's work"—the creation of home, the tasks of nurturance and nourishment—given less and less value, by men and women alike. We found people more and more leaving behind soil and community. We found the themes closest to the primal mysteries increasingly negated: birth taken from the realm of wonder and the community of women, and placed into a world of anesthetics, emotionally sterile hospitals and male doctors; death, whether in medicine or religion, becoming a non-entity, stripped of its emotional power as personal experience and its stature as formidable teacher. Within transitional reality, people find it hard to understand softness as anything more than passivity; surrender as anything but failure.

 Movement past transition in any formative process is marked by a gradual remembering of mystery and the Below, and a gradual infusing of this power into the whole of experience. We can usefully think of this as the

Integration primary task of the second half of creative cycle.

This manifests as we move into the second half of our lifetimes in the finding of the courage needed to meet the fact of our mortality. Death is, very directly, the face of mystery. Meeting it changes us in significant ways. It reveals achievement, appearance and popularity as transient—appropriate concerns, but clearly only part of the picture. It takes the certainties of knowledge and tempers and expands them with an appreciation for the unfathomable and for life's subtlety and immensity. It reminds us of the importance of connection—to friends, to family, to nature, to self and soul.

As I have suggested, culturally we are seeing today the beginnings of what seems a precisely parallel process. This century has had a dual trajectory—moving more and more isolatedly into the material, and at the same time making first steps into the process of larger integration. By its first decade, this second dynamic was already well in motion, evidenced by ideas such as Darwin's radical assertion of our continuity with even the "basest" of creatures, and Freud's contention that the invisible in us, far from being dead, often does a rather clever job of running things, despite its necessary anonymity.

In recent decades we have seen an interesting shift in our feelings about the dynamics of separation. Images of severance have always generated strong emotion, but in our past these feelings have been largely positive—the human triumph over nature, the subduing of "base" instincts, the defeat of disease. We increasingly hear them defined in much less pleasant terms—the subjugation of the feminine, the oppression of the underprivileged, the denial of our bodies, the destruction of our environment. Often such sentiments are voiced naively, as an enmasse condemnation of the formed—of institutions, intellect, the masculine. But even when what we see is just a flip-flop, the fact of shifting sensibilities is significant.

Many of the most important themes in cultural change can be understood quite directly as expressions of our present need to gradually reconnect into who we are as nature, source and mystery, and to experience the larger reality that this integration could make available to us. We see this most obviously in our growing ecological consciousness—a reverence for earth and nature that sees our environment not just as something to utilize, but as home, nurturer, friend and teacher. We see it in present efforts for world peace that have their foundation in a perspective large enough that human differences seem increasingly secondary to our kinship. It is there in the new feminine consciousness. And we see it in a growing sensitivity to aspects of experience that are particularly intimate to our primal natures—birth and death, the experience of children, our own bodies.

One way of understanding the new face of science is as an expression of how our experience of material reality changes as this pole of our being is reengaged. In the realm of "hard" understanding, it is becoming acceptable for truth once again to include the mysterious. It is not surprising that this larger scientific truth is often couched in terms we might think more appropriate to an imaginative child than a learned theoretician: charmed quarks, white dwarfs, red giants.

Some of our new theories are trying to look right down into the formative essence. While there is a point one can never see beyond —even the death mother can't accompany us to the source—there are some remarkable ideas emerging.

One of the most pertinent and amazing comes from the field of astrophysics. It is that stellar phenomenon dubbed with appropriate mythic reverence and foreboding: the black hole. Because black holes cannot be seen, they are incredibly difficult to study, but they are thought to occur when celestial matter collapses into an exquisitely compact state.

Gravitational fields curve space and time. Within a black

hole, space-time curves so far it becomes circular. And the gravitational field is so intense that everything that comes close disappears into it. A black hole is black because no light can escape.

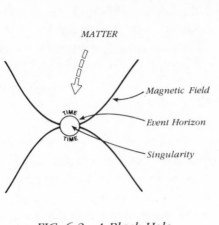

MATTER

Magnetic Field

TIME

Event Horizon

TIME

Singularity

FIG. 6-2. A Black Hole

At a certain point, called the "event horizon," the spatial dimension disappears entirely; only time remains. In theory, if you were traveling into the black hole, you could look back over your shoulder and watch the whole past and future of the universe pass by.

Beyond the event horizon is the black hole's center, the "singularity." Here there is, in theory, neither space, nor time as we think of it; it is pure energy concentrated at a point of infinite density.

Black holes are thought to function like great generating engines at the centers of galaxies. We are in our infancy in understanding their workings. To quote Cal Tech astrophysicist Anthony Readhead, "Fifteen years ago black holes were on the fringe of respectability. Now we must take them seriously. No other mechanism can explain the energies released by active galaxies. Nuclear explosions won't do. Throwing stars into black holes is perhaps a fifty times more efficient way to generate energy."

The similarity between the poetry of a black hole and the dynamics at the germinal pole of formative process is dramatic. Some physicists postulate that all of reality is pockmarked by mini black holes, which, functioning like their galactic big sisters, constantly create and recreate the reality we live in. It is a new area with many questions. The respectability of this kind of inquiry reflects the degree to which we are beginning to let the mysterious, as mystery, be a valid realm of study.

SOURCE, GROUND AND THE HEALING RELATIONSHIP

"First you prepare the ground well, then when you plant, the whole thing grows easily, and birds come to nest in it."
—James A. Michener

"This is one great obligation: to enable the human animal to accept nature within himself, to stop running away from it and to enjoy what now he dreads so much."
—Wilhelm Reich

*"... deep inside,
in that silent place
where a child's fears crouch ..."*
—Lillian Smith

In each stage, then, there is a specific relationship to the germinal pole in creation that is in fact creative. This relationship is an essential aspect of health. To the degree it is achieved, the moment is embued with a sense of time-appropriate connectedness: one feels "at home" in one's experience.

In the parlance of popular psychology, one speaks of a person who has this timely connectedness as being "grounded." While a useful term, listening to the different ways it is used, one might easily conclude that the notion has in fact very little real meaning. In one situation we speak of a person's ideas as being grounded, meaning well-tested in reality. In another we use the word to refer to a person's physical and emotional stability, their ability to "stand on their own two feet." Or we may use it in a very different way to refer to qualities like earthiness. While the term is often used loosely, the larger factor in the confusion, is, as I see it, the simple fact that the relationship with self and world that results in a feeling of "home" is relative in time. What gives this kind of experience, and the qualitities that experience will have, are functions of the defining creative stages.

This implies several things. Sociologically, it means that in different cultures, different factors are going to be most critical to feelings of safety and belonging. Psychologically, it means that the

151

elements essential to ground will vary markedly depending on a person's primary energetic. Ground is statement about creative balance. Right connection in the timeless is relative in time.

We can trace this progression by looking at how ground is experienced by people who hold the major part of their aliveness in different primary energetics.* Where there is a lot of early-axis in one's personality, good grounding will be experienced bodily as a sense of connection downward through pelvis, legs and feet, that extends and expands well into the earth. An example of a satisfying image for such a person might be a tree with ample roots reaching into moist, fertile soil. With a lot of lower pole in the dynamic, the image might become even more satisfying with the addition of, say, an underwater river—a primordial well-spring— or creatures burrowing amongst the roots. Such early-axis images of ground might also have attraction to someone with a different primary energetic whose personality was beginning to expand to include early-axis sensibilities.

Where middle-axis dynamics are predominant, the same images and bodily sensations would be expected to evoke very different feelings, home and safety definitely not among them. Here ground's most essential quality is solidity. A tree image could still be acceptable, but the soil would need to be firm and solid (and no rivers or creatures, please). Better yet might be an image like the stone foundation of a castle, or focused somewhat more on the nurturant, a country cottage with ample table and a warm fire. Movements that evoke feelings of ground here come more from the visceral body and characteristically involve an impactful relationship to the earth. (The dance forms of pre- and early-axis cultures involve foot and leg movements that caress or pat the ground. Middle-axis dance characteristically involves a more pronounced interface with the ground—the empassioned heel thrusts of flamenco

---

* I will most often leave out the pre-axial stage when discussing personality style. Within late-axis culture, a person who embodies this dynamic in any pure sense would be simply too unbounded to function. In Chapter 10 we will look in some detail at personality patterns. I will show then how we can understand psychotic patterns as expressions of dynamics embodied in very early substages of creation.

from the early parts of this stage, the very defined foot placement of Irish step-dancing, the stomp of traditional American squares and clogging.)

When we use the word ground to mean "well-tested in reality" we are speaking from the reality of late-axis. Here, home has less to do with downwardness than with connection in solid facts and social acceptance. A cement sidewalk is sufficient below; what matters is what happens on it. In movement work, once solidity is established, gestures that give a feeling of home are more horizontal—expressions of greeting, movements that place things about one. (The social dances of mature life in late-axis culture relate to ground, but more importantly, move across space, for example, a Viennese waltz.)

The kinds of things that can open the door into fuller groundedness are endless—connecting to a childhood memory, having the courage to be angry, letting oneself really feel pleasure, accepting deeper responsibility in one's life. In the following example from work with a client, the key was the courage to doubt and fear. (The dynamics are primarily middle-axis.)*

> I had worked with Mary for about a year. Much of the work revolved around questions of trust. One day she came to the session feeling sad and confused. Her lover had become seriously ill. It bothered her greatly to be so helpless and out of control. She could neither understand the illness nor change what was happening.
>
> At one point, in describing the situation, she mentioned the trust she had felt with her lover's doctor. I asked what it was that engendered this. She described a scene in which he emerged from her lover's room, his eyes moist and said simply "I don't know what is going on ... I will do all I can." She said that somehow, with those words, he became for her not just a technician, but a healer.

---

* From here on, when I share a clinical example, I will include some brief information about the person's primary energetic. I do this both so the reader can become more familiar with these diagnostic concepts, and so that the examples can be returned to, for further learning, once the concepts are more fully developed.

Then she realized the importance of this awareness for herself. In days ahead she played with letting go of her need to always understand. One day an image came to her of a wise old woman sitting, simply present, in her lover's room. She began to recognize how simple caring can transform. The image expressed both her growing ability to be a healing force for others, and the way she was risking to trust in, and thus heal, herself.

I commented earlier that each stage in formative process has certain, most characteristic, types of symptom patterns. We can differentiate this further by looking at patterns that effect variously from the different poles within a stage. With each polar bias we see two types of patterns: those directed toward self, and those directed toward external challenges to capacitance.

Patterns that function primarily from the lower pole are inherently tricky to grasp, since there is nothing to see. They work "under the table." In the same way that it is hard for us in our present culture to understand the richness of the lower pole, its less savory aspects easily leave us positively baffled.

In an early-axis personality, the most common self-directed, lower pole dynamic involves a dampening of the ascending impulse of aliveness so that the Above and the Below cannot connect. The resultant feeling is depression. Externally directed mechanisms include merging with and enveloping the challenging stimulus (that which is not different cannot have an effect) and certain kinds of undermining.

Early-axis being the least form-defined of common personality stages, these dynamics are the most conceptually elusive. We can get some help from the symbolic, the language that most directly voices early-axis experience. I think of two motifs here, each with a most potent place in myth. The first we could call the "suffocating" or "smothering" mother. Overtly she communicates selfless nurturance, but beneath there is passive violence toward any act of distinction—boundary making, any impulse toward independent life and breath. To the act of standing, she is quicksand. Internally, she swallows the new impulse to aliveness: early-axis depression has a characteristic "wet" quality, the person feels awash in the unformed. Externally, she merges with or sucks on the challenging form, acting to dissolve its boundaries and drain its potency. Relationships with the suffocating mother are sticky, undifferentiated, symbiotic.

Importantly, this figure is not *inherently* diminishing. She is diminishing because of the timing of her actions. The suffocating mother is simply the mother of original unity acting past her appropriate point in the cycle. One reason this kind of mechanism is so tricky to deal with is that ultimately what this figure is offering is simply love. The problem is that what she is offering is not the freeing, inspiration-based love of early-axis, but the love of the womb.

There is a Zoroastrian legend which describes the first parents of the human race as a single reed born up from the earth. Soon after its appearance they separated, then returned, and from this union, gave birth to two children. The children were beautiful. But the parents loved them so irresistably that they ate them up, the father one, the mother the other. It is said that God, to protect the human race, then reduced our capacity to love by 99 percent. Seven more children were then born and they all survived. It is this "tempering" of love that the suffocating mother has yet to learn.

The second image is one of the most fearsome in the mythic underworld. We could call her the "tooth mother." We know her in dream and fable as the haggard witch who eats children, or as the vagina with teeth that shreds its offspring in their attempted escape. While the necessary violence of the death mother returns rhythm to origin when it is time, the tooth mother goes for blood at that fragile and heroic instant when the moment first attempts to stand. Where the death mother brings the essential turn from summer to fall, the distorted potency of the tooth mother brings destruction to the young shoots of springtime. A popular Appalachian song includes these words:

"Don't sing loud songs, you'll wake my mother
She's sleeping here right by my side,
And in her hand a silver dagger—
She's sworn that I won't be a bride."

We are witnessing this fanged mother when we undermine our own inspiration or subtly undercut another's confidence.

In the lower pole of middle-axis, diminishing of aliveness takes one of two primary forms: passivity or passive-aggression. The essential issue of middle-axis dynamics is control, and these are mechanisms of passive control. Internally, we are all familiar with times when we are immobilized by the inertia and struggle of procrastination. More severely, these dynamics often play a central role in addictions and physical illnesses. Externally they manifest in such things as chronic lateness, abdication of responsibility, and reflexive contrariness. Where the dynamic is strongly held and the outer aspect of lower pole predominates over the inner, we may see outright anti-social behavior.

Common diversions to aliveness from the lower pole of late-axis are scattering and sexual seductiveness. Scattering often masquarades as feeling, as the subjective (the appropriate lower pole complement to achievement), but in fact is just irrationality. Sexual signals, as used here, promise contact, but are more truthfully a play for attention—and a diversion of attention away from more vulnerable issues.

All of these dynamics function in an essentially similar way. They diminish aliveness through the untimely dissolving of distinction and structure: merging swallows inspiration, contrariness undermines formed action, and scattering disrupts the structures of rational thought. Archetypally masculine violence, aggressive violence, is the violence of twoness. Archetypally feminine violence is the violence of untimely oneness. It functions by collapsing experience into the lower pole's esthetic of unity so that the creative connection between upper and lower poles is broken.*

The following clinical example is from work with a woman whose childhood environment was extremely invasive. Mythically, much of her early years had been spent coping with the "tooth mother." The example is a good illustration of the import-

---

* In something like anti-social behavior, we see a combination of these two dimensions of violence: with the outer aspect of the lower pole predominant, there is commonly an aggressive posture; but, the overall effect is to undermine established form.

ant role that difference plays in a timely sense of ground. (The dynamics include both early- and middle-axis elements.)

Jane was in her mid-twenties, a frail tense woman who lived alone in a small cabin and worked as a waitress in a nearby cafe. She was friendly, but had a subtly biting sense of humor that kept most people from getting too close. The closeness she did find tended to end fairly quickly in discord. When she became frightened, her pattern was to herself become invasive, using the person's response to her uninvited intrusion as a way to create both connection and distance.

In one session, she brought in a drawing she had done that seemed important to her. It was an abstract image that looked like a tall, thick-walled vase with a large, roundedbottom. I asked her to sculpt the image in movement. She found herself sitting on the floor, her body rocking gently, her hands stroking the carpet. She took time to sit and just feel this, commenting that she felt cradled by her movements. She noted that in speaking from this place, her voice had become more resonant, and also that her feelings were bigger and rounder, not as quick and sharp as usual.

After some time, she said she wanted to work further. I asked her if it was possible to connect with another person from the place she was feeling. She asked me to put my hand out and she would see if she could touch it and still keep that inner connection. It worked. She was pleased. She kept her image of ground, and with it a sense of inner directedness.

Then she reached out again, only this time pushing harder against my hand. She pulled her arm back quickly, her face pale and her voice high and sharp. "I can't push," she said, sounding both angry and frightened. And then even more scared: "When I bring my hand back, your hand is still in my image; I can't get it out." Her image of the vase had disappeared.

As she settled into herself again, memories came to her of her childhood. She realized that with her parents, acts of identity brought smothering, invasive responses. She had learned to hold herself above experience as a way to protect herself from this. She saw as well that she was often invasive herself.

Much of the work in months ahead focused on her ability to feel solid difference—between herself and her parents, herself and others, herself and her impulsive invasiveness. With this, her sense of ground, and her capacity to feel connection deepened dramatically.

What kinds of factors contribute to a healthy ongoing connection in ground? The list from my experience looks like this:

— a biologically sound embryonic development and a healthy birth.
— a close and consistent bond between mother and child.
— a father's capacity as co-nurturer.
— a strong respect for individuality and boundaries within the family structure.
— the existence of an extended family system and/or close community.
— consistency in living location, especially in early years.
— general acceptance and appreciation of sensuality and bodily function in the child's world.
— the ready presence of ancestral connection (grandparents, ethnic heritage).
— an equal appreciation of archetypically feminine and masculine qualities.
— a reverence for nature and time for exploring it.

The following exploration can help you connect more deeply in your own right relationship to ground:

Stand up and take some time just to notice how you are in your body. Note your breath and the degree of freedom and fullness in its rhythm. Notice your stance and your place in gravity. Just observe, don't change. Notice especially how your feet contact the ground—are you on the inside or outside of your foot. Are your toes open or bunched together? Notice whether your knees are locked or whether there is ample flex in them. Notice the degree to which there is a sense of space in your chest, belly and pelvis. Ask yourself where the center of gravity in your body feels. Put your finger at that point.

Now take a moment to let an image form for your relationship to the ground. Is it like skipping along a cement sidewalk, a foundation tilting in boggy soil, balancing on a tightrope, pilings driven deep into the earth beneath you? You might reflect back to your image of a bush or tree from the last chapter, and see how the feelings there relate to what comes to you here

Then explore what for you feels like the leading edge in this. Is it to find more solidity in this relationship? to let there be more sense of depth and mystery? perhaps to let the connection be more playful?

Take what you sense and try it out with movement. You may want to stomp the ground. Or perhaps to imagine you are digging your toes into dark, fertile soil. You might want to run briskly across the floor and feel your connection with the things around you in the room.

As you do this, notice any changes that occur both in how you experience yourself and your environment. Do you notice any changes in your body—how you are breathing, what is happening in your legs and feet, where your center of gravity seems to lie? Has your image changed in any way?

A Favorite Poem:

In a pine tree,
A few yards away from my window sill,
A brilliant blue jay is springing up and down,
On a branch.
I laugh, as I see him abandon himself
To entire delight, for he knows as well as I do
That the branch will not break.

—James Wright
from "The Branch Will Not Break"

CHAPTER SEVEN

THE MAJESTY OF ASCENT: INSPIRATION, DISTINCTION AND ATTAINMENT

"Awake, Awake, O sleeper of the land of shadows, awake!"
—*William Blake*

"Oh, children, no grave could've keep that body down
Ain't no grave gonna keep God's body down
When that first trumpet sound ..."
—*From a traditional song of the Bahamas*

"If I appear to see farther than others it is because I sit on the
shoulders of giants ..."
—*Leibnitz*

 Our focus shifts now from the voice of the unformed in the vertical, to that of the manifest, to the upper pole in creation, and the processes of ascent and distinction that give rise to its existence.

While the core motif of the Below was mystery, with ascent, our eyes turn specifically to the visible. The themes that now stand forefront are the wonder of new inspiration, the courage that gives inspiration form, and the glory of successful realization. Our attention shifts upward.

The beginnings of vertical distinction hold a powerful place in the human story. It is a common belief amongst early peoples that at one time the earth and the sky were fused. Creation began with the separation of the Above from the Below.

161

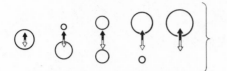

FIG. 7-1. Ascent as Creative
Relationship in the Vertical

Our cultural images for ascent and the ascendant trace a proud and dramatic lineage: the primitive's great bird of the spirit; the Greek sun god Helios or Apollo, driving each day across the heavens in a chariot with four great horses; Odin, wise and omnipotent, sitting upon his throne in the upper branches of Yggdrasil (an eagle beside him, a crown upon his head); the mountain as home of the divine—Qaf, Olympus, Sinai; the Word as God; the uplifting spire of European cathedral, Arabic mosque or Oriental stupa; the firmament of heaven; the lifted transept of the Latin cross; the nation as flag; Washington, Napoleon, Churchill; Newton's laws of motion; the Bill of Rights; the Empire State Building; a rocket shooting the first human onto the surface of the moon.

There are two essential themes in this progression. The first is most obvious: the magnificence and wonder of realization. The second, less obvious, is equally important. The impetus to manifestation is the force that ushers pain onto life's stage. A bird or beast may feel hunger or the sting of a wound, but only this erect being who builds civilizations knows longing, regret, or the death of a dream.*

Part of this is the simple fact that successful human creation never happens without struggle. To manifest as form we must leave behind the garden of eternal peace. Consciousness can be born only in the realm of opposites. And only when there is room left for the combat as well as the embrace of these opposites can the germinal impulse of creation become fully manifest.

* Recent research with higher apes and marine mammals such as dolphins and killer whales shows evidence of some significant degree of both the particular kinds of creative capacities that become available with the separation of consciousness, and the particular array of feelings that follow from this evolution. But it is in humans that this experiment has clearly been taken furthest.

Further, there is the essential truth that if we climb, some-times we fall. When one risks to create, sometimes one fails—and even more, sometimes one does harm. While a lion kills, only this *human* being—separable from nature—has the capacity to be truly violent.

Creation evolves as a play of polarities. Here, counterbalanced to the germinal pole's poetry of oneness, we hear the ever more de-fining voice of difference and distinction. It speaks forth that we might not just be, but be *something*.

ASCENT AND SEPARATION

"He has stepped out of the glowing darkness of chaos into the cool light of creation. But he does not possess it yet: he must first draw it truly out, he must make it into a reality for him-self, he must find his own world by seeing, hearing, touch-ing and shaping it."
—Martin Buber

"[A new theory] is rather like climbing a mountain, gaining new and wider views, discovering unexpected connection between our starting point and its rich environment."
—Albert Einstein

As we move through the stages of the first half of a creative rhythm, our relationship to, and as, the Above evolves in important ways. With each stage of ascent and separation the upper pole grows as a force—from early on, but a faint spark of light in the im-mensity of mystery; to later, in effect, the whole of truth. In addition, it changes in very specific ways, both in how we perceive it—its appearance in both our inner and outer experience—and the values and concerns its presence gives voice to and acts to manifest.

For our thinking here to be at all complete, there are a number of things it will be important to keep in mind. One is the inherently multi-layered nature of ascendant dynamics. The Above, like the Below, is not just one dynamic, but a structure comprised of multiple tiers of creatively interwoven relationships. Taking the experience of a child: just as below the individual ground of a child lie the cradling arms of parents as ground and source, and beneath that, the supporting lap of community and culture; so above the child's budding consciousness we find first parents as protectors and decision makers, then the stuctures and mores of the culture.

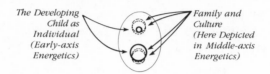

The Developing Child as Individual (Early-axis Energetics)

Family and Culture (Here Depicted in Middle-axis Energetics)

FIG. 7-2. Ascendant and Descendent Layerings in the Energetics of a Young Child

Each of these layerings defines, and provides context for, the layers within: a spark of new awareness differs in important ways in the experience of a child and in the experience of a young adult, as does the individual's conception of self in the childhood of culture and in modern times.

Equally important in thinking about ascendant dynamics is the ability to keep a creatively dynamic perspective. In examining ground, there was never a question but that we were dealing with something more than the simply material. With the Above, form now preeminent, it is not always so obvious. From within any isolated polar reality, the ascendant seems to all intents and purposes something quite independent and concrete: a king is a king, an idea is an idea.

To understand it as otherwise we must view from the perspective of the relevant creative whole. From here we can see that the forms and qualities of elements in the Above, far from being simple facts, are both relative to their place in this whole as an evolutionary process, and intimately co-generative with their polar complements. The Above and the Below not only create each other, each is necessary for the other to be something that can be experienced: the Above is our reality seen from below, the Below our reality seen from above.

Let's examine the evolution of our experience of the Above, focusing on two themes: first the unique qualities manifested by the ascendant with each stage, and second, the story of the evolution of conscious choice:

Pre-axis

In the most germinal substages of a creative cycle, the Above is at most a slight budding upward from the creative matrix. Consciousness waits ready, but has yet to make its appearance into, and as, the light. The young infant is conscious in a creature sense, but not yet self-conscious. Concomitantly, the nurturant and defining aspects of the infant's parental surround are felt as a single protecting blanket, not yet as separate forces. Culturally, symbols for the Above—a mountain, the sun, an eagle or hawk—have distinct qualities, but clearly speak from within the whole of nature. Similarly, while a leader, such as a tribal chief, is easily identified and revered, his power is regarded not as his own, something of will or personality, but as a manifestation of an immanent power of nature.

Early-axis

The Above, in early-axis reality, moves into and becomes the light. It is the magical residence of the newly created: the images that pour forth in a moment of inspiration; the child's bright curiosity and fragile but wondrous sense of identity born from the new-found gift of consciousness; in culture, the visible expressions of a new-felt impulse toward the "rise" of civilization.

The Above here is distinct in a sense not known before. Early in this stage, culturally, we see the sun, in figures such as Helios of early Greece and Ra of Egypt, coming to be worshiped not simply as the inseminator in nature's turnings, but as a throne of divine knowing. The simple fact of a shifting of interest in nature in the direction of the sun is itself significant. The sun, unlike the earth with its turning seasons, or the moon with its phases, is constant, immortal.

We can see this newly distinct Above as well in the evolving relationship of the child with its parents. To parents as nurturant ground, the child is held on high, a magical new joy and most appropriate center of attention. Simultaneously, the child stands below, eyes turned upward to an increasingly acknowledged and clearly powerful, mythic Above. Parents are to young children more gods than mortals, and the adult world as a whole exists as a sometimes feared, but ultimately wondrous, land of giants.

It is in this stage that consciousness first steps forth into the world of choice. The freedom declared is characteristically much greater than that which actually exists, but it is none the less most significant. The child begins to discover and express its preferences. The protecting and defining presence of parents is much the larger determining force, but simply the fact of conscious volition is a major step. Culturally, figures of leadership take on a new grandeur and prominence. While their power is regarded not as personal, but as a gift of the gods, this new visibility and autonomy of voice is none the less significant.

Middle-axis

In middle-axis, the Above evolves from something principally of light, myth and magic to become increasingly something of substance. Inspiration becomes realized as crude, yet clearly tangible, form. With this, the values represented by the Above evolve in distinct ways: concerns with numinosity and artistry are replaced by the elevation of such qualities as honor, might, perseverance, control and morality.

In a creative task, communion with visions of the possible here necessarily takes a back seat to the fact that realization requires sweat and courage. With adolescence, we see the child's identity of magic and make believe give way more and more to a self concept defined by bonds of emotional allegiance and convictions about what is good and what is bad. Along with this internal shift, we find parents, in their ascendant manifestation, leaving behind their roles as mythic gods, to become figures of authority: representatives of moral order, and foils for the important task of assuming control in one's own life.*

---

* As I alluded earlier, any stage in creative cycle itself cycles, going through each of the relevant creative realities. Besides adolescence, another place we see middle-axis dynamics is in that period we call with appropriate trepidation the "terrible twos." The period from a bit past age two through age four is the middle-axis substage within the early-axis developmental stage of childhood. (The creative substages in childhood correlate roughly with Freud's oral, anal and genital periods.) In chapter

New evolutions in the upper pole of culture have a similar flavor. The social Above now has two faces, each in its own way giving voice to a new more structured authority. In figures such as kings, emperors and dictators, we see culture's new powers of dominion: the capacity to bring together and take control over the politically chaotic and disparate, as Arthur did in uniting the warring clans of England. In the image of the church, and figures such as the Pope, we see symbolized the parallel imperative to keep dominion over the personal Below. The teachings of religion are increasingly moral, set in the language of good versus evil, and increasingly formal, written in scriptures and canons of holy law.

In all of this, we can see new pieces in the story of our evolving capacity for choice—choice over the impulses of instinct, choice in the matrix of family, individual choice in the body of culture. Culturally we see this in a part of the divine coming more into the realm of mortals, and in a new degree of ascent within the masses of humanity. In early-axis culture, at least in its early substages, the figure of leadership is regarded as an embodiment of the divine (the Pharaohs were seen as incarnations of Ra, a Tibetan Lama incarnates from a timeless holy lineage). Kings or popes are not ordinary mortals, but neither are they deities. They have Divine Right, but are not themselves divine. And while the social Above was before inhabited only by this omniscient leader and his priestly entourage, with feudal culture, and later developments such as the Magna Carta, we see privilege becoming available to a growing class of lords and nobles.

Late-axis

As we move into late-axis reality we see yet a further evolution in the appearance, values and functions of the Above. In middle-axis, the Above presented an emotion-charged countenance; here the posture is more measured. There is a new confidence in the security of the ascendant, and with this a shift in concern from questions of control to issues of order and refinement. The ascendant pole, the voice of form and dis-

---

twelve we will explore how such creative substages manifest in cultural development.

167

The symbology of ascent traces a proud and dramatic lineage.

ABOVE: *Georges Rouault.* The Old King. *1916-1936.* BELOW: *The space shuttle.* OPPOSITE, TOP: *Akhenaten and Nefertiti offering sacrifice to the sun. Egypt. 14th century B.C.* OPPOSITE, BELOW: *God as "Architect of the Universe." From a 13th century French miniature.*

tinction, is now unquestionably preeminent. The new ascendant values are such things as rational discernment, objectivity, appearance and materially measurable achievement.

In a creative project, the Above here is two things, each now a voice for this new esthetic of refinement. It is the project as form, here getting its finishing touches. And it is the creator's discerning eye, examining what must be done to bring the work to completion. In a lifetime, the issues are similarly ones of delineation and completion. The young adult, independent existence nearly won, looks now to more material measures for self worth: ideas, popularity, respect, "success." Authority is still the best word to describe the ascendant aspect in family dynamics, but the term takes on a new meaning; here authority is less a statement about who is in control, than a measuring rod for stature, maturity and achievement.

The story of movement into late-axis culture is now a well developed theme in these pages. The Age of Reason's atomistic, individualistic, materially causal world view is a direct expression of reality as perceived from the upper pole of this cultural stage. "Real" truth is now ascendant truth. And ascendant truth lies in the province of the intellect and conscious awareness, in rational thought and repeatable empirical observation.

Late-axis reality takes us an important step further in the journey toward the capacity for true choice. We see it in the young adult risking ideas that may be outside the pale of peer approval, and beginning to establish a life physically independent from the structure of the family. We see it culturally on numerous fronts: in the breakdown of blood-defined class structure and the emergent ideal of representative government; in the new contention in religion that the individual is the appropriate final interpreter of God's will; in the domain of learning, in the concept of universal education. The autonomy of the individual was a central rallying cry of the Age of Reason: we hear Voltaire proclaiming, "not until the last priest is hanged with the bowels of the last king will mankind finally be free." One of the strongest indicators of this evolution is the simple fact that we identify this new perspective with the achievements of individual people: Bacon, Descartes, Newton, Galileo, Luther, Washington, Jefferson.

Transition

As we move toward the transition point in creative cycle, we approach a reality in which the upper pole becomes in essence the entirety of existence. The journey of form-taking and emancipation from context is nearly complete.

A central myth of late-axis is that individual sovereignty has been achieved. In truth, within late-axis dynamics, individual freedom is yet much more an ideal and a rallying-cry, than realized fact. The young adult, while physically free, has yet really to individuate; parents and their values continue to occupy centrally determining places in the young adult's overworld. In a similar way, while the individual in late-axis culture gains new freedom in mobility and available life options, he is not yet psychically free. The referent is not yet the individual, but concepts and institutions: the knowledge of "experts," the hierarchy of the "ladder of success," and the defining structures of bureaucracies—governmental, educational, religious, corporate.

As we move toward the transition point in the creative cycle, increasingly the last obstacles to full distinction fall away: to completion of one's creative task, to full adulthood, to the realization of individual determination. Increasingly there is only the Above, and we are it.

And as we have seen, the dynamics of transition always have a hidden side. As we move through the midpoint of the creative cycle, we discover that distinction and freedom are not, as we had thought, the same thing. In one sense the journey is over, in another it is only beginning. Looking only at form, to finish the object is to complete the whole. But form is not the whole picure, just part of it. And that part by itself is not sufficient for enduring fulfillment, or for freedom in any meaningful sense. A world only of the Above is a world defined by difference. And difference, while an aspect of freedom, by itself is as easily isolation, purposelessness, and self-estrangement. We need interconnection—with others, with nature and cosmos, and with ourselves—to have real freedom: not just randomness, but purposeful choice.

In the second half of the creative cycle we search out a new, expanded connecting. We take this new, hard won freedom, and more and more ground it in the fact of life ... but that is a subject for later.

THE ESTHETICS OF ASCENT

"On the tree of life, there are two birds,
  one who eats the fruit, another who watches."

—Bhagavad-Gita

"Form acts the father:
  tells you what you may and
  may not do."

—Theodore Roethke

"For three or four thousand millions of years, life has been
  nipping away at the earth, constructing for itself ever more
  miraculous abodes."

—Paolo Soleri

What are the key themes that link the dynamics of ascent? What is it that each new thrust of visibility offers that was not present before? I think of three primary things. First, creative ascent gives us new perspective. With it we rise above, find a place that allows us to perceive the patterns of the forest where before we saw only trees.* Second, it puts new form and structure in our reality. To ascend is at once to climb a mountain, and to be creating that mountain. Each new level of creation offers a leap in monumentality and complexity. And third, it offers autonomy. To grow "up" is to define our natures as distinct.

A rich place to see this progression is in the evolution of ascendant symbolism. In each creative stage, ascent and the ascendant have characteristic symbolic qualities, this irrespective of whether the periodicity is a creative task, a lifetime, or civilization.

We can see important aspects of this progression culturally in the images presented at the beginning of this chapter. Here we saw an evolution from, in earliest times, nature images; to in early-axis culture, figures, which while decidedly archetypal, are now human

---

* There are two sides to this dynamic. We can look out over a greater distance, but at the same time, our amnesias blind us to much that before was obvious.

in form; to, in middle-axis culture, figures such as a king or a mono-
theistic godhead—still mythic, but decidedly more emotionally
manifest; to, in late-axis culture, symbols that are increasingly abstracted above the human, images such as the mind, progress,
science, institutional structure, and the dollar.

In order to focus more on the emotional qualities behind the
symbols, we might frame this evolution in terms of one specific
motif. As we used images of the primal mother as a "mythic shorthand" for addressing ground, so we can usefully think of ascent in
terms of a lineage of symbolic "fathers." While men and women
each embody the Above as well as the Below, there is an archetypal sense in which the tendency toward form is masculine. We
often speak of these as "patriarchal" times, referring to the fact
that the more form-defined pole of reality is preeminent.

The first such symbolic father I call the father of nature. This
is the father of simple awareness in life's turnings. The following
description by M. Scott Momaday, from his book *On the Way to
Rainy Mountain*, beautifully captures a sense of this part of us (this
from quite late in pre-axis).

> When I first went there to live, the Cacique, or chief,
> of the Pueblos was a venerable man with long, grey hair
> and bright, deep-set eyes. He was entirely dignified and
> imposing—and rather formidable in the eyes of a boy. He
> excited my imagination a good deal. I was told that this
> man kept the calendar of the tribe, that each morning he
> stood on a certain spot of ground near the center of the town
> and watched to see where the sun appeared on the sky
> line. By means of this solar calendar did he know and
> announce to his people when it was time to plant, to har-
> vest, to perform this or that ceremony.

The next figure is the inspiring father. This is the father for
the magical time of beginnings. He manifests as the god-king in
early culture, the guru in mystical spirituality. He is the first men-
tor to the creative act. He challenges us to awaken and models what
is possible. We are small children to him.

The father for the middle phase of creation is the father of dominion and authority. He has two kinds of tasks: he is the father
who protects, but also the one who judges. The father as authority is

the traditional "head" of the family. As "overseer," he assures that no one in his domain will suffer harm. He is also the master in any trade. It is him to whom one apprentices and from whom one must gain approval before initiation into a higher station. He is the father as limitation, Roethke's "father as form" who "tells you what you may and may not do." Sitting above the personal level, he is conscience. Above the cultural, he is an omnipotent and omniscient "God the Father."

The fourth figure in this great patriarchal lineage takes a position even higher than authority or moral dictate. He is the father of knowledge. We find him symbolized in figures of philosophy, education or science. His stance is that of cartographer to the great expanses below. When we salute the human mind and the powers of objective observation, we are paying homage to him. Above the cultural level, he is the father God of liberal religion—a God whose task has become less moral commandment than counsel and philosophy.

There is a further image, but it appears only after the midpoint of the cycle has been passed, and then only gradually. He is the father who knows the expansive magnificence of achievement, but who knows also limitation and the fact of mortality; the father who understands the mountaintop, but also the valleys and plains; the father who keeps company with the most learned, but cherishes equally the company of small children—the father of wisdom.

A fascinating place to observe the metamorphosis of ascent is the evolution of architecture, particularly architecture that is regarded by the people of its time as sacred or special. Particular shapes move us when they speak from how we are coming to shape ourselves. Let's take a moment with this progression.

In earliest pre-history, the most common ritual dwelling was the earth herself. The "medicine" of earliest stone age people—drawings and ritual objects—has been found most often in the recesses of caves. It was apparently these caves, and such sites as sacred wells and burial mounds, that

were the most common places for the shaman's "discourses" with earth as ancestor,
nature and the great goddess. Sculpturally,
the sacred forms in this period were spher-
ical containers or gentle mounds.

With early ascent, attention shifting
upward, ritual spaces increasingly became
ritual structures, and these structures specifically places for conferring with the heavens. The neolithic stone circles of Europe
are some of the earliest examples, while the
pyramids of Egypt and meso-America are
somewhat later, and the temples of early
Greece and the ritual dwellings of the
classical East—Buddhist stupas, Hindu temples—somewhat later still. The architectural mass remains in secure juxtaposition to
the earth's belly, but there is now a clear
verticality. Worshippers stand below and
look up to the divine.

Approaching middle-culture, places of
worship increasingly reflect an equal structural affinity with Above and Below. The
domes of the Byzantine period very nearly
balanced in their upward might the weight
of the foundation and sanctuary beneath. In
the uplifted towers and high rounded arches
of Romanesque architecture, we see the first
gestures toward real ascendant preeminence,
a statement made fully manifest by the last
centuries of middle-culture in the Gothic
cathedrals' surging buttresses and poetic
spires.

With the beginnings of late-axis culture, we find two important architectural
themes. The first is the continuation of upward movement. The second is the secular-

ization of the ascendant. The most powerful gods of industrial high culture are in the material realm, rather than the church. The key themes in architecture are a growing emphasis on the temporal, and a further elevation of structural mass. The culminating form of this period is the skyscraper. With its cubic glass and steel purity, it is a perfect monument to the abstract.

With transitional times we have taken one further step. The skyscraper continues to have an important place, but it is joined by an even more ascendant image: the spaceship. The spaceship is a "ritual dwelling" in which humans not only contemplate the heavens, they inhabit them.

Each stage in creation can be thought of as a particular sort of dance between one of our mythic fathers and a feminine counterpart. Depending on where in the creative cycle that dance is occurring, it may seem to express the essence of timeless love, or the most unforgiving combat. These dancers have been entrusted with the task upon which all else depends, and must not shrink either from the vulnerabilities of intimacy or the dangers of conflict:

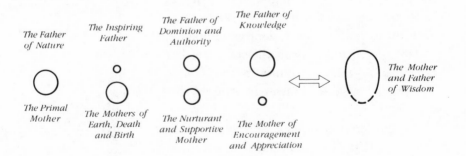

FIG. 7-3. The Mythic Parents

Shifting from symbols to emotional qualities, this polar progression charted for a simple creative event would look like this:

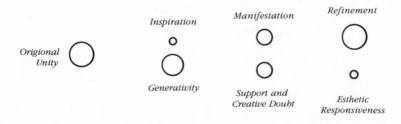

FIG. 7-4. Polar Qualities in a Creative Act

At each stage, for creation to occur, we must have both poles, and in their proper balance. In early-axis, if the lower pole is too strong, the impulse to form will choose ease over the struggle to manifestation. If the upper pole is out of proportion, the inspirational impulse "goes to one's head." Similarly, in middle-axis, there needs to be a proper balance between the courage to form-taking and creative doubt; in late-axis, between the drive to completion, and the esthetic sensibilities that let completion be not just mechanical polishing, but creative refinement.

If we compare and contrast all the various periodicities of creation, we can put together a more generic diagram. These are words that work for me:

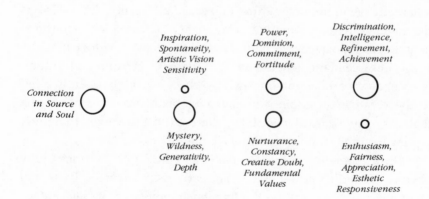

FIG. 7-5. Polar Qualities of the Creative Cycle in General

ASCENT AND CAUSALITY

"Nature rejoices in nature,
Natures subdues nature,
Nature rules over nature."

—*Ostanes*

"It almost scares a man,
the way things come in pairs."

—*Robert Frost*

"The young are both too down-to-earth and too spiritual ...
the teenager is almost gnostic in his dualism."

—*Galway Kinnell*

As I mentioned earlier, in looking at issues of ascent and the ascendant, it is easy to miss the fact that we are dealing with something that is creative. With ground, it was obvious that mystery and generativity played important roles. Because our focus with ascent is form, we easily treat the ascendant as simply what is, as fact, missing its place as just one part of a four-dimensional picture.

Three awarenesses are particularly helpful for keeping the larger picture in view. One is the simple, yet easily forgotten fact that ascent and separation are processes that require significant risk; they demand we face creative uncertainty. The second is the inherently evolutionary nature of ascendant reality. The third is the necessarily co-generative relationship of ascendant constellations and their polar counterparts. Let's take a moment with each.

With ascendant images—be they parents, cultural institutions, or ascendant parts within our own psyches—we are frequently blind to the creative uncertainty involved in their existence. We forget that they have not always been there. And we forget that their coming to visibility took significant courage.

But a moment's reflection makes this fundamental uncertainty obvious. To authentically ascend is clearly risky business. To ascend one must put one's soul on the line. Each move to a higher vantage requires that we challenge what before was Above—old ideas ideas, parental sanctions, peer codes, cultural customs, religious beliefs, political structures and world views. The essential recognition is that it is not possible to gain entry to a level just by memorizing its regulations; to open the door we must offer something that was not there before. We may fool the patriarch for a time with obsequiousness, but this will only keep us children. To make this passage, we must at once offer the gift of what is most intimate in us, and stand ready for mortal combat. When these risks are authentically taken, both the gift and the domain it enters are irrevocably altered.

The word combat here has a larger meaning than we customarily give it. Brute strength or willpower alone are not sufficient for this task. The risking must be deeper, more all-embracing. Willpower alone cannot bring about creative change: the only things we can will are things we can image and conceptualize, and the only things we can image or conceptualize are things we already know.

The second thing we must not forget is that while ascendant forms may look solid and absolute, they are always in evolution. From the perspective of the ideas here, this is obvious. But from within the isolated vantage of a particular creative moment, this is often a most elusive insight. As we have seen, we inherently have amnesia for the truths of past stages. And we do no better with the future. In the first half of the creative cycle, our images of possible change are limited to images that follow directly (causally— whether that causality is magical, moral or material) from what is known. Thus, while once past the eternal turnings of pre-history progress is a meaningful concept, our images of it are never more than extrapolations; it never occurs to us that the future might involve alterations in reality itself. Similarly, while a child understands it will grow up, if you ask it what that means you get a picture of a big kid, playing daddy or mommy. In creating a sculpture or a piece of music, even though I have made the cycle many times before, when I am in a particular stage of it, it's very hard for me to remember that my experience will change, much less how it will change.

Key in this is recognizing that creative change always involves not just gradual alterations, but qualitative change processes. Lest I forget this, I need only refer back to the last time I worked on a creative project. The common image of creative work is that we get an inspiration and then we carry it out—we take the image, compromise some in meeting limitations of materials and skills, then put it into the world. But in real life, it does not happen that way. Between inspiration and realization the original image always changes, and not just in being tempered by the hard facts of reality. It is transformed. Sometimes the alterations are small; often the original project is hardly recognizable. Always the changes are significant.

The third thing we need to keep in mind is the inherently co-generative relationship of creative poles. While the ascendant often seems to function autonomously, in truth how it appears and what it is capable of are intimately a function of its relationship with its descendant counterpart.

To illustrate the significance of this, we might play with a fascinating question from cultural evolution. I've commented that the rulers of early culture are usually perceived by the populace as superhuman, with the omniscience of the divine. Did they really have these powers? Within causal thinking we only have two op-tions. Yes, these figures had amazing, special powers. No, it was projection, cleverness, or psychological manipulation. Neither op-tion is very satisfying.

From a four-dimensional perspective there is a third possibil-ity. Because the leader and populace were poles in a creative rela-tionship, things were possible that would not be if they were iso-lated units. The god-kings words were not just those of an individ-ual, but expressions from the "intelligence" of the social whole as a creative system.

Because the juxtaposition of god-king and populace comes from a time when the esthetic of onesness predominated, this kind of co-generative effect is here particularly pronounced. But it is at work to some degree in any polar relationship, even when individuality is the much stronger bias. The teacher/student relationship makes good example. I am always aware when I teach of a certain sense that I am being entrusted with a sacred task. By virtue of the teaching relationship, I have a power, and even to some degree an intelligence, that is not solely my own. I am not just myself, but also a voice for this "body" of students as a growing creative organism. To me a big part of teaching effectively is being humble to this fact, and staying aware that the ultimate aim is the empowerment of the students.

Any parent knows something of how creative complementarities shape action. Parenting brings out particular parts in us (for good or ill). It also connects us into a whole larger than ourselves, and in the process often significicantly expands who we are. A wisdom and integrity often emerges in becoming parents that makes little sense in terms of our previous attitudes. We have become part of a larger system, and to a significant degree that system now guides our behavior. As with the early-culture populace and the god-king, the child expects the parent to be omniscient. And to a remarkable degree, parents, within the sphere of that relationship, succeed in fulfilling this humanly impossible heroic expectation.

ASCENT, SEPARATION, AND THE HEALING RELATIONSHIP

"The greatest revolution in our generation is that human beings, by changing the inner attitudes of their minds can change the outer aspects of their lives."
—William James

"In each of us there is a king, speak to him and he will come forth."
—A Norse Saying

Clearly, much of the healing relationship has to do with questions of ascent. We want greater awareness in our lives. In the best sense, we want to "grow up," to learn to act with greater integrity and responsibility. And we want to come more and more to know what we "stand for," and have the courage to stand for it.

In these dynamics of growth, the effective therapist at various times wears all the faces of the mythic "fathers." As the father of nature the therapist is simply present. As the inspiring father the therapist serves as a symbol for the capacity for ascent, a model for the ability to live a conscious and effective life. As the father of

authority the therapist challenges and encourages the client to per-
severe through the inherent battles of growth. As the father of
knowledge, the therapist is an educator, pointing out options that
may not have been recognized before as choices, offering ideas that
clients can use as maps for understanding their own experience. As
the father of wisdom, the therapist knows that truth is larger than
what can be said or striven for, and understands when to get out of
the way so the client can discover it.

The following exercise can help you explore some of your own
relationship to, and as, ascent and the ascendant:

Begin by lying on the floor in a posture that lets you
relax fully. Take a good bit of time there with yourself.
Then, when it feels right, simply stand up.

Now reflect back on this process of standing. What
part of your body seemed most to initiate it: your head,
feet, belly, shoulders, eyes, pelvis? What stages in it felt
easiest and most natural, which more difficult or conflict-
ed: getting started, rising, bringing your body to an erect
stance? What feeling qualities most characterized this
progression: excitement, resignation, determination, playfulness, recalcitrance? Try standing several times and notice everything you can.

Then, standing in your natural posture, let an image
form for this your "stance" in the world: is it upright, but
relaxed; fervent and enthusiastic; held back; held up;
overbearing; overburdened? What words or pictures best
describe it for you?

In chapter four, you explored imaging your life as a
journey. Were there any aspects of that image that spoke
to issues of ascent? Were there mountains, ladders, tall
figures to be dealt with? Notice your relationship to these
parts of the image, and the feelings they evoke in you.

In a similar way, reflect back to your image of yourself as a bush or tree from chapter five. Does it add any
additional useful information? What is going on in the
branches and leaves of you image? What is the overall
sculptural quality of your image: short, squat and protected; tall, thin and bending with the wind; massive and
square shouldered?

What seem the important ascent-related issues for
you? In them, what are the "edges," the riskings that

might increase aliveness? Just for fun, explore finding a way of standing that more embodies this larger possible aliveness. What would it mean to live your life more from this place?

Earlier I listed the developmental factors that I see most critical in the evolution of ground. Below are those that seem most essential in the dynamics of ascent and separation:

1. A solid and nurturant foundation in ground.
2. An environment with stimulation and challenge—physical, emtional, intellectual, spiritual—that is of high enough quality and diversity to engage the individual throughout the progression of developmental stages.
3. High quality ascendant figures at each stage to serve as models and mentors, people able to teach and to protect without restricting. These figures must be sufficiently strong in their own development to meet the critical points of struggle with integrity, neither shrinking from confrontation nor invalidating the challenge.
4. Opportunity at each developmental stage not just to learn from, but to engage and affect one's world.

Just as lower pole dynamics can manifest in violent ways, we often act from Above in ways that diminish aliveness. Again we can use the mythic parent as a symbolic shorthand. I think of six primary destructive faces for the mythic father, for each formative stage one who diminishes by opposing, a second by seduction.

Ancient Cronus, who ate his children so they would not supplant him, usefully symbolizes the first figure, the devouring father. Like the devouring mother, this figure consumes, but he does so for very different reasons. His fear is not of being abandoned, but of being replaced. He is the evil giant who crushes the tender shoots of possibility from fear of the change inherent in new life.

In the second destructive early-axis posture, one equally as violent, the father becomes a cultivator of charisma, intent on a collusion of lifelessneess: himself as knower, his followers as mindless children afraid to stand on their own.

The more active middle-axis destructive face is the tyrannical father. He sits in the place of the father of authority, but rather than using his position to lead and protect, he uses it to oppress. We know him within when discernment turns to self-condemnation, and without when the strong hand of dominion becomes the mailed fist of domination.

His more seductive twin is the leader who uses ascendant power to hide himself and others from vulnerability that needs to be faced. In the religious sphere, he is the moral absolutist; in the political arena he is the purveyor of simplistic answers and images of righteous superiority.

The first negative face of the father of knowledge can be seen in the popular image of the white-coated scientist, isolated in a sterile laboratory, and oblivious to the consequences of his work. He is less overtly destructive than the earlier faces, but in the end no less harmful. From his pinnacle of formedness and patriarchy, he does not need to devour or imprison the new creation; he can simply ignore it. Often he will simply label it subjective (tainted by the impurities of the feminine), barring contact with a single word. We know him within each time our thoughts become refuges from more personal kinds of understanding, and each time we dismiss new ideas that might challenge us. We know him without when ideas and institutions become outmoded and rigidified, shored up in defense against the emergent voices of inquiry.

The complementary late-axis face hides us from the whole by offering that the material alone is the solution. We know him as a constant presence in advertising, telling us that if we just buy this product or that, we will always be happy, never insecure. We know him more personally when we are able to convince ourselves that our "net worth," or how much we know, is sufficient to define our value.

I commented earlier that "symptoms"—responses designed to protect a system from new aliveness—can be either momentary reactions to an unusual challenge, or ongoing patterns of organization. In fact this is a continuum; we each have a certain tolerance for aliveness that once exceeded will result in symptoms. For some people, this point is rarely reached. For others, either because their capacitance is particularly small, or because their life context makes chronically high demands, it is exceeded much of the time. When the exaggerated separation that characterizes symptoms tends toward the chronic, I speak of there being *splitting* in the person's or system's primary energetic.

What do we see when there is significant splitting? The basic dynamics are the same as with more episodic responses, though because the person has greater opportunity to practice them, the patterns are frequently much more highly developed. As a polarity becomes chronically split, a number of things can be seen. First, the involved polar parts become significantly estranged. They lose their creative relationship. This happens in characteristic ways. Upper poles rigidify; lower poles lose substance and directness. Being "on top of the world" turns into a chronic state of "having one's head in the clouds;" the ability to "hang loose" becomes a feeling of being "down and out."

Second, there is increasing tendency toward a polarized identification in the energetic. Both halves of the primary duality are still present, but the distance between them becomes sufficient that it is increasingly difficult to act in a way that acknowledges both at the same time. With this, some people come to identify with the same pole in most all situations—an upper pole chronic "know it all," a lower pole posture of eternal victim. Other people may flip-flop depending on the context (i.e., taking one exaggerated polar posture in the role of parent, the opposite when talking to the boss at work). Whatever the posture, the complementary polarity— even though vehemently disowned—is always present and actively a part of the dynamic. Beneath the bravado of the tyrant is a frightened, insecure child. Hidden from view in the person who feels constantly maligned is a figure who feels superior to everyone, particularly anyone who might be critical.

Third, to the degree a polarity is chronically split, unconscious mechanisms for protecting the system from new aliveness play a larger and larger role in that system's functioning.

When I sense a person's aliveness coming from a partiality in the whole, there are four kinds of questions I ask myself. First, is this partiality simply a reflection of a person's place in a presently important rhythm (i.e., just starting a new relationship, being an adolsecent, etc.) or is it part of ongoing bias in the person's primary energetic? Second, if it is the latter, is this bias simply an expression of the part of the whole the person most comfortably embodies, or does it reflect as well some diminishing of aliveness? Third, if there is diminishing, is it in response to a particular challenge, or is it a chronically held posture? Fourth, if it is more chronic, what is the degree of splitting in the dynamic? (For example, a person with a slight disturbance in early-axis, upper pole, might have a tendency to feel "spaced out;" a person with a similar more serious disturbance might become grandiosely delusional.)

What do we see when there is splitting and the primary identification is with the upper pole? We have many colloquial terms that describe different ways we hold ourselves artificially aloft. We speak of someone going around on their "high horse" or acting "above it all." We may say that one person's speech is "stilted," another's thoughts "flighty," that a third acts as if everything is "below their dignity."

Whether the predominant identity in an ascendant posture is that of a perfectionist, classicist, moralist, inspired creator, tyrant, political dogmatist, spiritual superior or materialist, the common energetic results in similar core features. Central is the need to be on top, both in the sense of keeping control of oneself and in maintaining ascendency in the situations around one. Alertness is essential. Defending the self from the seductive pull of gravity requires constant vigilance. We can let down only if our interpersonal, institutional and philosophical supports are firmly in place.

When we hold our aliveness artificially aloft there is often an appearance that we are without needs, that we are fully "self contained" and have it "all together." In truth, to the degree our stature is artificial there is a fear of intimacy—real closeness requiring surrender and uncertainty—and simultaneously a strong tendency toward conformity and other-directedness. Real autonomy and individuality involve spontaneity, passion and indefinability, things that easily lead to the "downfall" of an identity that is not organically supported.

The following clinical example is from work with a woman whose dynamics had significant splitting and ascendant identification. (Her primary energetic was centered about midway between middle and late-axis, with about a 50/50 balance between upper and lower poles.)

When we began working together, June was 52 and a professor at a local university. She was a striking woman—tall, an impeccable dresser, and extremely articulate. She entered therapy after noticing how great a gap there was between her ideas about the friendships and intimacies in her life and the degree of closeness she was actually allowing. It was also a time in which her work seemed to be increasingly losing passion for her.

In exploring feelings, she recognized a significant pattern in her relationships. In almost all her life, her role was in some sense the expert: she was a teacher and faculty head, knowledgeable mother to well-behaved children, wife to a husband who was quiet, submissive and not really her equal. She realized that she became anxious in relationships with equals, and for the most part avoided them.

In one session, I suggested that she let an image of herself in her present life situation come from her unconscious. Her image was unsettling to her: a small evergreen in a wooden planter set high atop a Greek column. From the image she was able to see the degree she used her position in the university—her "ivory tower"—and her generally posture of superiority, to hold herself up. She recognized that when she was in a superior position, she was relaxed. When she was in social situations with equals, she would hold her body tightly, muscularly creating the support her identification with her "high" position usually provided. Looking back, she saw that earlier in her life this dynamic had provided safety and excitement. But as time passed, it left her isolated from others, and from her own passion and vitality.

She was in therapy the better part of a year. In the office she explored feelings and memories, while outside, she risked the equal relationships that she feared. As she worked, the image of the column gradually changed. The wooden pot fell away and the tree's roots and trunk began their movement downward, eventually making connection with the earth. At once she found herself experiencing herself both physically and emotionally in new ways. She was struck by a new sense that her body could really support her, that she didn't need to rely on anything or anyone to hold her up. She began taking dance classes and discovering for the first time the joy of movement. In her daily life, she was becoming a markedly more dynamic, engaging and spontaneous person. She was recognizing, in ways she had never acknowledged, how much of a feeling person she could be and how much she cared about others. In exploring her lower pole, she was both connecting with her deepest needs and values, and mining the trust that would allow her to risk acting on them.

The feelings that arise from artificially descendent postures range from selfless devotion to helpless dependency to chronically feeling "under the weather" to "getting the short end of the stick." Intrinsic to these postures is the attribution of ascendant power to forces outside the self (the cruel hand of fate, people in authority, the other sex). There is also often the manipulation of those who—because of their own artificially ascendant posture—are disarmed by the descendent's invisible potency. A visible, overtly effective, straightforward stance in the world is not an option. Since closeness requires the ascendant dimensions of initiative and responsibility as well as passion and release, when there is marked polarization, real intimacy, as well as autonomy, is again difficult.

In the following example we see splitting with primary identification in the lower pole. (The client's primary energetic centered in the early part of middle-axis dynamics, with about a 40/60 balance between upper and lower poles.)

> When I worked with Bill he was in his late thirties. While very talented and intelligent, he never seemed able to make anything of himself. Both his schemes and his loves characteristically began with a grand flair, and ended in apathy.
>
> His feeling was that life never seemed to give him a break. More accurately, he would feel an impulse, become excited by it and make plans, then procrastinate until the idea had lost all vitality. While most of Bill's activity was sedentary, his body was tensely muscular and block-

like; his upper and lower halves were held in chronic isometric tension.

During one session he recounted a dream in which he saw himself as a small red haired boy holding himself in a stance of intractable defiance. In talking about it, he described how his impulsiveness and oppositional posture during his school days had created frequent conflicts with school authorities and police. Beneath these memories came floods of feelings toward his parents who, while caring, expressed their need for control by demanding high standards from his work while withholding validation. He had responded to them by reactively opposing their control. In working with these feelings, he was able to recognize how his procrastination now was a parallel defiance of his own upper half.

We worked by bringing each of these halves into the room, allowing them both to express their identity and purpose, and offering the opportunity for communication between them. In this process, his upper pole softened its control and the impulse to dominate gradually transformed into strong, creatively useful, powers of discrimination. Parallel with this, the spunkiness of the little boy bit by bit evolved into a potent source of creative conviction.

The symptoms we see with splitting at any stage can be understood simply as polarized and caricatured expressions of the qualities that normally define that energetic. Below I've outlined some of the more common symptom qualities when splitting is relatively severe (we'll look at such patterns in more detail in chapter ten):

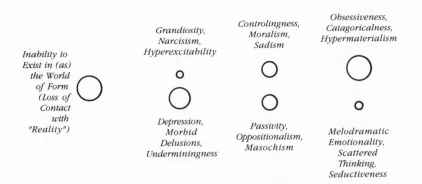

FIG. 7-6. Some Examples of Polar Qualities as Symptoms

The recognition that identity grows as a play of polar dynamics can help us understand many common, but logically baffling psychological phenomena. For example, when we feel fragile, we quite reasonably assume that what is needed is to ascend—to be strong, to fortify ourselves. In fact, while this is frequently the case, just as often the opposite is true. We feel weak because we've been trying to hold ourselves up past the timely point of release. When the feared surrender is risked, we experience a revitalization, and new ascent follows as a natural continuation of rhythm.

Similarly, when we feel tense, we usually assume that what is needed is to learn to relax. But not infrequently the solution lies in quite the opposite kind of response. The tension comes from the fact that there is some challenge we need to face that we are keeping at bay. When we risk the struggle it asks of us, we gain a new level of internal structure. With this new solidity, we find the desired release coming naturally.

Another place a grasp of polar dynamics can help is in understanding shifts that often occur in people between highly disparate kinds of behavior. It is not uncommon to find a dogmatic atheist becoming a religious zealot, or a juvenile delinquent emerging as a vigilant advocate of law and order. From the outside these seem like dramatic changes. From the perspective of energetic patterns, we can see that what is changing is less person than attire. Shifts of this kind happen readily between two elevated or depressed patterns in the same energetic stage, or between one pattern that is elevated and another that is depressed in the same stage. Whenever we see the startling qualitative changes of a "conversion"—be it religious, political or philosophic—it is this process we are witnessing.

A sensitivity to polar dynamics can also help in understanding many initially confusing personality constellations. For example,

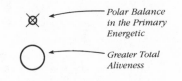

Polar Balance in the Primary Energetic

Greater Total Aliveness

even when a person with a bias toward early-axis in their personality is strongly balanced toward the upper pole, their fundamental values will almost always be much more matriarchal than patriarchal. If we are seeing the whole energetic, this makes perfect sense; no matter how great the shift, the greater aliveness here is in truth below. We see the reverse situation in a person with a largely lower pole, late-axis personality. Even though the polarity is descendent and organized

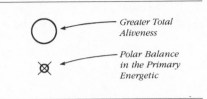

genitally, such a person will frequently seem bubbly in their personality, and if there is significant splitting, in touch with their sexuality in only the most superficial ways. No matter how decendent the polarization in late-axis, the great preponderance of aliveness is ascendant.

Working actively with polar dynamics is one of the most powerful levers for change I know of. I commonly have people dialogue with and between parts of themselves as "inner characters." In dreams and myth, the symbolic naturally represents the different parts of who we are as personified images. We can similarly access this kind of material in a waking state. Working with it is not unlike doing family therapy, only here the parts in the system are the members of a person's "inner family." My concerns are very similar to those that pertain when working with a real family. To the degree it is possible, I want to include everyone, and I want to open some degree of communication between them. Importantly, this communication need not be pleasant—expressed difference is as or frequently more important than agreement. Growth emerges out of the courage to creatively take part in reality as it exists.

One way of thinking of the process of growing is that it is simply the willingness to risk honoring the multiple relationships between Above and Below, Within and Without, that at any point in time are most generative. This risking takes place at a complex interplay of levels, from the moment to moment rhythms of activity and repose, to the various inner tensions of growing up, to the particular juxtaposition of mystery and majesty that defines the edge of one's historical reality.

CHAPTER EIGHT

A STEP BEYOND: EXPRESSION, PENETRATION AND BOUNDARY

"Three kinds of prayers;
I am a bow in your hands, Lord,
Draw me lest I rot.

Do not overdraw me, Lord, I shall break.

Overdraw me, Lord, and who cares if I break."
—Nikos Kazantzakis
Report to Greco

"But such is the irresistible nature of truth, that all it asks,
and all it wants, is the liberty of appearing."
—Thomas Paine

"I will act as if what I do makes a difference."
—William James

THE HORIZONTAL

 We move now from looking at the creative cycle as a dialogue between the Above and the Below, to exploring how it manifests in the horizontal: as an interplay between inner and outer aspects of experience. Before turning to specifics, we should take some time with horizontal dynamics as a whole. The details will at first inevitably seem abstract, but as we progress this overview will help keep us in touch with how the elements we are exploring fit into the larger creative picture.

Though we are addressing the vertical and the horizontal separately, it is, in starting, important to recognize that these dynamics are in fact always intimately related. For creative rhythms of any great periodicity—such as those of a creative task, a lifetime, or the evolution of culture—the vertical and the horizontal organize within us as a single pulse. By virtue of our erect posture, they concern themselves with somewhat different aspects of our experience, but the themes are integrally related, and the dynamics are part of an integral process.

The shift in focus to the horizontal is a shift then in emphasis more than in domain. But it is a definite shift. We are leaving behind our primary concern with the internal workings of systems, and bringing to the foreground questions of relationships between systems. The vertical and the horizontal each embody both internal and relational dynamics, but the simple fact that we engage each other most often face to face, and belly to belly, places relationship most strongly in the horizontal domain.

With interaction now forefront, we need to understand a bit more about the creative workings of relationship (a topic we will examine in detail in chapter eleven). I distinguish three primary kinds of interactive patterns in human relationship. None ever exist in isolation; they are overlapping mechanisms. But recognizing how they are different can help in making important delineations, both in how various systems interact, and in how they change creatively through their interactions.

The three kinds of creative interface are distinquished by the nature of the parts that are interacting.

In the first, the units exist in a parallel relationship and are, for the most part, whole systems. We see examples of this in the meeting of two people who do not yet know each other, or in interactions between two similar social systems, say, two similar cities or organizations.

$O \Leftrightarrow O$

Parallel Relationship

In the second, the systems, besides having individual identities, function as polar complements that together define a larger system. The relationship between a king or queen and the royal subjects is such a relationship manifest predominantly in the vertical. This kind of dynamic can manifest as well in the horizontal. An example is the traditional family of not too many years back, in which the woman, in spending most of her time caring for home and children, acted as the primary keeper of the inner aspects of the family system, while the man, in "going off" to work, was primary keeper of the outer.

Polar Relationship

In the third kind of interactional dynamic, one system functions as the generative context for the other. This type predominates in the relationship of a child to its family as a system, or in that of any creative project to the individual or group who brings it into being.

Contextual Relationship

A deeper understanding of the horizontal aspects of relationship and change will let us think in more creative detail about relationships of all types, and particularly about those aspects of relationship that happen between horizontally analogous systems or parts of systems. It will as well help us better understand both personality styles and the roles we take in systems. Just as we differentially embody upper and lower realms within ourselves and the systems we take part in, so we also inhabit variously domains that are closer to the intimate core of experience and ones that are closer to its more manifest periphery.

To begin thinking about the horizontal, we might examine how it manifests bodily. If we are sensitive, we can notice that in the course of any formative rhythm, something very similar to what goes on between Above and Below happens between the body's vertical axis and the body surface. A very specific kind of wave propogates in, and shapes, our bodily experience. This progression is structurally identical to the vertical one, except that in the vertical progression the path etched is bipolar (the upper pole ascending, the lower pole moving downward), while in the horizontal progression the less form-defined pole is fixed at the bodily axis.

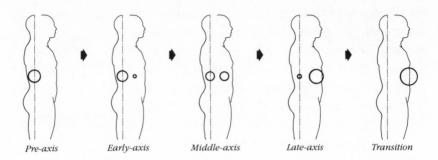

| Pre-axis | Early-axis | Middle-axis | Late-axis | Transition |

FIG. 8-1. Basic Progression in the First Half of Horizontal Rhythm

The essential variables in these changes are identical with those in the vertical. First, there is a separation of the whole of experience into inner and outer aspects. Second, the outer aspect becomes increasingly form-defined. And third, throughout the first half of rhythm, there is a gradual shifting of emphasis from the more unformed pole to the more peripheral and delineated half of things.

Our growing up is at once a growing out, a shifting of attention from a primary focus on inner experience to ever greater interest and effectiveness with more worldly concerns. Below is the diagram I presented earlier showing the vertical and horizontal propagating as a single pulse:

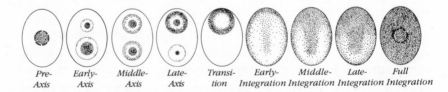

| Pre-Axis | Early-Axis | Middle-Axis | Late-Axis | Transition | Early-Integration | Middle-Integration | Late-Integration | Full Integration |

FIG. 8-2. Vertical and Horizontal Rhythms
Together as a Single Cyclic Progression

How do we experience our horizontal creative polarities? We refer to their juxtaposition in a number of ways in our common speech. We talk of having a private self and a public self, an inner world and an outer world, a self of being and a self of doing.

But they are more than just intrapsychic dynamics. Just as the Above and Below are resonant statements about each of the creative wholes of which we are a part (our relationship to the Above and Below in family, society and planet/cosmos, as well as in ourselves), so are the inner and outer aspects in creative organization expressions not just of the Within and Without in ourselves, but of the Within and Without in each one of our spheres of creative involvement. In any creative whole there are inner and outer elements, parts that feel most intimately internal and parts that feel most external. For example, in a family or neighborhood there are qualities of feeling and action that lie clearly in the domain of hearth and home; and there are others, equally critical, that reside more peripherally, in the workplace, and in social structures that both protect and provide expression from these more inner domains. At the level of culture, our embodiment of inner and outer aspects are mirrored in polarities such as those between sacred and secular, or art and science.

Where we experience ourselves in this polarity is a function of a multitude of factors. Often, depending on the moment, we can experience ourselves from each side in the same general context. This is particularly common when we are dealing with a situation where one system is serving as the generative context for another. For example, for a child playing safely in the family house, the parents are outer: they protect, and they are the keepers of the unknown beyond. When that same child ventures from home and gets lost, the image of parents shifts inward. Now they symbolize the known, and the warmth and acceptance of home. In contextual relationships, we see shifts of polarity as well as a function of the germinal system's development. As a child grows up, it is more and more able to assume, and increasingly committed to assuming, outer, more form-defined aspects of the relationship.

Just as with the Above and the Below, if we wish to think creatively, we must look at more than just the poles, since the poles alone are static. We must look at the generative movements that link them, and issue forth from them. Systems are alive by virtue of being constituted not just of parts, but of creative interfaces between parts, and further creative interfaces between these systems as parts in further systems.

In the vertical dimension, the creative movement most related to form-taking was ascent. Its horizontal analogue is the *expressive*. Our expressivity is our ability to affect our world actively, by making form toward and into it. Like ascent, it gives preference to the language of the many over that of the one. We express to "make a difference." The horizontal analogue to ground is the *receptive*. Our receptivity is the dissolving, opening aspect of the horizontal, our capacity to be touched, to be moved.

Importantly, as with ascent and ground, with the expressive and the receptive we are dealing not with simple vectors, but with statements of creative relationship. These are four-dimensional concepts. At its most basic, we see this living dynamism in the simple fact that neither the expressive nor the receptive ever function in isolation. An integral part of the receptive is responsiveness; without it, all we have is the deadness of passivity. And only when we are receiving at the same time we are expressing are our words or actions anything more than empty, reflexive externalizations.

We will see the implications of this in much more detailed terms in exploring how the creative relationship between horizontal poles defines not just the felt quality of an act of expressing or receiving, but *what* is possible to express or receive, and even *where* in the body we experience expressing and receiving as happening.

This last notion is worthy of a moment's attention. It helps fill out our picture of how the horizontal organizes in, and as, the body. The interplay of several factors determines within what layers, from core to periphery, we will most feel a particular interaction. One factor is simply what is being related about, from issues about which one is vulnerable at an intimately personal level, to more surface concerns. Another is the back-and-forth inherent to any exchange. In alternating between expressing and receiving, there is a slight shifting outward and inward in the balance between Within and Without that defines any moment of interaction. A further factor is the relative juxtaposition of systems that function as complementary parts within a larger creative system. We may see quite polarized energetics when that complementarity is the preeminent reality, for example, in a teacher-student relationship at test-time, or between husband and wife in a traditional marriage at moments of close intimacy. The degree of polarization may depend strongly on the situation: take either person out of that particular space and time context, and you may see a very different sort of balance.

The above factors affect relative inner and outer balance within a particular stage. The following affect not just this physical locale, but also the bodily reality that is interacting. Just as with vertical rhythms, each horizontal rhythm is relative within each of its larger defining rhythms. Both what one is moved to express or receive, and how that expressing or receiving organizes in the body, are functions of all other relevant periodicities: the developmental stage of the relationship one is interacting within, how far along two people are in a project they are working on, and lifetime and cultural rhythms. All of these things together define the "us" that is there to interact.

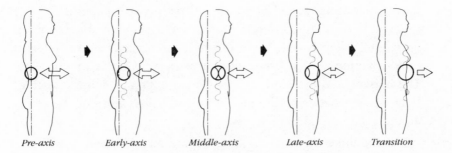

Pre-axis   Early-axis   Middle-axis   Late-axis   Transition

FIG. 8-3. *Expressive and Receptive Acts Made from Different Stages of Horizontal Rhythm*

The further a system's relevant creative periodicities have progressed into the first half of cycle, and the greater the identification in that stage with the more form-defined polarity, the more peripherally in the body the dynamics of relationship will be experienced. I have depicted this evolution within a single rhythm above, indicating the balance point between inner and outer poles, the average felt "self" of interaction, with a circle. (The line dividing the circle indicates the relative balance of inner and outer qualities embodied here by virtue of the stage in creative cycle.)*

To be complete, this depiction must include the vertical as well as the horizontal. When it does, the picture looks like this:

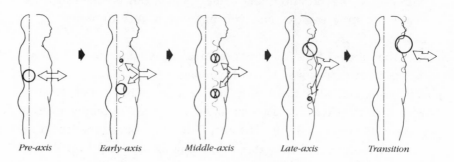

Pre-axis   Early-axis   Middle-axis   Late-axis   Transition

FIG. 8-4. Expressive and Receptive Acts Made from Different Stages in a Contextual Rhythm

Both the embodied reality and the layering in which relationship is most strongly felt are also affected by a person's primary energetic. The variables here are both the dominant stage in the primary energetic and its relative balance between polarities.

We have many common words for describing differences in horizontal balance. We speak of one person as reflective, internal or introverted, and another as extroverted, worldly, or outgoing. The horizontal dimension of our primary energetic defines much of how we experience both who we are, and the nature of the world around us.

If the inner aspect is dominant, more receptive values will predominate in our feelings and actions, and the world will seem to reside distinctly "out there." If this kind of balance is relatively healthy, our outer experience, while not as familiar, will still be a source of gratification. If there is significant splitting, the world may easily seem overwhelming and fearsome, or exciting but out of reach.

_____

* This shift in the bodily locus of aliveness with movement through the creative stages is not as pronounced in the vertical because of vertical rhythm's bipolar structure, but there is still some effect.

If the energetic is balanced more externally, we will tend to identify more with the manifest. What will seem most other is not the world, but the inner self, and the kinds of connectings with people and nature that require a deeper, more intimate kind of resonation. If the balance is timely, worldly concerns will mean most to us, but when we need to tap into more personal levels we can do so. If there is significant splitting, we may feel an estranged "outsider" to ourselves and to meaningful connection with others.

Related to the question of the pole one is most likely to inhabit is the question of the pole one is likely to perceive as most importance. The key variable here is how far along one is in the relevant creative progressions. Early on, we are most likely to attribute power and truth to the Within; later, in the more form-defined stages, to the Without. A simple place to see this is the already-mentioned tendency of people in early stages of culture to view the world of essence and spirit as the "real" reality, and that of things as very secondary, or even illusionary. This is in sharp contrast to more form-defined times where "the actual is the factual."

The horizontal, then, describes who we are as creatively relational beings. Formative progression in the horizontal defines both how relationships grow and change, and how we grow and change as embodied participants in them. In this chapter, our interest is with the form-creating, difference-establishing voice in creative dialogue; in the next, with the complementary voice of form-release: receptivity and dissolution of difference.

EXPRESSION AS CREATION

"I actually felt that I had a great river thrusting for release inside of me, and that I had to find a channel into which its flood-like power could pour. I knew I had to find it or I would be destroyed in the flood of my own creation."
—*Thomas Wolfe*

"When I am a man, then I shall be a hunter.
When I am a man, then I shall be a harpooner.
When I am a man, then I shall be a canoe-builder.
When I am a man, then I shall be a carpenter.
When I am a man, then I shall be a artisan.
Oh, father! ya hahaha."

—*A Kwakiutl Indian Song*

Who are we as the expressive? As with ascent, there are major aspects of expression we can address quite well with our usual language: much of it is quite "straightforward." Our concern is with movement toward form, with acting and doing, and thus the language of form, of goals and linear causation, can embrace a good part of what is important in understanding.

But if we spend any time with what really happens in an act of expression, we discover quickly that our usual language is hardly enough. Any act of real expression is a fully creative dynamic, a generatively interactional process both within the system doing the expressing, and with the system which that expression engages. As with ascent, to understand four-dimensionally, we must read between the lines of our usual assumptions.

What does it mean to move outward into formedness? Myth offers us some good beginning images. The expressive embodies in myth and legend in the image of the hero, and specifically in the hero's active aspect—the hero as wielder of the sword, utterer of the incisive word. This active aspect of the hero can personify in an infinity of forms—the poet, the warrior, the inventor, the magician—but the essential quality is quite specific: the capacity to penetrate reality. Anything that can actively alter the world can do the penetrating—the spoken word, a gesturing hand, a brush, a fist, a pen, a phallus, a carpenter's hammer, a sewing needle, a knife or sword.

The common thrust of such images is that in some way they speak of taking the impulse toward life and selfhood, and propelling it to the forefront, visible and external, committed to whatever may happen.

Our colloquial language is rich with phrases that speak of who we are when we "put ourselves forward." Some simply describe movement outward or how movement outward penetrates another's reality. We speak of "getting through to someone," of making "a point" or "an impression," of "getting something across," or "speaking out." Others emphasize the finality intrinsic to expression: we "put our cards on the table." Many such figures of speech give voice to the inherent vulnerability of expression. We speak of "going out on a limb," or of putting ourselves "on the line."

To fully appreciate the transformational nature of expression, we must take these images and move with them beyond the bounds of usual material thought. Limited to Cartesian/Newtonian understanding, expression is a mechanistic act, simply externalization. Our thoughts and feelings are "things" that we have, and when we choose, we send them out into the world in the form of words or actions. They either impact or they don't, and that's that.

For many purposes, such a vending machine image does not get unduly in the way. But it clearly stops short of embracing the wonder of human expression. Real expression is never just manufacture; it is a critical, integral part of generative reality.

The words and feelings we express are not static, but ever-growing and evolving dynamics; and they are not just things that grow in us; their growth is us. Even when we think we have learned something we express from someone else, to the degree that it is alive for us, we will find it has been carefully selected from a miriad of things we might have gleaned, and subtly reshaped and re-animated in the process of our ongoing self-creation.

And more than this, the act of expression is itself a critical part of that self-creation. Our usual notion is that we first devise something, then express it. But in truth, the impulse or image that starts an act of expression is rarely, if ever, a finished creation. What we express always grows and changes through the act of expression, often dramatically. This book is different in very important ways from the book I started seven years ago. In a similar way, in getting up to speak at a meeting, while there are certain things I know in advance, much that I say always surprises me. As I see it, we really can know little about who we are or what we know until we express it. Expression is not an appendix to knowing, but an integral part of the process by which something becomes knowing.

Expressive acts penetrate reality: They act to make a difference.

ABOVE: *Madame Curie.* BELOW: *"How Arthur drew froth ye sword." From* King Arthur and His Knights *by Howard Pyle. 1910.* OPPOSITE, TOP: Pictish Warrior. *Watercolor by John White. c. 1590.* OPPOSITE, BELOW: *Krishna playing his sacred flute for the animals. Indian miniature. c. 1770.*

It should be clear from this that there is no such thing as expression without uncertainty. Expression inherently makes us vulnerable. To express is to put ourselves on the line, and never as something complete once and for all, but as process. And this is a process which, because it is us, we can never fully understand. Any real act of expression—be it only a nod or a touch, a letter to a friend, or Michelangelo's David—is ultimately a leap of faith.

In risking to express, what kinds of things can happen? Certainly we can be rejected. We can risk to initiate, speak our minds, or share what excites us and find ourselves facing an impenetrable wall. Or we can extend our aliveness and find it met by forces bent on destroying it, forces of all sorts, stated symbolically, from Above—clubs or cleavers; from Below—openings girded with teeth or a path suddenly turned quicksand; from Without—imprisoning walls or the knife blade of attack; from Within—a seductive offering of ease or false grandeur. When we offer our aliveness into the world, we always risk that it may enter a trap born from the fear that such aliveness might manifest. A further kind of danger seems on the surface less a peril, but in truth it is what we fear most—this is that in putting ourselves into the world, nothing will happen; there will be no response at all.

Meeting such fearsome forces need not be negative; often they are just what we need to challenge us to more significant and developed expression. And not infrequently, the specters we fear, on actual encounter, transform to reveal themselves as very different from our imaginings.

But the dangers in expression are real as well, and we can be fully potent in our words and actions really only to the degree that we accept that expression is indeed a risky endeavor. Every real act of expression—putting ourselves into the world—involves the fundamental danger that some part of what is most essential in us, of who we are as self and soul, will not survive. To risk full expression is, on one hand, very ordinary, just being who we are; and at once it is something for which the dramatic symbolism of the hero is fully appropriate.

I mentioned that the thing we fear most is that our acts or ideas will "fall on deaf ears," that there will be no response, that

our words will move through space and touch nothing. This observation nicely introduces a further piece in understanding the creative nature of expressive dynamics: the relational nature of
expression.

If our expression is part of us, that we might fear violence
toward it, at least when it is not yet fully formed, is understandable. But what about rejection or unresponsiveness? Why should
these be anything more than just a signal to try again?

The essential awareness is that, as living beings, we have
existence only to the degree that we have relationship. And without expression—and by this I mean expression that has effect—
there is no relationship. Risking the vulnerablity of expression is
much more than a matter of choice; to the degree that we wish to be
alive, it is an imperative. We can only live in a world we can connect with and affect, and not just from rote or reflex, but in a way
that speaks from the full and unique passion of our being.

Observations of young children show that if no one sees their
tears or smiles, if there is no holding, warmth, or excitement in
response to their sounds and movements, they begin to give up life.
They become depressed, and some just die. Life is a meeting of self
and world. Ultimately, we can be vital only to the degree that our
words and actions creatively engage and effect the living reality
around us.

A nice place to see the relational nature of expression is in the
ultimate inseparability of the content of expression from its relational context. We usually assume that while we may choose to say
different things in different situations, what we think and have
available to say is relatively independent of the setting. If we
examine what actually goes on, we notice something quite different.
What occurs to us to say and do, and often even what we find ourselves capable of saying and doing is intimately a function of who
we are saying and doing it in relation to. Expression is not just some-
hing we do to another; it is born from our connection with that
other. Not only does the voice affect what the ear will hear, but
the "ear" affects as well what the voice will say.

This co-generative aspect of expression becomes most visible in
settings where the esthetic of unity is strong. A simple place to see

it is in lovemaking. Most often, when we talk about what happens in lovemaking, we frame it in causal terms: I do this, he or she gets aroused. But clearly, this hardly explains what happens. In truth, what occurs to us to do, and our ability to do it, are each intimately a function of that arousal. The expression in lovemaking involves two individuals, but to the degree that it is alive, it is well beyond simple intention; it is a dance in which each movement creatively calls forth the next, often in most mysterious and unexpected ways.

THE VOICES OF EXPRESSION

"I see the thing I have made coming out of the women's bush. It is now a proud man jina (guardian spirit) with plenty of women running after him. It is not possible to see anything more wonderful in this world. His face is shining, he looks this way and that, and all the people wonder about this beautiful and terrible thing. To me, it is like what I see when I am dreaming. I say to myself, this is what my neme (individual guardian spirit) has brought into my mind. I say, I have made this. How can a man make such a thing? It is a fearful thing I can do."

—*Gola Maskmaker (Liberia)*

"To speak the truth, to maintain the right, to practice courtesy, to despise the allurements of ease and safety, to maintain honor in every perilous adventure, to uphold Christianity, to destroy tyranny wherever it might be, to defend and protect to the uttermost women, the poor and the oppressed."

—*The Oath of the Round Table*

What and how we express is a function of the stages we occupy in our various major rhythms, and our balance within the energetics of that stage. Expression is not arbitrary: it manifests from, and as, the particular truth that we are at a specific moment.

We could go through each of the major periodicities and talk about the changing faces of expression within them. For brevity's sake, I will choose just one, that of cultural evolution. Our interest here will be with the progression of expressive identities that become defined with the growing "cultural body."

In speaking of these dynamics, I will discuss two ascendant and two descendent faces for each stage, one each for the outer and inner aspects. I will indicate them diagrammatically as in the figure below. I have drawn the two horizontal polarities as a single locus to indicate that it is their rhythmic interface which serves as the point of organization for the smaller rhythms of expressing and receiving.

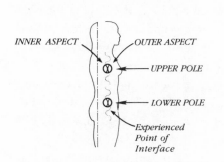

FIG. 8-5. *The Voices of Expression*

It is not precisely accurate to talk as if the inner and outer poles are each expressive. More accurately, any system at a point in time has a certain balance between internal and external organization, and this balance determines both what will be discussed, and the distance from core this expression will travel. Where the balance is more toward the outer pole, the system will be organized more around external concerns and be most overtly expressive. Where the organization is more internal, a more unitary esthetic will prevail and receiving will outweigh expressing. In looking at inner and outer "expressive" poles we are in fact talking about relative balance between expressive and receptive dynamics.

The basic sensibilities expressed at each stage should be familiar. The inner and outer faces at each stage are simply the more worldly and more intimate aspects of the ascendant and descendent dynamics that we have previously explored.

At the point of original unity, we can think of expression in two ways. If our focus is on the new creative rhythm, we would say there is no expression yet—nothing has become visible. Putting our focus on that rhythm's context, we recognize abundant expression, but it is "second nature," just part of the accepted ebb and flow of the system.

In earliest pre-history, the expressive element is simply the outer rhythmic edge of the tribe as organism—extending by day into nature's larger surround with stone, spear, basket, or trap to gather sustenance for the tribal body or to protect its perimeter, returning by night to the tribal circle. There are differentiations in role here—the more ascendant voice of a chieftain, the piercing gestures of the warrior, the special intimacy with nature of gatherers and hunters, the bridging between Above and Below of the shaman—but at least in the earliest emergings of pre-history, these differentiations are more nuances in a single gesture than the dynamically-charged polarities we find with later stages.

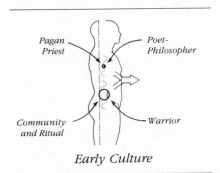

Early Culture

Expression, as we move into early-axis dynamics, becomes more delineated, but according to the still very permeable laws of magical causality. Mythically, the upper pole is occupied by the god-king and those close to him. There are two sorts of voices. Within are those figures whose tasks are meditative and priestly. Without we see the poet-philosophers and those concerned with the functions of governance, offering words and images for the new truth. They are like the juxtaposed faces of awe and excited utterance in the child.

The more overtly expressive face of the lower pole is the warrior, guided by emergent numinosity but taking his power more from the wildness of the descendant. Within we find the expressive functions closer to the core of family and community, and to mystery—sustenance, ritual, communion, the erotic.

Especially in the early parts of this stage, the distinctions between expressive figures are rudimentary. Not uncommonly the more peripheral structural/governmental tasks of the ascendent sphere and more inner spiritual functions are assumed by the same figures. And while today we would ascribe such concerns as defense and the erotic to quite different realms, here such lower pole distinctions are much more fluid.

Descriptions of how the ancient Celts approached warfare offer striking illustration. Warriors and poets each had roles. The warriors, often nude with bodies painted in frightening colors, would lead with screams and thrusts of the lance. The poets would stand amidst the fury, commenting on particularly valorous acts and crafting images to describe what was taking place. The battle could end because one side had clearly prevailed with the sword, or because the words of a poet had rung with particular eloquence. Warfare here was less a method of dominion, than simply part of life's passionate dance.

As we move toward middle-axis dynamics, the tension of polar opposites at its strongest, expressive roles become increasingly delineated. There are now two distinct voices in the ascendent as-

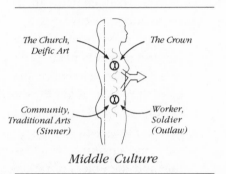

Middle Culture

pect of the horizontal. The King, Czar, or Emperor, and his court, utter the dictates of the secular; religious heads those of the divine. They work together, but there is an increasing tension over just what belongs to Caesar and what to God.

As truth shifts upward and outward, the sensibilities of the artistic shift to the inner and lower realms. There is a strict differentiation. Looking upward, we see the devotional monumentality of religious art. At the same time, more abundant, but less acknowledged, there is the craftsmanship of traditional "folk arts."

The relationships between Above and Below, Within and Without, are ambivalent. The lower poles each contain two sorts of faces, one an ally to established power, the other a thorn in its side.

Without, and in allegiance to the Above, we see the soldier and the worker. War is now fought for state supremacy and moral order; the warrior is no longer primarily a voice of mystery and the untamed, but like Roman legionnaire or medieval knight, a servant of ascendant right. The worker, serf, or slave offers the sweat and toil out of which the structures of power rise.

But certain elements of the lower pole's voice of creative doubt and germinal wildness remain, kept at a distance, but never fully out of the picture. We see this part of the outer Below represented in "folk heroes" like Robin Hood or Jesse James. As James once said, "All the world loves an outlaw. At least for some reason they remember 'em."

Within and Below, the voice of mystery is more and more muted, still heard in ritual, but increasingly contained in its manifestation. Qualities such as constancy and forbearance are more and more valued in the actions and toils of home and community. When the dark forces of mystery and chaos are too strong, this domain speaks as the voice of sin, a force ardently condemned, but by this very ardency, revealed as having powerful importance.

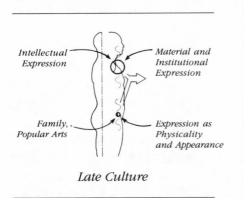

Late Culture

As we move into late-axis culture, the dominant forms of expression shift more and more upward and to the peripheral. The major heroic figures in this stage are the creators of invention and the voices of rational determination. Expressive power has ascended above dominion by force or even moral decree, and is becoming increasingly secular in focus. The pen now is indeed mightier than the sword. The other expressive domains are present, but increasingly ordered by this ascendent/peripheral esthetic and given ever-decreasing status.

The ascendant functions closer to core, at least in the early part of this stage, maintain a relatively prominent place. But their power is waning. The church continues to have a place, but its role becomes more and more secondary to secular government, and within it, philosophical ideas increasingly replace the more direct voice of ritual. Similarly, the arts that attend to the ascendent play an important role early on. With the Renaissance we see the great flowering of high culture forms—opera, ballet, symphony, the work of the great masters. But while this is happening, art is also gradually leaving behind its connection in the primal source. The voice of high art is increasingly material. In the later parts of this substage we see art for the first time openly regarded as a commodity in the marketplace.

The lower expressive realms are now fully secondary to the higher. The soldier is strictly a functionary of the state; the inner domains of home and family exist to serve the patriarchal order. As ascent becomes more and more complete, the sanctions against the more wild sides of the descendent are somewhat loosened if these parts of us are expressed in appropriately circumscribed locales: on the sports field and behind closed doors in the bedroom. We give the body more freedom but increasingly regard it as a purely physical object.

In the later part of late culture, with the disappearance of the community foundation necessary for traditional art forms, we see the emergence of the "popular arts." While symbolizing the ultimate arena of pleasure and release for many, again we are seeing a descendent domain for which the greater part of the energetic is in truth ascendent and peripheral. What before was participatory becomes something to purchase—"entertainment"—and something intended to touch only the most surface layers of our being.

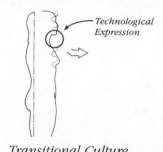

Technological Expression

Transitional Culture

As we move past late culture into transitional times, the expressive, like the ascendant, becomes permeated by contradiction. The outer pole is becoming more and more peripheral and ascendant. With this, on one hand, we find the expressive becoming ever more sophisticated. New information technologies dramatically increase the volume of communication. Computers process as much information in a few minutes as was exchanged in the whole history of written language. Communication satellites encircle the earth.

And at the same time, the connections necessary to make this technology serve the human soul become more and more tenuous. The possibilities are wondrous, but side by side with this amazing potential, one sees a frightening paucity of substantive expression. Politicians find that media time is better spent polishing their image than addressing issues. Televisions sit in nearly every living room and offer little but psychological junk food.

The lower poles similarly reflect this irony and perturbation. In one sense, they have simply ceased to exist. The hero is hyper-mechanized man, flesh replaced by its bionic equivalent. In another sense, the longing for passion and the untamed is so great that it becomes amplified by distortion. Hollywood "stars" and sports celebrities get million dollar salaries and unending publicity. They are dramatically visible, but increasingly empty and superficial images: symbols with only the thinnest veneer of substance.

What lies ahead in the expressive domain? While the times ahead will not necessarily be easy ones, we should, if we prevail in them, see exciting new possibilities emerging in our expressive potency. We should see continued development of new tools of expression. And we should see a new and growing ability to use our expression to address living concerns. With this we should see an emerging capacity to bring the forces of expression that were before isolated to particular stages into a larger expressive sensibility, and an expansion of each of these earlier expressive realities—a poet who is at once a scientist becomes a different kind of poet. But again, these are concerns of the second half of rhythm and this book's final chapters.

BEING AND BOUNDARY

"The No, as the Yes, is power and is the truth of God, or God himself. He would in himself be unknowable, and in himself would be no joy of elevation, no feeling, without the No." —Jacob Boehme

"Always be ready to speak your mind and a base man will ignore you."

—William Blake

*"Don't hem in on me, don't hog, don't crush, don't bird
dog, don't trail me, don't crawl under my fence, don't
squeeze in my chipmunk hole, don't suck my popsicle, keep
your greasy fingers to yourself."*

—Susie Rutherford

We found in considering the vertical that we could not talk
about ascent without simultaneously speaking about a second process: separation. Similarly, when we examine the form-taking half
of the horizontal, we find, along with expression, a second critical
dynamic: boundary-making. To express is to distinguish.

Boundary is an essential part of formative process. We are
often unconscious of its role, but its place is pivotal. It is what
makes interface not just merging, but meeting. It is the essential *no*
that makes possible the *yes* of living interrelationship. Relationship and change require difference—and not just static borders, but
dynamic points of challenge and interplay.

Expression and boundary making are inextricable dynamics.
The warrior carries not just a sword, but a shield as well. The
tribesman is not just the hunter, stalking game for tribal sustenance,
but the tribe's defense as well, by his movements defining the
tribe's periphery and by his actions protecting it from invasion.

As boundary making is a function defined by form, again the
conceptual challenge in understanding it lies less in recognizing the
fact of boundaries, than in understanding how they work as creative dynamics. Our usual images for boundary are decidedly
static—a wall, a sheet of glass. Living boundaries are vital
entities, and entities that grow and change as integral parts of
creative progression, evolving both in quality—how we experience
them—and in function—in what, both within us and without, they
serve to delineate.

To begin exploring the dynamic nature of boundary, we might
take an image from biology, that of the cell membrane. The first
time we look at a cell through a microscope we easily overlook this
plain-looking bag surrounding the cell, drawn to more exotic sights.
But we can't spend much time observing the life of a cell without
being awed by the membrane's special magic.

The cell membrane is extremely thin, only a few molecules of protein and lipid thick. But it accomplishes one of the true miracles of life. Mythically, the cell membrane speaks the lines of both intimate and warrior. It is the gatekeeper: inviting entry for things essential to the cell's growth and well being, keeping out what might be harmful, and expelling whatever has become toxic or lost its usefulness. It keeps a dynamic difference of incalculable complexity between Within and Without.

Biologists speak of the cell membrane as "semipermeable." In its full sense, this refers not only to the complex discriminations that occur at this interface, but also to its inherently transformational nature. The membrane is alive and ever-evolving. Its capacity for dynamic responsiveness is critical in every aspect of the cell's life as change: from the internal shifts born from the cell's growth, to fluctuations in cell size and shape, to dramatic alterations in the makeup of the cell's external world, to an ever-evolving parade of potential threats to the cell's integrity. The cell membrane is both entryway and city wall to a teeming metropolis that is never in two moments the same.

In a similar way, it is through the creative forming and unforming of our boundaries that—as individuals and groups—we establish both discrete existence and our relationships to things around us. It is through boundary that we are able to say, "This is me, and that's a stone, and that's my friend John." We have many different types of boundaries. The outer surfaces of all of our cells and organs, and that of our physical body as a whole, each form obvious, selectively permeable, interfaces. As social beings, we recognize critical interplays of interface with words like "community," "friendship," "home," and "intimacy." Finally, there are the psycho-physical interfaces within that delineate what we respond to as parts of our being: the dimensions of our feelings, the roles we assume, the categories of our thoughts, the cast of characters that move in the terrain of our symbolic experience.

Boundaries are creative functions. They are not just walls, but living interfaces. As with all living processes, they can exist only to the degree we can risk uncertainty. As with expression, there is no guarantee that risking to make a boundary, even when timely, will in fact bring fulfillment. If it is made in relation to a system that cannot yet tolerate this degree of difference, a boundary can as easily bring attack or abandonment.

The creative nature of boundary becomes most explicitly understandable when we can begin to recognize its inherently evolutionary workings. The boundaries that delineate experience are very different at different points in evolutionary processes, different both in their felt qualities and in what precisely they delineate.

Take a few moments with the following exploration. It is an exercise often done in psychology groups, and is powerful in that it can help one get a directly palpable sense of the workings of boundary.

> Find another person and have him or her stand about twenty feet away, facing you. When you are ready, have that person begin walking slowly toward you. Keep in touch with your body, and when you get a response that tells you they have reached your boundaries, gesture for them to stop.
>
> Notice all you can about your experience in this. What was the first signal you got that the right distance had been reached? How and where did you experience this in your body? As you made boundary, what feelings came with it—decisiveness, rigidness, hesitancy, warmth? Let an image come for the quality of boundary that you eventually made—a wall, a feather, a pointed stick.
>
> Try this with a number of different people in different situations. Notice what patterns you can find in how you make boundaries.

In doing this exercise, you likely noticed that both the distance at which you made boundary, and the quality of boundary were different with different people. How we make boundary is relative to a number of things: to time (where we are in the evolution of relationship with that person and in other pertinent periodicities); to place (where we each reside within different social wholes), and to our primary energetics.

The kinds of boundaries we need at different times can be dramatically different. For example, when I am doing new creative work, working close to core, I can be like a mother bear with new cubs. I don't let people get too near to me. Things are still too fragile, and I don't want to need good judgement. I need room to be un-balanced. At a later time, even with the same creative work, but now more formed, my boundary needs change, and I want people close to share what I have created.

Boundaries go through a specific developmental sequence as part of the evolution of any creative dynamic. The details in this evolution are most easily grasped if we think in bodily terms.

We experience our social boundaries in two ways. We feel them as something out there, as an interface with our world. And at the same time, we experience them as a particular relationship within ourselves. In the exercise, as your friend walked toward you, there was a point where they "over-stepped their bounds." There were two parts to this experience. First, there was the specific distance between you defined by the boundary. Second, there was a specific response in your tissues, a palpable, localizable, kinesthetic "no."

The place in our bodies where we feel this response, the felt quality of the response, and the distance at which it occurs are all time-relative within our various periodicities of formative process. The response is felt at that interface which I spoke of earlier as the energetic balance point. In the course of a creative cycle, the place where we feel boundary propagates first outward from core toward periphery, then, in the cycle's second half, integrates to become po-tentially available at any layer as different situations warrant. In terms of quality, boundary moves from being quite diffuse early in cycle to becoming increasingly solid and delineating as creative cycle progresses through its first half. Then, through the integra-tive stages, we see a growing resolution of "hard and fast" bound-aries into more "semi-permeable," organic, and situationally flex-ible interfaces. The distance at which boundaries, if made overtly, manifest is inversely proportional to the distance from core at which they are experienced, and to their degree of definition. When boundaries are fragile and there is little safety zone between them and one's inner self, potential threats must be kept at a con-siderable distance. With more developed boundaries, the system is better protected, and systems perceived as other can come very close and present no great risk.

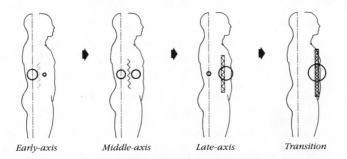

Early-axis   Middle-axis   Late-axis   Transition

FIG. 8-6. The Evolution of Boundary
in the First Half of the Creative Cycle

As one would expect, these boundary differences manifest not just through the course of evolutionary processes, but also as a dimension of a system's primary energetic. A major part of what we are seeing when we say two people have different kinds of personalities is how they deal with boundary and difference.

For example, people with strong early-axis elements in their personality tend to be capable of very close interaction if the context is safe, but keep people quite distant if it is not. If they experience those around them as part of their system, the esthetic of oneness prevails, and boundaries are very permeable. If something changes so that those close by become "other," their proximity will present a major challenge to capacitance, and the person will either have to flee or create symptoms so as to diminish the amount of living connection. There are similar boundary dynamics in childhood relationships. The child functions well with its parents present (they provide boundaries), and with other children (a shared reality of fluid boundaries) but must make radical adaptions if left to go it alone in the adult "world of hard knocks." If the system's capacitance is significantly limited, it may need to make specific adaptations to compensate for this insufficiency in boundary capability. Common approaches are to devise a carefully structured lifestyle to provide some of the boundaries not organically present, or to choose a social niche that allows a largely solitary existence.

Sometimes in response to the need for primal closeness one enters into relationships where the bonds are primarily of a parent-child or child-child sort (e.g., a dependent marriage, a religious cult).

We see opposite kinds of boundary predicaments in people with strong late-axis elements in their personalities. Here there is no particular problem being in proximity. The problem lies in how to have proximity translate into closeness. The late-axis, upper pole person, especially where the outer aspect is pronounced, can function well in a crowded office, and is sufficiently "thick skin-ned" that few things another might do or say are likely to cause real damage. But relationships, even with those one is closest to, will tend toward the business-like; however good one's intentions, it is hard to connect deeply and personally. The predicament of the person with isolated late-axis lower pole dynamics may look very different, but in fact is not dissimilar. Such people are often extremely gregarious, the "life of the party," but because it is hard for them to get beyond the superficial in relationships, they often, in fact, feel very isolated.

In talking about the specific distances at which boundary manifests at different stages, I carefully included the phrase "if made overtly." One of the primary functions of symptoms is to serve as covert boundaries. They let us have proximity without being affected. Intellectualization takes us above the plane of experience; playing victim drops us below it; scattering makes us untrackable targets; smothering or mergence makes it so there is no other, and thus no real possibility for contact.

One of the most common interventions that I make in working with couples is simply to help them be more overt with their boundaries, for example, to honestly own how much time they want to spend with each other and how they want to spend it, and to shape their relationship from this. Many "problems" in relationship can be usefully seen as simply ways we avoid the vulnerability of honest boundary. When a couple has never-ending arguments, the content that is being argued about is rarely the real issue; indeed, in a fundamental sense there may not even really be a conflict. More often, what we are seeing is an unconscious collusional pattern in which apparent conflict is used as a mechanism to fulfill basic needs: for contact, difference, and excitement. The couple has found a way to keep close (they never stop thinking about each other), that at once guarantees safe distance (anger is a great buffer), and supplies constant, but highly predictable drama (it provides a ready source of pseudo-excitment to mask the low level of actual aliveness).

To the degree such a couple can risk to be overt with their boundaries, the fighting will stop. That this is not as easy to do as it might sound helps us to see further into the creative nature of boundary dynamics. The covertness of boundary here is not something "broken" that needs to be "fixed," rather simply a reflection of the amount of real aliveness that at present this couple is able to tolerate in their relationship. To make boundaries more overtly will involve major risks on each person's part—the risk of being more honestly in contact with the other, the risk that without the fighting there would be nothing left, the risk that without this emotional hook the other person might just leave, the risk of not having preoccupation with the other as a diversion from being honestly in contact with oneself.... The making of overt boundaries requires more than just awareness or will; it requires that each person is ready to take on an increase in aliveness.

One of the most striking things in working with people around issues of boundary is noticing just how similarly any one individual manifests all the vastly different kinds of things that fall into the generic category of boundary. In an important sense, boundary is boundary. We are dealing with much more than just an isolated behavioral phenomenon: we are looking at a key aspect of how, most fundamentally, a system organizes its reality.

Thus we find that a person whose boundaries in interpersonal relationships tend toward the porous, will most often have as well loose categories of thought. We will also find that their tissue structure will tend toward the unbounded, having less than average tone and delineation. In addition, if we work in the symbolic, for example, with inner characters, we will find that the person's inner relationships quite directly mirror in quality their more flesh-and-blood counterparts.

In a similar way, when a person's boundaries tend toward the rigid, this balance in the direction of the formed and particular, and away from permeability, will be felt underlying creative organization in every sphere.

We see this multiplicity in another way in the fact that a person's ability to deal with boundary is always mirrored in the way they deal with limitation, be this limitation as the basic truth that others have boundaries as well, or simply limitation in the sense that what is possible, and what one might wish, are not always the same thing. Again, with questions of boundary, we are dealing simply with a system's creative relationship with, and as, difference.

EXPRESSION, BOUNDARY, AND THE HEALING RELATIONSHIP

"If you bring forth what is within you,
what you bring forth will save you.
If you do not bring forth what is within you,
what you do not bring forth will destroy you."

—Gnostic Gospels
Gospel of Thomas (14.29-33)

"My sacred sword's invisible:
Let go, it's light as straw,
Gripped, it jets with flame,
Protecting me these years,
It showed itself today—
Let Mara's army come!"

—*Ingen*
17th Century Japanese Zen Master
(trans. Lucian Stryk and Takashima Ikemoto)

"If your heart catches in your throat ...
ask a bird how she sings."

—*Cooper Eden*
Remember the Night Rainbow

Questions of being in the world in a way that meaningfully affects it are ever-present in the healing relationship. The healing

222

relationship can usefully be thought of as an alliance through which everyday life comes to be lived a bit more heroically.

What sorts of approaches work best in helping people develop their expressivity? While many techniques can help, in the end, I think, we always arrive at this: we learn to express by expressing. We learn by risking to put forward what we care about as it feels timely, and dealing with the consequences. There are a few things that a therapist can offer: a setting in which to practice expression and learn about how we have come to organize it, some perspective on the vulnerabilities in expression, and perhaps, in his or her own actions, something of an example. But ultimately a person expresses because they risk doing so; there is no way another can do the doing.

The following clinical example offers a nice illustration of the creative nature of expressive growth. It comes from my own therapy, from a time a number of years ago when I was in a relationship that seemed perpetually stuck for no reason I could understand. If the therapist had simply offered the outcome of this work as advice, I would have likely discarded it. The work came out of a combination of where my relationship with that therapist had grown to, and a natural next step in my own creative development— a deeper accepting of the validity of middle-axis aspects of expression and boundary. (My "native" primary energetic has an early-axis bias. Upper and lower poles, and inner and outer aspects, are relatively balanced.)

> In a dream, an image had come to me of walking down a country path. The path led to a place where an old-fashioned split rail fence blocked my way. On my side of the fence was a broad grassy field. On the other, I could see the enticing form of a majestic old castle on a distant hillside.
>
> Working with the image, I first approached the fence in an easy and relaxed manner, expecting little difficulty getting over it. I was fascinated at what the fortress ahead might offer. On reaching the fence, I carefully lifted, and one by one set aside, the split logs of which the fence was built. I stepped through, and replaced the logs behind me.
>
> But, to my surprise, I found that I was again where I had begun. The grassy field was before me and the castle

223

still stood on the other side of the fence. I again approached the fence and once more began dismantling it, only in
retrospect recognizing the resentment that was building
within my mellow exterior toward this uncooperative pile
of sticks.

After my third such attempt at gentle persuasion, the
dam broke. I went into a rage, wanting to smash everything around me. Suddenly, in my image I had hopped into
a caterpillar tractor and was driving headlong into the
middle of the fence, splinters flying in every direction.

The act gave an immense satisfaction, and of course
when I turned off the tractor's motor, there was the castle
before me, ready to be explored.

As I stood there, the image of the castle faded and I
found myself viewing a montage of memories from my
relationship. The theme was obvious. I simply was not
acknowledging the passion of our differences when this
was what I felt and needed to express. The fence and how I
approached it represented my old way of making boundaries. The fence was pleasant to the eye, and my approach
was gentle and balanced. On the surface, this way of
making boundaries looked good; beneath this appearance
lay a fear of acting from what I truly felt. It was a time
when I frequently mistook the holding back of important
feelings for kindness and love. It was clear that if I was
going to be in the world with any potency, I would need to
find the courage to live and love more directly.

In workshops that I lead, the exercise that people most often
later come back to me and say really changed their lives is an immensely simple one. I ask people to spend some time examining
what means the most to them—what they really most care about.
Then I have each person step before the group and express—with
words, with movement, with song, whatever—what this is they
most "stand for" in their lives. After each person's sharing the
group gets a chance to play devil's advocate, to question and challenge. Much is revealed: what in fact we want to express, how we
caracteristically shape our expression, and what we must mobilize
in ourselves if we are to most fully manifest from this that moves
us. We rarely in daily living take the risk to ask this fundamental
question—and clearly there is nothing more important to ask. You
might try it with a few friends.

Often the most powerful way to creatively facilitate the expressive is to place our attention not there, but on vertical aspects of our formedness. We can express only to the degree that we have the ground to express from, and the stature to stand behind what we have to express. The relationship between expression and our vertical rhythm is ultimately not causal but creatively complementary: with any increase in depth or stature, we see new aliveness becoming available for expression; similarly, when new expression is risked we see with it lifting, deepening, and filling out along the bodily axis.

Just as often, the most direct door to expressive potency is the receptive. Frequently when expression is blocked, the problem is simply that the person is not listening deeply enough in themselves to have anything of significance to say. The task of opening more fully to self and/or world may be a scary undertaking, but once it is confronted, the desired expression happens quite spontaneously.

There are few themes in therapy more evocative of change than that of boundary. As I have commented, a frequent part of therapy for me is helping people to see the covert ways they make boundaries, and challenging them to make these boundaries, if not overt, at least conscious. The task of making overt boundaries inherently confronts people with fundamental fears—annihilation, rejection, abandonment, being hurtful, being wrong, making commitment, being free—the list is endless. To the degree that a person can confront these fears and make their boundaries clearly, they discover life becoming suddenly much simpler—not easier, in fact much more challenging—but decidedly more direct and immediate. Life's complexities are very often simply ways we keep the profound potency of life as simple, direct relationship at bay.

The following example demonstrates the use of preverbal work to explore a boundary dynamic. It also illustrates a process of owning and integrating a polar dynamic opposite to that of one's primary identification. (The client's predominant energetic is late-axis, with about an equal balance of upper and lower poles, and, horizontally, an identification with the inner aspect.)

Kathy was 40 years old, a therapist, and a vivacious and strong-willed woman. In this session, she was working with her fears of intimacy. In earlier sessions, she had gotten images of herself as a child in a tall glass cylinder and a girl locked in the top of a stone tower. As she talked I noticed that she was using her hands to protect the mid part of her body.

Charley: "I notice your hand is over your stomach, what are you feeling there?"

Kathy: "Nothing ... [closes her eyes] ... well it's like a hole, it's raw, it's like in growing up it was supposed to close up and it never did. There is just a thin piece of skin over it. I'm protecting it from being hurt."

Charley: "By what?"

Kathy: "I don't know."

Charley: "Just let images come, let them surprise you."

Kathy: "A can opener ... a hammer ... a butcher's meat hook, this is silly... god that's scary ... a man's fist."

Charley: "How do you protect yourself?"

Kathy: "I don't let people too close. I keep hunched over, to keep hard in front. I don't rely on anyone."

Charley: "Try placing the objects you imagined in front of you, then choose one you feel comfortable in exploring further. [She chooses the can opener.] Now hold it and move it as if you were using it. [She begins small hand movements, breath held, belly tight.] Now explore using your whole arm in that movement. [She begins moving spontaneously, her breath deepens.] Try letting your belly direct the movement; let the impulse start from there."

Kathy: "Before the image of the can opener was very loathsome to me. Now I find it interesting and somehow important. [Her hand has moved away from her stomach and her abdominal muscles have relaxed considerably. Her breath has moved down into her belly.]

Charley: "You don't seem to be protecting your belly."

Kathy: "I don't seem to have to. I feel safe. But that's crazy. I'm not weak. Everyone knows I'm someone who can protect and take care of myself."

Charley: "But before you did it with the cylinder."

Kathy: "And that's lonely and hard. I was safe but I really couldn't let anyone in, or myself out. I think I'm risking a different kind of protection, one I can pick up or put down as I need it. One I can take part in."

What contributes to a healthy ability to express and make boundary? We learn about and shape ourselves as expression in every creative moment of our lives. Environments that are generative to expression are themselves authentically expressive, and at once able to deeply receive. When our attempts to reveal ourselves as form bring fulfilling responses in our world, our ability to express grows, shaped by, and as, the unique aliveness of those meetings. Where attempted expression leads to a diminishing of aliveness, we learn to restrict its range and spontaneity—constricting our throats, holding back free movements in our arms and shoulders, restricting our pelvic mobility.

We learn about, and expand, our capacities for boundary each time that we are confronted with issues of difference. Our experience at each of our infinite peripheries of interface contributes to our organization of boundary. In that it is as children that we make our first differentiations of self and other, it is there that the most critical experiences lie. We learn about creating boundaries from each of the protecting and limiting forces in our environment: parents, siblings, schools, social structures. Our feelings about those who make boundaries around us are always ambivalent, for our protection is also our containment. Through this creative ambivalence, we grow our unique relationship to, and as, interface. When these structures honor what is alive, the boundaries we develop are similarly most likely to be vital. And then too, sometimes precisely because a boundary we meet is not vital, we are challenged creatively, and respond with a sensitivity and power that would not have been possible otherwise.

As with dynamics in the vertical, when a system is challenged with too great a dose of aliveness, or where there is chronic splitting, expressive responses that would otherwise be catalyzing can become distorted and serve to divert attention away from what is real. A pair of seemingly opposite yet energetically closely related patterns can be seen in scattering and compulsive categorizing. With scattering, what appears initially as expression becomes so diffuse that any thread of meaning is lost. With compulsive categorizing, we create boxes around expressivity so that spontaneously living movement is not possible. Another form of such pseudo-expressivity can be recognized in the utterances of the dogmatist. Whether loud and pushy or smooth and articulate, he/she is engaged in "communication" that allows for only a predetermined outcome.

Expression can also be used, either overtly or covertly, to do harm. Whether the vehicle is a gun or a well-chosen word, the purpose is the same: to diminish the aliveness that is challenging that system to be more.

Ultimately, as with aliveness in general, there is no litmus paper test for determining whether an act of expression is the real thing—heroic and vulnerably present—or is in truth a fraud—irrelevant or even harmful. There is no way to tell simply by the visible form of the act. Hard-nosed criticism is often the greatest gift that can be given, and while we may condemn warfare, it has in its timeliness been an essential, and I would say, even beautiful part of the human story. In the end, the only measuring device we have is our best sense of what is in fact right and timely.

CHAPTER NINE

A STEP WITHIN:
OPENING, ALLOWING,
AND RECEIVING

"We must neglect nothing that could give the truth a chance to reach us."

—*John Stuart Mill*

"The first hole through a piece of stone is a revelation. The hole connects one side with the other ... The mystery of the hole—the mysterious fascination of caves in hillsides and cliffs."

—*Henry Moore*

"The sound of the gates opening wakes the beautiful woman asleep."

—*Kabir*
trans. Robert Bly

 This chapter will complete our exploration of the first half of creative rhythm, and the complementary dynamics that comprise it. Here our interest turns to the dissolving aspect of the relationship of the Within and the Without: the receptive.

Just as the ascendant and the expressive can often be treated as a single function, the receptive is intimately related to the dynamics of descent and ground. Again, this is a dynamic where connection is primary—in which wholes are preeminent over parts, in which the one becomes figure, the two ground: to receive is to resonate with. The expressive side of boundary speaks the language of sep-

229

aration and difference; the receptive speaks the language of meeting. One speaks the creative no, the other the creative yes.

As with ground, we can talk only inferentially about what is primary in the receptive. The more surface aspects of the receptive, those that are most form-defined, are not difficult for us to grasp: intellectually, the ability to comprehend another's ideas; bodily, the dimension of experience we call sensation; emotionally, the ability to empathize with another's feelings. But the more we move inward, the more our accustomed rules of understanding abandon us. Again, what most defines these dynamics is the disappearance of the definable. The softer half of reality demands a comfort with the poetry of mystery if we are to enter her in a way that will at all reveal her nature. That a model such as this is beyond depicting with our usual images is simply a reflection of the fact that it includes, as an integral part, this more elusive half of things.

THE POWER OF THE RECEPTIVE

*"The softest thing in the universe, overcomes the hardest
thing in the universe."*
—*Lao Tsu*

*"I have been drowned to your sweet odor alone, as the
unicorn falls alseep under the influence of a maiden's
fragrance. For this is the nature of the unicorn, that no
other beast is so hard to capture, and he has one horn on
his nose which no armor can withstand, so that no one
dares to go forth against him except a virgin girl."*
—*Richard de Fournival*
Bestiaire d'Amour (13th C.)

Since it won't be possible to define the receptive by "making a point," we will begin with a montage, a few images that together may serve as an invitation to this dimension in experience.

An initial image comes once more from the legend of King Arthur. With his sword broken in battle, Arthur is led by Merlin to the shore of a small body of water. In it lives the beautiful Lady of the Lake. From her Arthur receives the mighty sword Excalibur and its scabbard, the sword and the scabbard with which he will found the great Round Table. The sword is broad and sharp, embellished in gold. Engraved on one side are the words "take me," on the other, "cast me away."

Standing before him, Merlin asks Arthur which he likes better, the sword or the scabbard. "The sword," is Arthur's quick choice. To this Merlin responds, "In that you are unwise. Excalibur is a good sword, the best in the world. But the scabbard is worth far more. For however sorely you are beset in battle, you'll not lose a drop of blood as long as you have the scabbard with you."

A second image comes from the mythology of the unicorn. Tales about him can be found in both East and West in times of early and middle culture. Then considered a creature of flesh, not fancy, he was described as a handsome and inspiring beast. It was said that he could run faster and farther than any other creature. With a single coiled horn protruding from his forehead, no creature, be it ferocious like the lion or great in stature like the elephant, would dare challenge him. He could not be captured alive. Kings paid high prices that one might be brought to them, but traps could not hold his might, and spears could stop him only at his death. If ever there was a symbol of the impassioned spontaneity of pure expression, the unicorn embodied it .

Many descriptions of the unicorn contain a highly moving and poetic scene. It is said that if a maiden, pure of heart, ventures alone deep into the woods, and finding a quiet place, sits very still, a unicorn will sometimes come to lie beside her, and placing his head in her open lap, fall fast asleep. Depending on the bent of the writer, the emphasis might be on the power of innocence, or the fact that this scene often led to the creature's demise. It was said that hunters would bring a virgin maiden to the forest and when a unicorn appeared, with guns and arrows slay him.

A last image is from the beloved European folktale of Beauty and the Beast. We engage the story as Beauty, having run many hours through the entangled forest, finds the Beast outside his castle, his breath gone, the spell having done its evil work. Through her tears, moved by the love that has been growing within her, she embraces his terrible image. At that moment, the interminable spell that has imprisoned the prince is broken.

What is the mysterious power that runs through this montage: that could keep Arthur safe from injury; that could meet the strength of the unicorn, bringing (depending on whim) tranquility or destruction; that gave Beauty the capacity to transform? The power, I would suggest, is simply the willingness to be affected. What is being symbolized here is the act of risking to be touched and moved—in its four-dimensional sense, to receive.

Because this aspect of our power is so elusive to thought, we most often refer to it by saying what it is not, or by alluding to it indirectly. We frequently use sensory metaphors, though the five senses may not literally be central. As "pores" in the "membrane" that is our body's integument, they are useful images of the greater process. We may say we "got a taste" of an experience, or that we "drank in" what someone was doing, that we were "touched" by someone's feelings or that we "saw" what they were saying. The reference to receptivity is often kinesthetic. We may speak of being "moved," "inspired," or "turned on." Frequently our words reflect the surrender of control intrinsic to the receptive moment. We speak of being "amazed" (from the same root as maze) or "taken" by the experience. Our words may reflect the letting down of boundaries, that we felt "open," or that someone was able to "get through" to us. Or they may be descriptions of our bodily experience when we can do so, such as feeling "warmth" toward someone. Words like caring, curiosity, fascination, appreciation or love reflect some of the feeling states that accompany the receptive. We have many ways of talking about it, but always they speak in indirect ways.

We customarily associate "power" with action and might, but in fact the receptive holds a power equal in magnitude to anything which the warrior has to offer, and a presence no less heroic. Indeed, it could well be argued that receptive risks are more powerful (and empowering), for their significance and vulnerability are magnified by their relegation to our cultural hinterlands.

An African tale I heard as a child gets close to the transformational kernel in receptive power. The story begins with a young girl coming to her mother crying. She says that a boy has been throwing stones at her. Her mother tells her daughter to catch one of the stones, and to tell the boy how beautiful it is. The young girl reluctantly returns and does as her mother says. But when she catches the stone and starts to speak, she realizes that the stone is indeed beautiful, the most beautiful she has ever seen. The girl and the boy become inseparable friends, and with time the depth of their love inspires the entire village.

When we risk receiving—appreciating, caring, wondering, being touched—new life is created in ourselves and in the world around us. When a child draws a picture which somehow touches the magic within us, what we give the child with our silent sharing of this awe nourishes and enlivens in a way no words of praise or advice can approach. Any time we risk really hearing someone, letting who they truly are dance against the intimate core of our being, what we give that person is the gift of themselves. When the space in us is an invitation, we find things around us answering by coming alive. It is in the nature of things that a beautiful opening inspires us to find something of equal beauty to put within it.

THE DYNAMICS OF RECEPTIVE POWER

"Learning to draw is really a matter of learning to see and that means a good deal more than merely looking with the eye."
—Kimon Nicolaides

"... and then I asked him with my eyes to ask again yes and then he asked me would I yes ...
and first I put my arms around him yes
and drew him down to me so he could feel my breasts all
*   perfume yes*
and his heart going like mad
and yes I said yes I will yes."
—James Joyce

"Know that when you learn to lose yourself, you will reach the Beloved. There is no other secret to be learned, and more than this is not known to me."
—I Ching

We commonly equate the receptive with the weaker end of a linear scale of expressive potency. It should be clear here that passivity is as much an opposite to receptivity's transformational power as it is to expressivity's more visible potency.

Receptive   *Passive*   *Passive*   *Expressive*

The critical difference between receptivity and passivity is readily evident bodily. Passivity is a state of cellular inertness. It manifests either as tissue too rigid for impulses to penetrate or too flaccid to interface or significantly respond. Receptivity, on the other hand, is precisely a tissue's degree of excitability. It is a statement of our vital responsiveness, of who we are as a unique meeting with our living existence. Our receptivity is our readiness to possibility. It is Sleeping Beauty at the moment of the Prince's kiss.

What do we derive from the receptive? If the purpose of the expressive is actively to affect, how might we best describe the "purpose" of the receptive? Clearly that purpose will be far less definable in terms of destination. Perhaps the simplest way to say it is that our receptivity is how we derive our human sustenance. Just as the primitive cell opens the pores of its containing membrane to draw in vital nutrients, likewise our receptivity brings in the emotional, physical, and spiritual "nutrients" of our complex human "diets." We are fed by each aspect of real contact we allow— by a friendly touch, by a new idea, by each part of the physical environment we choose as our "infusive" surroundings. When our "diet" is appropriate and sufficient our life feels "full," when it is not, we "hunger."

But we must remember that the process by which we take in these human nutrients is much more than just consumption. It is one half of the living dialogue by which we expand into and create our worlds. The receptive is the entry way for life as challenge. When we receive, both ourselves and what touches us are indelibly altered; to receive is to take part in reality as living change.

To receive is always a vulnerable thing. We are inviting another to enter a room of our psychic house, knowing that with this visit the room will never again be quite the same. And there is no guarantee that what is offered by the visitor will be positive, either nourishing or creatively challenging. It could be that this visitor comes on false pretences, intending instead to rob, destroy, poison, or violate. As with expression, receiving is always in the end a leap into the unknown. However deep our grounding and thus our power to sense harmony or disharmony, however ascended our consciousness, and thus our vantage over potential harm, however keenly developed our expressive abilities to do battle, ultimately we can never fully know the effect of an experience until we have risked its transforming touch. To receive is to risk annihilation; yet how fully alive we are is precisely a function of how deeply we can trust in, and engage, that risk.

An essential part of understanding the receptive is grasping its essential relationship with the expressive. Neither the receptive nor the expressive exist in isolation. They are the animating voices that link the formed and unformed in creation. We could argue well that either causes the other, that we can speak "because" there is someone to hear us, or that we can be touched "because" there is someone who risks touching. The larger reality is co-generative. The fact of, and the living permeability of, interface is a statement of the larger process that these two faces together embody. Put together, they are life—who we are as living, evolving relationship and identity. Take one away, and not only does the other cease to exist, but reality ceases to exist.

One of the simplest ways to understand receptive power is in terms of its "effect" on the expressive. The receptive has an important significance in and of itself, beyond just its role in the process of creating form. But, because it is form we presently best understand, and because form is something we can see and describe, this role makes a valuable window.

A time I am especially aware of the power of the receptive is when I play music for others. I don't have to play for long to realize that it is not just me that will be determining what happens with that music, and how alive it will become. Other people in the room and the potential spaces that exist or can be evoked in them are equal forces in the creative process. I sometimes imagine the music I am playing as a colored ribbon coming from my mouth and hands, extending toward those present. Where there is little receptivity, if I do not compensate with increased receptivity to myself, the ribbon's initially fluid dance becomes brittle, faded, and ungratifying. Where there is true hearing (not necessarily agreement or approval) I feel as if the ribbon is being taken and gathered in, its colors and textures weaving, its shapes swelling and coalescing as it plays in the unique inner space of each person. What happens often deeply surprises me. It is almost as if, to the degree it can be received, nearly anything can be brought into being.

This kind of dynamic is present in any expressive act not done in a mechanical way: teaching, public speaking, dancing, or just talking with friends. While our most ready recognition conventionally goes to the doer—the eloquent speaker, the skillful actor—it could well be argued that the person who can hear eloquently, who can be vitally moved, is rarer and more significant. I am aware that the people I most cherish almost always have the gift of appreciation, fascination, and awe. If the receptivity of a situation is strong enough, it is nearly impossible for beautiful and potent expression not to manifest, and often from the most unlikely places.

To receive is to connect with. An important question in looking at any receptive act is what specifically any particular opening is connecting us to. Depending on the context, it can be very different sorts of things, and interestingly, often many sorts of very different things at the same time. When we receive from our more form-defined layerings, our connectings are often quite specific—to a particular person, to a particular idea or feeling. As we move inward, they become less so. The further toward the unformed a receptive act is embodied, the more elements become involved: to receive is to become permeable, and the deeper this permeability the more pan-experiential it becomes. Deep receptivity can manifest at once in a multitude of ways, ways that would seem to have no connection limited to our usual ways of thinking.

We see a first layer of this in the simple awareness that to some degree any receptive moment is not just an opening to our outside world, but to ourselves. When we soften a boundary between ourselves and a particular situation, we are always, at least in some small way, also softening a boundary within our own being. We cannot really receive without discovering new things about ourselves in the process. Sometimes the outer softening seems to come first, sometimes the inner: we may risk hearing a friend's words and in the process hear ourselves more deeply, or we may risk connecting in a new way to our inner self, and discover that we are also hearing others with a new depth.

Looking a bit deeper we can see that there is an important sense in which any receptive moment is, at least to some small degree, also an opening to experience as a whole. Ultimately, to open is to open. This is more pronounced the further one moves toward the unformed. Here the receptive increasingly transcends not just the dualities of self and other, and inner self and outer self, but also that of self and existence as a whole. Close to the embodied core, being is simply wonder, and there is nothing which wonder does not embrace. This is why the poetry of the receptive often has a powerful mystical or spiritual ambience. *

---

* Are such experiences a literal connecting into something larger than oneself, or just a subjective sense of union? Often they are clearly much more the latter (or perhaps more accurately, there is a connecting, but it is in fact happening within a very limited, and largely internal sphere). But, there are situations where what is happening seems to be more than this. Much in human communication is mysterious to us. We know very little about what orders experience in the deeply unformed. It is interesting to note that the contexts where events that seem to violate usual laws of physical connection are reported are commonly ones where the esthetic of unity is naturally predominant. Two of the times when "paranormal" kinds of experiences are most often described are near death and in moments of extreme emergency. More simply "intuitive" experiences are similarly most frequently described in "unformed" contexts—for example, in the "twilight" time between waking and sleeping, in moments of deep intimacy, or in the kinesthetic connectings that link parents and young infants. Consistent with this, the people who most frequently describe intuitive kinds of knowing are individuals with primary energetics that embody in the early parts of the creative cycle. (In theory, these are the people who should be both most capable of this kind of receptivity, and most likely to imagine it when in fact it is not present.) This is another area where it is important that we be humble to how little we know.

Understanding receptive power requires that we turn much of our usual thinking around. Logically, to receive is to take. Yet, in practice, nothing lies closer to the essence of giving. Authentic receptivity empowers all who come near it. On the surface, the receptive seems a most transitory thing, something defined only by the moment. Yet, at once, one could say it is what defines true permanence. When we risk to be touched by something—a person, an idea, an image—we come to have that thing. And it is having in this sense that ultimately endures. As Emerson said, "We have what we enjoy."

FACES OF THE RECEPTIVE

"He who without the Muses' madness in his soul comes knocking at the door of poetry, and thinks that art will make him anything fit to be called a poet, finds that the poetry which he indites in his sober senses is beaten hollow by the poetry of madmen."

—Plato

"As the mirror to my hand, the flower to my hair ... musk to my breast ... ecstasy to my flesh, as wing to bird, water to fish, life to the living—so you are to me. But tell me, beloved, who are you? Who are you really? Vidrapati says, they are one another."

—Vidrapati

"She sums up all that men can never get the better of and is never done coping with."

—C.G. Jung

As with the other directions of creative movement, the receptive can be understood as an array of dynamics that manifest sequentially through the creative cycle. Through the course of creative progression, both what is possible to receive and where and how we receive it changes in characteristic ways.

We have touched on all the major themes in these changes earlier. First, through the first half of cycle, the bodily layer where receptivity is felt to occur gradually shifts from near core outward, toward the bodily periphery. Second, there is a gradual evolution of what one can receive from things of essence and the un-formed through each of the layerings of bodily reality—from the magical, to the moral and emotional, to the material. Third, our receptive dynamics become more specifically focused and focusable, concerned more with distinct aspects of experience. And fourth, there is a gradual shift toward more ascendant receptive concerns.*

Before we turn to looking at the receptive developmentally, you might want to take some time with the following exercise. To understand the receptive in any differentiated way, it is essential that we have a good grasp of what it is as bodily experience, and some sense of how that experience varies relative to the situation.

Place yourself near a person you care about and take time to simply take them in. They can be doing any-thing—moving, talking, humming to themselves, sitting quietly. Notice all you can about how it feels to be with them and how you are with yourself in doing it. Be aware of what senses are most activated for you—sight, smell, hearing, the kinesthetic? Be sensitive to where in your body you seem most in contact with that person—belly, head, pelvis, heart, hands or legs? As well, ask yourself where, from core to periphery, you seem most to be exper-iencing. Is it different for different levels?

Turning to the symbol-making part of yourself, let an image come for the quality of feeling you most deeply ex-perience coming from that person. Let a second symbol come for how you are responding to it, how you are taking in or repelling that feeling. Try this experiment with dif-ferent people, and in different kinds of settings.

I have outlined the main themes of receptive progression below. As I did for the expressive, I will speak of inner and outer re-ceptive dynamics. Again, it is not really that we have two sep-arate kinds of receptivity, rather that receptivity is a function of

---

* Each of these variables are relative to our situation within the dy-namics of larger defining cycles, and are influenced by the bias of our pri-mary energetic.

The power of the receptive lies in the risk to be touched, to be moved The receptive aspect of the creative is frequently represented in feminine images.

ABOVE: *From India, a coco-de-mer, worshipped as the vulva of the goddess.* BELOW: A *Muse playing a lyre. Greece. First century B.C.* OPPOSITE, TOP: *Moritz von Schwind.* Knight's Dream. *1822. The ascendant receptive as an image of idealized virtue.* OPPOSITE, BELOW: *Auguste Renoir. Study for* The Bathers. *1884-1885.*

balance between these poles, and we tend to take polar roles in embodying this relationship.

In rhythm's boundless beginning, in one sense everything is the receptive: all is openness. But in another, just as there is no discrete expressivity, equally there is not yet the receptive; to receive in a generative way requires difference. Receptivity, as creation first begins, is nearly osmotic. The embryo takes in all from the mother, the early tribe all from nature.

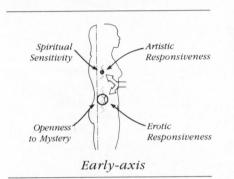

Early-axis

With first separation and movement into early-axis dynamics the receptive becomes more overtly recognizable, and with this something more and more cherished. In this stage the archetypically feminine is the seat of power, and its horizontal voices speak some of truth's most important themes.

I call the ascendant aspect of this first manifestation the inspiring face of the receptive. We know her in modern times in the image of the artist's muse. The muse emboldens and arouses the creative spirit, but not by example or challenge, rather through the simple act of being touched by it. "She" inspires the artist (her image is usually feminine, but not always) through her responsiveness. The potential beauty invites the artist to create equally beautiful means for penetrating it. When the balance is shifted toward the outer pole, we feel her most in terms of creative expression; when it is more inner-directed, she is the listening ear of the meditative aspects of the spiritual. She is the most numinous face of the receptive.

The complementary lower pole figure I call the passionate receptive. Her power is linked with the chthonic knowings of the mother of death and birth. Where the balance is toward the inner pole she speaks of the fluid mysteries of unity—culturally in ritual, personally in moments of surrender to the inner unknown. With movement outward, she is the pagan warrior's erotic connection in battle or the delicious chaos of Bacchanalian abandon.

Just as in the expressive we found only the most rudimentary differentiation between the warrior and poet faces of early-axis, so do we see an often very close alliance between the passionate and inspiring faces of the receptive. In the spiritual/erotic art of Tantra, they are often embodied in a single figure. In Greek myth, we can see important aspects of each in the figure of Aphrodite.

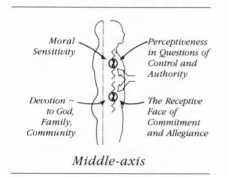

Middle-axis

With middle-axis the ascendent receptive moves decisively above the chaotic and erotic, and comes to reside in a new more worldly domain. Here she speaks for virtue, purity of being, and the ear of moral conscience. In the legends of middle culture we see her in the image of the princess, beautiful and chaste, fair in all her dealings. When she becomes queen, she balances the king's concerns of power with her sensitivity to moral right. In adolescence, it is her we put on a pedestal. Where the balance here is primarily outward, we feel this part of ourself as a commitment to fairness and balance in our dealings. Where it is shifted more towards the inner, it has a more religious and moral flavor. The Statue of Liberty symbolized this part of the whole for the United States in the middle-axis stage of its growth as a nation.

As with the expressive, the lower pole here is viewed ambivalently. We can think of this by depicting two layers of descendent faces. The first, especially in its inner aspect, is closely allied with the nurturant mother. She is good, God-loving, basic in her values. This is the receptive face of home, family, community—of love as devotion and communion. She is close to the earth, but earthy in only carefully circumscribed ways. With the outer aspect, concern shifts more to the kinds of receptivity needed for perseverance and constancy, qualities relevant equally to the home and to the battlefield.

We can think of the second layer either as the hidden face of

243

the lower pole, or as the ascendant's attempt to deal with the still tempting/taunting forces of early-axis. Here there is a bit too much of the untamed for the ascendant's comfort. Without, she is the comely wench with a predilection for revelry; Within one who is a bit too mysterious and brooding. Where the descendent element is stronger still, she may be symbolized as a whore or witch.

Again, as with the outlaw in the expressive, while these less refined aspects of the receptive are commonly condemned as evil, the truth is much more creative than this. Thus, we see stories like Cinderella in which the real princess is found covered with ashes and dressed in rags, and tales in which the fairest lady of the land leaves her wealthy husband for the prince of the gypsies.

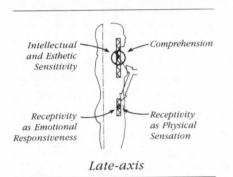

Late-axis

In the later stages of separation, the receptive plays an ever diminishing role. In the creative act—whether painting, lifetime or culture—form has been established. Questions of mystery and wonder no longer have their critical place, either as doorways to inspiration or potential destroyers of the fragile birth. There is still a need for the receptive—the tasks of refinement require some subtle sensitivities—but the esthetics of form increasingly predominate over those of formlessness.

From Above, the receptive is the ear of understanding. For the outer pole, this is simply comprehension, rational discernment and the accumulation of new factual information. Within, the receptive organizes from a more personal place. Here the material is tempered with humanistic sensibilities. Culturally this manifests as liberalism in politics and religion. We see this also in the esthetic ear of the high arts.

From Below and Without, we see the receptive aspects of our active physical natures. The body speaks to us here in the language of sensation. Within, the voice of feelings predominates. Toward the end of this stage, lower pole sensibilities manifest in a new emphasis on the erotic and dramatic aspects of the receptive (the distance is sufficient to make this safe). This may look like a return of the more chthonic responsiveness of early-axis, but in fact, as exemplified in the Hollywood stereotype, what we are seeing is taking place primarily within the surface layers of experience. This part of the creative is the receptive source for the popular arts.

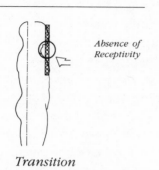

Absence of Receptivity

Transition

With the first half of the transitional phase, as aliveness approaches the turn toward reintegration, the receptive in effect ceases to exist. Separation is now total. Creation has become form and that form has been smoothed and polished until it shines in triumphant glory. A shiny surface does not receive: it takes the light and immediately reflects it away. Form at this stage is there to be seen, not to be changed. There will be time for questions later.

CREATIVE RHYTHM AND SEXUAL DIFFERENCES

"What's this generation coming to? I bet the time ain't far off when a woman won't know any more than a man!"

—Will Rogers

We might take a moment to address more specifically the question of gender differences in creative dynamics. Psychologists often argue about whether the development of men and women is essentially a single process (with conditioning adding a few minor variations), or whether in fact there are two distinct developmental stories. The model suggests that each view is in one sense true.

In the thinking of the model, a single dynamic, formative process, is seen as organizing reality, irrespective of whether one is a woman or a man. But, men and women tend to take part in this single developmental story in different ways. Within any stage, women tend horizontally to embody somewhat more of the inner pole and the receptive; vertically they embody preferentially the lower pole and the energetics of ground. For men the situation is reversed. While there is immense individual variation, on the average, the gender balance between poles is about 60/40.

This normative complementarity can be observed fairly easily in our body organization. If we look at how men and women hold their aliveness, we see an average two to three inch difference, relative to height, in the body's energetic center. Men tend to carry more emotional "weight" in their chest and arms, women in their pelvis and thighs. In the quality of skin surface, connective tissue, and muscle tone, good indicators of horizontal energetics, we again see differences. Even when men and women engage in similar activities, women's tissues tend to remain softer to the touch, men's more solid.

Consistent with all of this, we see that patterns of splitting for men more commonly involve artifically ascendant and outwardly-held energetics, for women descendent and inwardly-held postures. There are great individual differences, but this is what normatively prevails.

This gender bias in the primary energetic is reflected not only bodily, but also in the qualities (and commonly genders*) of the symbolic figures that emerge in dreams and imagery. A particularly fascinating dynamic in this regard can be seen at the midpoint of major creative rhythms. Here figures of opposite quality—and often gender—to the prevailing balance in the person's personality often quite suddenly take on great importance, frequently seeming to function almost as guides to the integration process.** This dynamic is quite understandable within the structure of the

---

* Lots of things go into determining the gender of a symbolic image: relative polarity is one, but our own gender and associations with actual people also play a part.

** Carl Jung talked about these opposite sex symbolic guides as the anima and animus and saw them as having central roles in the aspects of integration he called individuation.

model: integration begins with a glimpsing from across the mote of separation of the pole opposite to one's primary identification.

In thinking about gender in this way, it is important to distinguish between roles on the one hand, and as I am doing, questions of energetic organization. Within most times in history, the roles perceived as appropriate for men and for women have been pretty clearly distinct. The important recognition here is that even roles that are perceived in highly polar ways organize from relationships between polar dynamics.

Significant changes are happening culturally in these times in how we think about and experience both gender and gender roles. In chapter 11 we will look at what the model has to say about the significance of such changes, and what further changes likely lie ahead.

RECEPTIVITY AND THE HEALING RELATIONSHIP

"When you come to be sensibly touched, the scales will fall from your eyes; and by the penetrating eyes of love you will discern that which your other eyes will never see."
—*Francis Fenelon*

"The passive are first bewildered, then malicious."
—*Theodore Roethke*

The dynamics of the receptive permeate every moment of the healing relationship. Each time we risk being more alive we embrace ourselves in some new way, and open to new connectedness in our worlds.

And there are specific things that are particularly evocative of growth in the receptive. The most powerful tools a therapist has in this regard are not techniques, but simply his or her own expressive and receptive rhythms. As I have commented, the ability to hear always lies at the heart of the healing process. A person risks sharing what is most deeply meaningful and discovers not only that they have not been destroyed, but that they have become more. Often little more than this will ignite an incredible complexity of change and enlivenment. The therapist's ear both invites clients to hear themselves, and serves as a model for the beauty and potency possible in being touched by others.

In a complementary way, the therapist's role as expresser can evoke the receptive. The experience of letting another in, and finding fulfillment instead of violation, can catalyze a rich flow of sensitivity and receptive possibilities. Often the content of the therapist's expression is less important than simply the client's growing capacity to be present with the therapist as an expressive person. As the client deepens in ground and expands in awareness, he or she becomes increasingly able to meet the therapist with authentic responsiveness. The need to block, elevate or depress the therapist's expressive potency gradually diminishes. Full passage into adult vitality ends with two powerful people, each embracing the other's unique capacity to express and receive.

As I commented in the last chapter, not infrequently the most direct route to helping a person learn to let others in is to help them to recognize their boundaries and to set them consciously and overtly. Our "blocks" to receiving are ultimately simply the ways we have learned to make boundary in covert ways. In taking responsibility in our "no's," we gain both a greater sense of safety, and thus trust in receiving, and a greater ability to be selective in what we let in: to at once keep what would be unhealthy well distant, and to reap the rewards of deep closeness when that is safe and right.

Often one of the most powerful ways to facilitate the receptive is simply to engage the layers and languages in a person that most understand and value receptive sensibilities. I am aware, in using as I do active, preverbal approaches (like imagery and movement) along with more conventional modalities, that just the fact of the work, separate from any specific content, often serves as a powerful vehicle for opening new levels of receptive sensitivity.

What kinds of things most contribute to the development of our personal patterns of receptive potency and sensitivity? The basic configurations get established very early, in those first germinal interfaces between ourselves and our parents and family. These interfaces shape this growth in a number of ways. First, they are the initial boundaries for the child's yet poorly differentiated world. The borders of the mother's belly for the fetus, a protecting hand in the infant's first explorations, a firm "no" for a youngster's playing at a busy intersection—these give the child its first opportunities to model protective interface. Second, since the parents are also the first major expressive forces in the child's world, they help form the first "concepts" about the experience of being entered. Are the associations of these primary experiences principally ones of laughter, love and learning, or are they overshadowed by feelings of violation? Third, the parents, as the child's first "muse," model what degree and what kinds of receptivity are safe and appropriate.

In the following clinical example, we see growth happening both in relation to the receptive, and to its ever-present co-theme, the owning and manifesting of boundary. (The primary energetic here is predominantly late-axis, with a slight bias toward the inner and lower aspects.)

When she entered therapy, Anne, a therapist herself, was 40. Her desire in the work was to learn how to let others be closer to her, and as well to be more intimate with herself.

She began one session with the sharing of a dream. In it, she was in her childhood home, at her present age, and her mother was there. Her father was deceased. She was standing behind a twelve-foot-high iron gate, held closed by a great tangle of padlocks and chains. She felt protected: since her father was no longer there to protect her, this gate kept her safe.

In the session, she returned in imagery to the place of the dream. This time she found herself about eight years old. She described other children playing outside the gate. When I asked her feelings toward them, she realized there was fear, but also a longing to join them. I asked her how the gate got there. Her words came with an autonomous urgency: "My father put it there, my father is dead and I have no one to protect me."

I asked her to repeat her words. In tears, she found herself in a conversation with her father's image. "Father, the gate feels cold. I don't want its protection now." Her words were very faint, from deep within her. I asked if her father could hear her. "He's crying," she said. "I feel myself taking in, filling. These feelings are very important."

There was a long pause and she opened her eyes. She sat and looked at me, her body much softer than it had been when the session began. "I'm going to see him," she said. "I've never been to the cemetery. I've been afraid even to go through the gates. I am going there now."

The discovery of a new receptive place, the finding of new permeability in boundary, often brings tears. There are tears of release, for any rhythm toward core involves letting go of known forms. As well there are tears of wonder and thankfulness, tears that speak a nameless kind of gratitude for life's mysterious beauty. Our eyes soften and moisten, and our chests open and fill, making room for new breath.

The opening that organizes new receptive capacity may be a general thing, or it may be felt most in the rhythms and knowings of a particular part of the body. We may see it most in one person in a new-found flexibility and responsiveness in the pelvis; in another in a relaxing of the chest; in a third, in a willingness to let laughter and spontaneous feeling ripple through the tissues of the belly. We may notice it most in an awareness that our hands are alive and sensitive in a new way, or that our senses—the messengers of reality—are becoming more keen. However it manifests, when we risk new receptivity in the world, we are always in some way also risking receiving ourselves in new and more potent ways.

Just as the most direct route to receptive potency is often expression and boundary, similarly, when a person seeks help in being more effectively expressive, it is frequently the unformed side of things that holds the treasures. What is required may not be more force, but the willingness to hear and question. When this is risked, one discovers (always to one's surprise) a new vitalization of the power to penetrate. A new and larger reality is opened, which gives a whole new meaning to the place and purpose of expression.

The following case example tellingly illustrates this process. (The client carried his aliveness primarily in late-axis, with about a 75/25 bias toward both the upper and outer aspects, and mild splitting.)

> Several years ago I worked with a man whose initial goal in therapy was to be more aggressive in his work. Though early on he had risen very quickly in his profession, he felt that now he was somehow getting in his own way. He worried that he might be "afraid of success." In describing his feelings, the image came to him of a thick impenetrable stone wall standing before him.
>
> In one session, while expressing his frustration with what was happening in his life, he noticed that a glass doorway, like one in an office building, had appeared in this wall. His response in the image was to rush immediately toward the door, try to turn the handle and push through. But the doorway would not budge. He found himself standing outside pounding on its intractable surface and yelling uncontrollably, tears beginning to stream down his face.
>
> Then his body began to release and he started to share his feelings more deeply: self-doubt, uncertainty, estrangement. He began to breathe more deeply, and after a while, simply closed his eyes and was silent. He said nothing for almost twenty minutes, when suddenly the room's silence was broken by a laugh. He opened his eyes and spoke, his voice holding a subtlety, depth, and humor that had not been present before. He said, "You know Charley, I didn't really look at the door before. There is a sign on it.... It says 'pull'."
>
> The touching between us at that moment was very special, and marked the beginning of powerful work for him. In it, he refound the expressive potency which he cherished, and which had previously gone dry for him. He came to see how his growing ineffectiveness had been a function not of stopping short in creative rhythm, but of pushing beyond its point of necessary return. In risking to

251

listen to himself, to take time for silence and play in his life—to breathe in as well as out—he was able to reengage that passionate generative impulse from which true expression must ultimately spring.

In the same way that present cultural energetics blind us to the positive power of the receptive, they also shield us from its less savory aspects. When we think of deceit, we tend to envision active falsehood and invention. When we think of violence, we most readily imagine physical or psychological assault. Yet there is unquestionably as much potential violence and deception in the receptive half of rhythm as in the expressive.

As with each other polar dynamic, we can identify responses that function not to engage aliveness, but to diminish it. Again, such "symptoms" can be seen either as effective self-protection, or pathology. They manifest when, in response to a challenge to aliveness, a system creates an artificial split between Within and Without, then acts from the false unity of the inner aspect. Some of these patterns are simply pseudo-receptive, inviting penetration— through an apparent offering of friendship, interest in sharing ideas, a sexual allusion—with no real opening to receive it. Other patterns are more specifically destructive, offering invitation with the intent of doing violence to incoming expressive potency.

Pseudo-receptivity can take many forms. In passive patterns, there is invitation and apparent penetration, but when the guest enters, there is no one home. What appears to be receptive softness is, in truth, only malleability.

A second type is like a mirage. Here attempted penetration brings disappearance—either physically or in an evasive flight of emotionality or intellectual self-contradiction. Where such patterns are pronounced, the person may be intellectually, emotionally, or sexually seductive, repeatedly offering a "tease" or "come-on," before their emotional departure.

In patterns of receptive violence, we hear echoes of those destructive descendent forces which I called the suffocating mother and the tooth mother. In the first kind of pattern, the apparent receiver is a bit like Brer Rabbit's tar baby. Expression brings not responsiveness, but entanglement and insatiable need. Rather than being received, we are consumed—"sucked in" and "sucked dry." The snare may be the intoxicant of short term ease, guilt, or the implied knife blade of melodrama. As with the tar baby, often the more we try to free ourselves, the greater the entanglement becomes.

The parallel face to the tooth mother is the venemous seductress. Mythically, she is the "femme fatale" who, like the flame for the moth, attracts only to sear. This figure is often attracted to people of significant expressive potency. She derives her own sense of power from controlling the power of others. If we fall for the bait in her trap, we get hauled around by whatever sticks out—our ideas, our genitals, our caring.

As with other kinds of symptoms, there are certain kinds of needs that are effectively fulfilled by pseudo-receptive or receptively violent energetics, and other needs that are impossible to fulfill in these ways. In their ability to draw the attention of others, pseudo-receptive postures often function to guarantee that we will not be physically alone. In addition, through this same dynamic and through the dramas they often generate, they offer a way to maintain a state of apparent excitement. One way of looking at pseudo-receptivity and receptive violence is that they are ways to attain the creative energy of another without reciprocal vulnerability. A third covert gain is power. If successful, one is able to control and utilize the expressivity of others without taking any responsibilty for it. But to fulfill our needs for proximity, excitement and control in these ways, we must forfeit needs with which these dynamics are mutually exclusive: the intimacy of real softness, and the experience of beauty and growth that is inherently a part of honest and open interaction.

Having now completed our journey through the first half of the creative cycle, we might take a moment to review. The following chart summarizes the key variables in the dynamics of creative differentiation:

SUMMARY OF THE FIRST HALF OF THE CREATIVE CYCLE

CREATIVE STAGES:

	Pre-Axis (Original Unity)	Early-Axis (Early Separation)	Middle-Axis (Isometric Separation)	Late-Axis (Ascendant Preeminence)
STAGES IN THE MAJOR PERIODICITIES:				
Period in a Specific Creative Event	Incubation	Inspiration	Perspiration	Finishing & Polishing
A Lifetime	Prenatal Period & Infancy	Childhood	Adolescence	Young Adulthood
A Relationship	Pre-Relationship	Falling in Love	Time of Struggle	Established Relationship
The History of Culture	Pre-History	Early Culture (The "Golden Ages")	Middle Culture (The "Middle Ages")	Late Culture (The "Age of Reason")
CHARACTERISTICS OF EACH STAGE:				
Ordering Causality	Animistic	Magical	Moral	Material
Energetics	Matriarchal	Focused on Emerging Ascent, but with Values Essentially Matriarchal	Matriarchy & Patriarchy in Opposed Balance	Essentially Patriarchal with Secondary Matriarchal Influence
Issue which Defines Identity	Inclusion	Centrality	Control	Mastery

		circles around me."	therefore I am."	structure "), therefore I am."
Elemental Fear	Exclusion (= non-existence)	Reabsorption (= annihilation)	Loss of Control (= a fall into evil)	Failure (= impotence)
Manifest Qualities: *~ archetypically masculine poles (upper & outer)*	Manifestation from Source and Soul	Inspiration, Spontaneity, Artistry, Vision	Commitment, Power, Dominion, Fortitude	Intelligence, Discernment, Achievement, Refinement
~ archetypically feminine poles (lower & inner)	Manifestation from Source and Soul	Mystery, Earthiness, Generativity, Depth	Nurturance, Constancy, Fundamental Values, Creative Doubt	Enthusiasm, Fairness, Appreciation, Esthetic Responsiveness
CREATIVE LANGUAGES: (* = Primary Organizing Language)				
The Body	*The Creature Body, the Body as Nature	The Body as Essence, the Body of Ritual, the Spirit or Dream Body	The Visceral/Muscular Body, the Body of "Heart and Guts"	The Physical Body, the Body as Appearance
The Symbolic	Animism ~ the Symbolic as a Language of Nature	*Myth ~ the Symbolic as a Language of Ritual and Inspirational Relationship	Legend ~ the Symbolic as a Language of Moral Order	Fantasy ~ the Symbolic as a Language of Romanticism and Idealism
The Emotional	Feeling as Harmony with Nature	Feeling as Inspiration, Essence and Primal Passion	*Feeling as Visceral Emotion	Feeling as Sentiment and Pleasure
The Intellect	Participatory Consciousness	Magical and Esthetic Thought	The Logic of Right and Wrong	*Rational, Mechanistic Thought

THE MODEL : PART III
A LARGER VISION

We turn our attention now to the second half of the creative cycle, to the dynamics through which form and context integrate into a new and larger whole. We will give special attention to the implications of movement into this second half of things for the evolution of culture.

CHAPTER TEN

THE
SECOND HALF OF CREATION:
INTEGRATION, EXPANSION,
AND PARADOX

"Suppose you polish your skin till it shines, but there is no music within, then what?"
—*Kabir (trans. Robert Bly)*

"This is the sort of world we live in—a world of circuit structures—and love can survive only if wisdom (i.e., a sense of recognition of the fact of circuitry) has an effective voice."
—*Gregory Bateson*

"We all go on the same search, looking to solve the old mystery. We will not of course ever solve it. We will climb all over it. We will, finally, inhabit the mystery."
—*Ray Bradbury*

 The second half of the creative mechanism is the story of how the newly generated forms of creation reintegrate with their generative contexts, in the process both expanding those contexts, and being expanded by them.

Understanding integral dynamics with any depth is inherently challenging. This is in part a function of our particular place in the evolution of culture, in part just the nature of the task.

Turning first to the cultural component, if we look closely at transitional dynamics we can see that in them much of integration is simply cancelled out: integration requires the voice of mystery equally with that of the manifest, and at the peak of transition mystery essentially disappears as an ingredient in our perceptions. Often integration simply doesn't happen to any significant degree. When it does happen more deeply, we often have a difficult time understanding it, or knowing how to manage the experience.

A simple place to see this is in how we view and relate to the various life stages. In present times, we find it hard to conceive of our mature years as anything but a time of decay and degeneration.* We idealize the vigor and assurance of young adulthood, and fend off the second half of the life-time journey. Truth and power at the peak of transition is that which can be measured isolatedly as form: physical strength, beauty, the surety of factual understanding. Wisdom, the kind of knowing and power that more and more permeates our being as integration progresses, is both difficult for us to connect into, and hard for us to know what to do with when we do find it.

This has not always been so. When mystery had a more central place in reality, the second half of creation was both acknowledged and given most high regard. The ancient Greek, Chinese or Celt saw the later years of life as a time to cherish. Then it was elders who were venerated; wisdom was expressly valued. When the dimension of time has a significant voice, the second half of life, the period when the sensibilities of time become reintegrated in the whole, is felt not as loss, but as a new expanding of possibility.

But understanding creative integration with any completeness will require that we do much more than simply reconnect with earlier realities. There are a couple of reasons for this. First, integration within present reality, at least for creative processes that are relatively complete, occurs from a point markedly further along in the creative cycle than it did in those times. As a result, it requires qualitatively greater capacitance—to understand as well as to realize—and includes essential dynamics that then were simply not a part of reality.

----

* Until very recently, our developmental psychologies didn't even deal with the second half of life. They stopped at best in one's early twenties.

Second, the dynamics of integration have never been easy to grasp, even in cultural times when they were valued. The Zen master's koans were as baffling to the average person five hundred years ago as they, or the formulations of quantum mechanics or relativity are today. Because integration takes us beyond the reality of isolated polar truths, movement into the second half of the creative cycle inherently challenges us with knowings that are elusive and paradoxical.

Of what specifically is the second half of the creative cycle comprised? In a creative project, it spans roughly from the time a work first finds completion as form, to when the dynamics that the piece has been about are fully integrated into the person's experience. It most often commences with the first sharing of a work with its "audience," but this can vary greatly. For example, one can hold back a painting or a poem, letting it mature and ripen before it is shared, or conversely, offer it when it is still at a germinal stage. In new learning, integration begins about the time new facts or skills are first mastered, and extends through to the time when these new capacities are finally "second nature," both integrated into the person's whole of understanding and ability, and complete in being creatively altered through contact with the learner.

In a lifetime, the second half of rhythm begins at the point where the basic forms of adult existence have been established, and goes on to the end of one's life. When this point occurs is a function of the stage in cultural evolution within which one's personal development is happening. Since each stage in cultural development adds a new stage to the first half of the personal journey, passage into full adulthood takes place somewhat later with each succeeding stage in culture.

In pre-axial times, the major parts of this transition happen in conjunction with the passage rites of puberty. These rituals take one from childhood directly into an essentially pre-established adult reality. When truth is regarded as an eternal turning, there is no need to have generative stages between childhood and adulthood—either personally, for development of uniqueness in individual identity, or culturally, as a mechanism for the creative challenging of social norms. But as progress and individual identity become more important ingredients, this changes. Each cultural stage adds new personal stages. By middle-axis times, in addition to infancy and a now clearly distinct childhood, one must complete a period of apprenticeship in order to be ready for full participation in the adult world. In late-axis reality, this apprenticeship stage becomes adolescence, and a new stage of further education and experimentation is added, what we call young adulthood. In present transitional times, the age when integration concertedly begins can vary considerably. It can start as early as the mid twenties, or for some, in effect, never be reached at all. For most, integration first becomes deeply engaged in one's thirties or early forties, during that newly recognized time of passage we call the midlife transition.* We can move into full adulthood only after the form-defined goals of our youth have had some time to be lived out.

I have previously outlined how I see us as a species at the beginnings of the second half of the creative cycle in culture.** The new frequent stressfulness of the midlife transition in our times—making it not just a transition, but a midlife "crisis"—is, I think, a direct function of this fact. Always before the passage into adult maturity took place into a reality with clear truths: we exchanged personal parents for cultural parents. Today, to make this personal passage, we must do so into a cultural reality that is in the midst of an analogous passage, a reality that itself is leaving behind form-defined truth.

---

* The term "midlife transition," as commonly used, can refer to several different things. It can, as here, refer to the end of the primary formative stages in development. It is often also used when speaking of that period, usually in one's forties or early fifties, when one starts to deal with such things as children leaving home, and one's work entering its mature stages. The latter period also involves transitional dynamics, but in the creative tasks of parenting and profession, rather than in the lifetime rhythm as a whole.

** It could be argued that we can't really know that integration is what comes next culturally. Since the number of stages in cultural evolution defines the available stages in smaller periodicities, there is no way to be sure there aren't differentiation stages we don't yet know about. While we can't really be certain this is the case, the evidence suggests that integration is already in progress.

THE SECOND HALF OF CREATION

THE DYNAMICS OF TRANSITION

"In the middle of the journey of our life, I came to myself in a dark wood where the straight way was lost."

—*Dante*
The Divine Comedy

"... (to be) pure in spirit ... isn't the same as goodness. It is much more difficult, and nearer the divine. The divine isn't only good, it is all things."

—*D.H. Lawrence*

"One who is not alone has not discovered his identity."

—*Thomas Merton*

Before we turn to looking at the whole of the second half of the creative cycle, its stages and organizing dynamics, we should take some time to examine more specifically the processes that define the cycle's midpoint. The transitional stage is both a very profound, and easily very confusing and disturbing time in the creative story.

In one sense, the second half of the creative cycle is simply a continuation of the first: each stage, as in the first half of creation, simply adds one further increment to the system's capacitance. In another, it challenges us with something fully different than we have encountered before. This difference has two aspects. First, while each stage before was new—indeed qualitatively new—it always took us further in the familiar direction of form and conscious clarity. Here the trajectory changes: the new expansion is as much down as up, as much in as out. Second, while each stage in the first half of cycle demanded that we understand new kinds of answers, there always were answers; as long as truth is polar, we can define things, speak of them in the language of "this as opposed to that." Here the security of such ready handholds gets left behind.

Our first response on sensing the profundity of these changes is often anything but positive. The more form-defined side of our natures, having seen the first half of cycle as a struggle toward the realization of a dream, easily feels confused and betrayed. The dream has finally been realized—the project completed, identity established, relationship cemented, or individual freedom and sovereignty achieved—and now the rules are being changed. The less form-defined parts of ourselves, though easily at first intrigued, on beginning to sense what these changes are really about, commonly change their tune as well. The stages ahead offer neither just a time to bathe in the glow of projects completed, nor a new supremacy for the unformed, a "second coming" or a simplistically conceived "new age." The second half of the creative cycle is fully as challenging as the first.

We frequently respond to this unexpected threat to our known reality by trying to keep the process of passage at bay. In the lifetime rhythm we cling to our youth or we get "set in our ways." In relationships we hold more firmly to our roles and our ideas of what should be. In creative projects we may avoid that last step of putting what we have created into the world, or we may choose projects that don't involve enough of ourselves to be of any significant risk. As I will outline, many of the things we are presently seeing in the social sphere can be understood quite specifically as fear responses to the insecurites and confusions inherent to this most pivotal of times.

As a way to see some into the inner workings of transition, we might turn again to the language of the symbolic. Once more it can serve us as a kind of creative shorthand for describing processes that are immensely complex and elusive to our usual thinking.

Mythically speaking, once we have completed the journey of ascent and separation, what next? To find out, we might start by consulting with our familiar keepers of truth from the journey's first half.

First we ask the mythic patriarch. With pride and majesty in his voice, he tells us that from here it is "onward and upward," that our task is to continue as we have toward ever bigger and better things. He turns to a blackboard behind him and draws the second half of cycle like this:

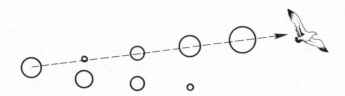

*FIG. 10-1. The Mythic Patriarch's Plan
for the Second Half of the Creative Cycle*

Expansive with excitement, we leave the patriarch, and go to see what the matriarch might have to add. But from her we hear a very different story. Form and separation, she says, were mistakes from the beginning. They just made us ambitious and greedy. Because of them, she says, we have come to forget exactly what is most important. She tells us that the patriarch is misinformed; the real course of the second half of cycle is a return to the things of earth and tradition from which we were born. She draws a very different diagram:

*FIG. 10-2. The Mythic Matriarch's Plan
for the Second Half of the Creative Cycle*

As we listen, we begin, reluctantly, to realize that from here on in our journey, neither the voice of the patriarch nor that of the matriarch can serve to guide us. The patriarch's vision of a rhythmless ascent into space is ultimately cold and sterile; it can describe only mechanical continuation, not living creation. And the matriarch's vision is no better. Her vision of rhythms is one of endless repetition; what she thinks would bring eternal peace is in truth a formula for decay and stagnation. Neither of these images will do. Either one by itself would destroy life—not create it.

265

We begin to realize that the journey is demanding that we bid farewell to the predicatiblity and safety that the archetypal parents have offered. If life is to continue, we must leave behind both the patriarch's finely etched maps and ready answers, and the matriarch's ever present table and unquestioning love. The journey from this point will be different. We must risk a leap.

As we turn to walk on, we sense a new kind of presence standing before us. At first all we can see is darkness, then the faint outlines of a cloaked figure beside a doorway. He speaks to us, saying simply that he is the gatekeeper, the guardian to the doorway of passage.

The gatekeeper is a kind of figure we have not seen before. His image is elusive, yet at once profoundly present. He speaks not just from one part of creation, but from many parts as he chooses. He has many faces, many voices. He understands the partialities of both the patriarch and the matriarch, and can be seduced by neither.

He will be met in new and more powerful ways with each step in integration, but this first meeting is easily the most unsettling. The gatekeeper stands before us and says these simple, stark words: "If you wish to make passage, there are three things you must accept. First, that from here on you are alone. Second, that you will no longer have answers. And third, that even though you will often not know what is happening, you are responsible for whatever transpires." The gatekeeper is something of a trickster, for each demand has an opposite that is also true. But for now, these things are not revealed (and would not be understood if they were).

The gatekeeper's three demands can be felt at the point of transition in any periodicity. Let's take several examples:

Imagine that you are just completing work on a painting or piece of sculpture. You've worked on it over several years, taking it through each of its stages. You've sat with it through the germinations of its fragile infancy, played with it and protected it through its wide-eyed childhood, met it with sweat and tears in the trials of its adolescence, and stuck with it to give it final finish and form.

Now it is time for the unveiling—time for others to share in the beauty and heroism it took to bring it into being, and time for you to step back and let the piece itself tell the story. The journey is finally over.

But it isn't, not really. There is much yet to come. Not expecting this (and in a way one never does), you easily feel that these new challenges are an unkind payment for such long struggles. It should be a time to celebrate, to chalk up a victory—not one to feel sadness, fear, questioning.

The first inkling that something more is up comes with the recognition that along with the celebrating, there is also a certain grieving. The work was part of you—an inner child. And the image of its potential being had for a time been a central goal and "answer" in your life. Now you must go your separate ways; the piece, your child, has grown, and if it is to stay vital, it must step forth into the world.

You also notice some fear. You feel it first as simply nervousness about what will happen with the piece. You remember just how different the world the piece is entering is from that of your studio. There it was your special child. Now it will be just one creation in an easily indifferent world full of creations. You must let go of it, having no idea what its fate will be. And whatever happens— good, harm or indifference—even though in a sense you understand the piece no better than anyone else, you are responsible; it is you it came from.

As you stand there a bit longer you realize that the unease you feel isn't just about the piece. You find yourself reflective. You remember back to starting the piece, and begin to ask why you were driven to do it. You realize that, in subtle ways, in creating the piece you were at the same time creating yourself. And you realize as well that what you have to learn from the process of that creating is far from over. Indeed, in a certain sense, it is just beginning. You see that the creative process, rather than ending, has simply shifted its focus from the piece to you. You acknowledge how little you truly know the piece, and realize that to the degree you can really let it in, it, and what will happen with it, will challenge you to the roots of your being.

The issues of transition in a lifetime are not essentially different. We are dealing with a longer periodicity, and our perspective is somewhat different: we are less the creator, and more the created. But the specter and challenges of transition are identical.

In the lifecycle, too, these changes can be most disturbing. Depending on our courage in meeting them, we can find the second half of life a time of rich seasoning, or an arid wasteland.

If we have reached cycle's midpoint in relatively good shape, it is a time for appropriate pride. We've spent long years in learning and exploring. We've traveled along the treacherous path toward individual identity, and while some ideals have had to be tempered along the way, major goals have been realized. By all rights, the last half of life should be simply a time to let some of this fill out, and to reap the rewards of our diligence and courage.

But such is not our fate. As young adults, hurrying forward in the tasks of our identity, we are sure in our steps. But approaching the midpoint in our lives, things begin to seem much less certain.

The gatekeeper stands by the doorway and we hear his first demand. "To go on, you must accept that you are alone. There will never again be anyone whose task it is to always be there for you, to always understand you." The guardian is in fact offering us the key to mature intimacy, but we are unlikely to understand the gift.

The second demand is equally disturbing: "And you must give up the idea that life has 'solutions'." As children we always had answers: we had parents. Later we internalized them and added new images to them. We lived them out in adolescence as codes of good and evil, as causes and romantic dreams, and later, in our goals and ambitions. But from here, answers will not be enough. Being "good" (or "bad") will more and more often be as much a denial of self as an expression of rightness. Causes and ambitions that before seemed unquestionable will begin to seem much less black and white, and often may get in the way of doing what in fact could bring change. And our images of love will increasingly do more to blind us to the fact of love than help to bring it into being.

This loss of answers is often initially very disturbing. We easily reach for anything to fill the void—perhaps a new, more virtuous goal: to perfect oneself, to do God's will, to make a better world. But these, past the timeliness of form-defined answers, work no better. They simply turn into further attempts to prove something when there is no longer anything to prove, nor anyone really to prove it to.

The gatekeeper's third demand is no less challenging. The call to be responsible has been there with each previous stage. But this is responsibility of a new sort: not just for what we do and intend, but in all of what we are.

The parallels with our present time in the evolution of culture should be readily apparent. The major form-definable goals of civilization have been realized. While in our beginnings we were at the mercy of nature's whims, we live our lives today in amazing independence of her influences. Where before the globe was a vast uncharted mystery, today we can reach any part of it in a matter of hours. We have left behind slavery and caste systems to realize a profound degree of individual freedom. And where only a century ago, physical labor consumed the majority of our energy, now most manual tasks are done by commonly available technology.

And once again, just as we approach what would seem rightfully to be a time of reward—a time to sit back and be served by this world we have created—we find ourselves confronted by a whole new set of questions. We clearly live in a time of immense tension, uncertainty and potential tragedy.

While the ascent of civilization has been a most courageous and wondrous process, if our eyes are at all open, we recognize that we cannot simply follow its past trajectory. Our cultural rules are changing in inescapable ways. The goal of defeating nature, while heroic when timely, when past its season evokes the image of a madman destroying his own home in a desperate attempt to affirm his own might. The goal of dominion and supremacy, similarly courageous in its time, in the context of an ever smaller world changes into a formula for global destruction. Progress defined isolatedly in the language of economic and technological growth, while a powerful battlecry for the material age, as a credo for today can only lead to ever greater alienation from the human dimension. The journey can go on only if we are willing to examine closely our roles as creators, both in the whole of our world and in the whole of ourselves.

The gatekeeper stands at the doorway and says simply: "If you wish to proceed, you must accept that from this point forth, things will be different, and different in ways that may at first be difficult to understand or accept." The demands are the same. First, as cultural wholes, national and ethnic "bodies," we must surrender our myths of specialness. All peoples believe in some way that they are chosen. To initiate war, we must believe we have "God on our side," that we are the special children of the Great Parent. As cultures, we must now risk final separation, to face our aloneness: we are each simply creations, no one particularly more divine or absurd than the next.

And we must leave behind our isolatedly form-defined answers. The new criteria for truth—quality of life, a sense of purpose, integrity in wholes of self, community and planet—are necessarily beyond definition in our usual sense. The guardian offers a simple warning: to the degree we cling to what can be held to in the old way, passage will be impossible. Our new "answers" must be large enough to embrace life.

The gatekeeper's final demand is again a challenge to responsibility, here culturally to be accountable in the planetary whole. Self-centeredness was a natural part of our cultural childhood, as was righteous moralism a natural part of its adolescence, and ambitiousness of its young adulthood. But these things, untempered, are no longer consistent with survival. We no longer have the option of projecting our darkness onto other peoples and self-righteously unleashing our might upon them. We have lost even the option of simple economic domination: when there are losers in a global economy, ultimately we all lose. It is being demanded that we understand a new kind of fully planetary accountability.

We easily retreat from the challenge. Around us we see being resurrected timeworn creeds of political absolutism and religious dogmatism, fervently frightened regressions to past solutions. Along with this we see an ever-mounting proliferation of pseudo-excitements: new artificial highs are being produced at a phenomenal rate—new things to buy, new substances to ingest, new media

270

sensations to consume. They express the hope that if we move fast enough, and stay high long enough, the threatening tasks ahead will just disappear. If a product claims to be an antidote for any of the guardian's three demands—if it says here's the answer, if it hides us from our aloneness, or if it lets us avoid responsibility for our lives—it is guaranteed to have a market.

Whatever the context, then, movement into the creative cycle's second half challanges us deeply. While what we imagine in anticipation is often much more fearsome than what we in fact encounter, these challanges are none the less always immensely significant. The second half of cycle demands of us new, dramatically more dynamic, kinds of understanding, and more personally vulnerable kinds of courage.

And the rewards ultimately are fully commensurate with these challanges. When we can begin to hear and accept the gatekeeper's demands, we discover that they have much fuller meanings than we first imagined. The gatekeeper is not the stern and uncaring figure he seems in anticipation. He is, in fact, the keeper of wisdom. His words are stark because wisdom is not easy stuff. But his message is not that reality is stark. Quite the contrary.

As we get to know him, we learn gradually how each of his demands has a second meaning. When we risk our aloneness, we bit by bit discover new capacities for mature connection, both within ourselves and with others. When we leave behind answers as form, we discover new, more living ways of understanding what it means to have answers. And when we risk accepting responsibility, we discover how, while responsibility in its fullest sense is not an easy thing, neither is it a burden; in it lies the gift of our empowerment.

To understand something of the mechanism of these paradoxes, we might turn again to our images of the mythic parents. In approaching the doorway of passage we bid them a final farewell. But as we step through, we discover that they have not in fact been lost. Indeed, in an important sense it is only now, in having completed the first journey, that we can really know them.

The parents are the same two figures we knew before, and they are not. Two things have changed. Rather than being external forces, they are now simply parts within ourselves. And with this, their relationship has begun a most important kind of transformation. More and more it is becoming possible for the dance between these polar archetypes to be an overt and conscious process of collaboration.

This new kind of relationship demands major sacrifices on the part of each of the mythic parents, sacrifices of exactly those things that in the old reality each figure would have been least willing to relinquish.

The patriarch must accept that there is more to reality than what he has been seeing. In addition he must concede that there are some places that he will never be able to penetrate, and that even what he can penetrate, he will never be able to completely control.

To the degree that he can make these sacrifices, there are rich rewards. There are awarenesses about things that he never before dreamed of, and with this, understandings about kinds of power more fulfilling than control. Where before he was glorified in his lofty mountaintop abode, his rewards were always really less than they appeared; separation's layered clouds isolated him from much of what went on below. Eventually, although he was blind to the fact, all he was really able to see were the hilltops. With integration, these clouds bit by bit begin to clear. He can now see more and more into the Below, and now and then to even make excursions into it.

The matriarch must also make sacrifice. Her story before was that truth was unity—unity of spirit, unity of community, the unity of release in ease and pleasure. Here she must accept that the two—as the secular, as the individual, as struggle—is as much a part of truth as the one. She must also accept that her words, far from being ever pure and loving as she has claimed, carry a capacity for violence fully equal to that of her polar counterpart.

And she too is richly rewarded for her sacrifice. The things she cherishes—values like depth, receptivity, beauty and instinct—come to play an increasing role in life's workings. And she finds she no longer needs to wield her power covertly; her concerns, while no longer "the truth," as she thought before, are increasingly things consciously valued in the whole.

THEMES IN THE SECOND HALF
OF CREATIVE CYCLE

*"In the midst of the world, the creator said to Adam, I have
placed thee, so thou couldst look around so much easier, and
see all that is in it. I created thee as a being neither celestial
nor earthly, neither mortal nor immortal alone, so that thou
shouldst be thy own free moulder and overcomer ..."*
—Pico Della Mirandola

*"Before I had studied Zen, I saw mountains as mountains,
waters as waters. When I learned something of Zen, the
mountains were no longer mountains, the waters no longer
waters. But now that I understand Zen, I am at peace with
myself, seeing mountains once again as mountains, waters
as waters."* —Ching-yuan

"I got plenty 'o nuttin, and nuttin's plenty fo' me."
—Porgy, in George Gershwin's Porgy and Bess

What are the key themes that emerge in meeting the
challenges of integration? I think of seven primary motifs. None of
them can be fully separated from the others, but each clarifies an
important aspect of the process as a whole.

With each stage in the second half of the creative cycle we
see: 1) a growing ability to be conscious in creation as a process, 2)
increasingly post-material definitions for truth, 3) an increasing
integration of previous defining polarities, 4) reality becoming
more relational, 5) a growing ability to remember into the realities
of previous stages, 6) the growth of a new, more relativistic kind of
identity, and 7) a more dynamic capacity for boundary. Let's take a
moment with each:

1) A Growing Ability to be Conscious in Creation as a Process.

In the first half of creation it is very hard to stand back and see
that one is in fact involved in a process: each stage has its own reality and there is amnesia for what has been and blindness to what

273

lies ahead. As we move into a cycle's second half, this changes. We begin to be aware of the larger process that our more circumscribed perspectives have been parts within. In a creative project, where before we were immersed in the tasks of each stage, we find ourselves now more and more able to get perspective on the place and importance of what we have been doing, both in ourselves and in the world the work will impact. In a relationship, we begin to find the ability not just to love, but to understand our love as something that grows and evolves, and within this to better understand its appropriate proportion in the whole of our lives. In our lifetimes, we begin, in a new way, to be able to not just live our lives, but to see and live from a larger picture of what our life is about, something which frees us both to take the individual events of our lives less seriously, and to live the whole of our lives with ever greater purpose and commitment. In our cultural history, we begin to be able not just to create culture, but to stand back and examine the function and effect of what we are creating.

It is this process that lies behind the gatekeeper's demand that we take final responsibility. Both awareness and responsibility here have different meanings than we usually give to them. Awareness in and of the whole in a creative process does not render all things clear and obvious; indeed, the more we live with awareness in this sense, the more we appreciate just how unfathomable life really is. Creative responsibility is, in a similar way, less a question of liability in outcome, than of courage to be conscious and accountable in a reality that is by its nature indeterminate.

2) Increasingly Post-material Definitions of Truth.

This has been a central theme in looking at culture, but it is equally relevant to all our smaller periodicities. Past transition, truth shifts away from the form-defined world of "up and out," more and more becoming the greater whole of whatever the encompassing creative process has been. Because such truth includes the whole, it is necessarily beyond definition in our usual sense.

In a creative task, we leave behind defining value in terms of the acclaim an act brings, or eventually even in terms of whether what we created "worked," to ask instead how, and to what degree, it made life more. In relationship, we find ourselves less and less concerned about the form and appearance of what we do—whether it fits the other's expectations, who thought of it, what others will think—and more and more valuing of the very "ordinary," yet infinitely subtle and vulnerable art of simply being ourselves together. In the cycle of a life, we see that the things we can define—what we achieve, what we look like, what we believe—are but one part of life's picture. In culture, we are challenged to face the fact that our inventions will not save us, that indeed if we can't see beyond them to the larger picture of which they are a part, they will be our undoing. Past the point of transition, creative truth becomes the living whole of the creative process, and within this, our integrity as a participants in it.

3) An Increasing Integration of Previous Defining Polarities.

The new creation is now sufficiently formed that the danger of it being reengulfed is past. With this, it becomes increasingly possible to acknowledge that the relationship between the formed in creation and its polar counterparts* is, and in an important sense always has been, complementary, and to develop that relationship in ever more integral ways.

We experience this process of one plus one becoming more than two in a multitude of manifestations. As polarities organize every aspect of creation in cycle's first half, we could make endless lists: right and wrong, new and old, or fact and feeling for a creative project; love and hate, romanticism and pragmatism, or masculine and feminine for a relationship; work and play, success and failure, or moral and immoral for a lifetime; our side and their side, mind and body, or art and science for the evolution of culture. The common thread in these changes is that parts that before appeared, if not opposite, at least contradictory, begin to reveal their nature as creatively related elements in some larger process.

This meeting and expansion of polarities is what lies behind our need to speak in paradoxes if we wish to address truth in a liv-

---

* The less form-defined pole, in its various permutations, expresses what remains of the original connection in source and context.

ing way. Past the point of transition, truth spoken from just one side of an either/or can no longer satisfy. We must experience in terms of the creative whole. From here, for any absolute we utter, there is always some antithetical absolute which is also in some way true.

4) Reality Becomes More Relational.

This growing awareness of the creative interrelationship between parts in systems applies not just to polar parts, but parts in general. Past transition, atomistic images of reality become unsatis-fying. It is not that now relationship becomes primary: we are not just replacing all is two with all is one. We are simply remembering and integrating the place of relationship in reality.

We can see this in the second half of any formative dynamic. As we begin to sense more deeply the *why* as well as the *what* in creative projects, the often disparate-seeming parts of what we have created begin to "make sense"—that is, to reveal the fact and patterns of their interrelationships. Similarly, as we move past life's midpoint and begin to more deeply understand "why we are here," the connections between the different things we do and have done increasingly "fall into place." In relationship, this is a time when there is commonly a growing depth of appreciation, both for the other, and for the various parts of one's self. In culture, we can see this dynamic manifesting in myriad ways, from a recognition of the importance of the interdisciplinary in education, to ecumeni-cism, to the post-atomistic thinking of quantum mechanics and modern ecology.

5) A Growing Ability to Remember the Realities of Earlier Stages.

Becoming aware in the creative whole is much more than just a process of becoming conscious. There are two parts to this "more." First it is more than simply looking back from the reality of a later stage—like remembering one's fifth birthday, or an archeologist digging up bones and sending them off for carbon dating. It is a reconnecting into those earlier stages as unique ways of ordering re-ality. And second, it is more than a simple acceptance and inter-nalization of those stages: it is a process through which each be-comes more than it was before. The wisdom of an elder is much more than a simple additive product of earlier life stages. It is a statement from the larger generative whole that together they comprise. Similarly, adding up the beliefs and practices of shamans, gurus, kings and scientists won't lead us to the edge of cultural knowing. Even if it might, we would be stopped before we could begin: how does one "add" different realities? The continuing growth in capacitance that marks the formative cycle's second half reflects the creative expansion needed to simultaneously and integrally embody these realities.

6) The Growth of a New Kind of Identity.

With the second half of creative cycle we begin to glimpse a new way of understanding who we are and our proper function in ourselves as creation. Prior to the point of transition, identity is a thing, one's self-definition. Once integration begins, this starts to change. Increasingly the "who" of who we are is not just what has been created as form, but our whole being.

This larger understanding redefines not only who we think we are, but as well the functions of this "who." From the third space in experience, both what we should do, and what is possible to do, come to look quite different to us. We glimpse aspects of this new role in the figure of the gatekeeper. The gatekeeper is less the definer of what will be created than simply one who knows enough about creation's workings to voice its imperatives. From a more integral place, the conscious self becomes a kind of "creative manager," a combination catalyst, facilitator, and stage director among the living parts of the whole.

This evolution happens in some way in every creative periodicity. As it occurs, it inherently challenges us from each side of our usual polarities of determination. For example, as we move into the second half of our lives we more and more have to face that life is much more than just a matter of conscious choice; many things are simply out of our hands, and as much as we would like to believe otherwise, most that is worth having is not obtainable by the simple application of will. But it becomes equally clear that we are not simply leaves blown in creation's winds; we are much more than just victims of the fates.

Then who are we? And how can we be it most powerfully? While we cannot determine the precise course of creation, we can know a lot about its workings, and we can become very good at creating contexts in us and around us for creation to happen in. We can invite it; we can also protect it, challenge it, poke and prod it. We can learn to listen to it as aliveness, and honor the engagement that it needs at different stages in its development. The ability to do this is what wisdom and mature power are ultimately about.

Identity in this sense defines a new kind of leadership. It is what, past the point of transition, we must realize internally if we are to be the most powerful "leaders" in ourselves. It is as well the kind of leadership we will need culturally if civilization is to continue to flourish. It is a less visible sort of leadership than we are accustomed to, one with less fervor and rhetorical drama. But in the second half of things, it is not only the most powerful kind of leadership, it is the only kind of leadership that works.

7) A More Dynamic Capacity for Boundary.

In the first half of creative cycle we develop the ability to set increasingly differentiated and solid boundaries. Past the point of transition, boundaries evolve further, becoming more and more dynamic and "semi-permeable." With our growing sensitivity to process, what were before "hard and fast" distinctions can become more time- and context-relative.

This alteration manifests in every sort of interface. Importantly, the fact of this new permeability in no way implies that there is less boundary. There is in fact greater capacity to make a hard boundary when necessary, and more willingness to do it. The elder has lived long enough to know what she likes and doesn't like, and years ago saw through her need to please. Once a creative piece has had time to mature, I can talk pretty openly about it; I'm also increasingly able to be in touch with when I really don't want to talk about it, and more willing to say so.

From this new place, boundary becomes a subtlely relativistic concern. The ability to be in touch with the myriad things involved in healthy boundary is a pivotal part of effective "integral leadership."

The changing face of international relations provides a good illustration. It is increasingly clear that it will no longer work for major powers, such as the Soviet Union and the United States, to view one another as incarnations of the devil and make our boundaries like stone walls. Yet, it is at best naive, at worst very dangerous to do the opposite, to deny the fact of difference, to act as if we are just one big happy family. One of the most important parts of learning to relate in mutually rewarding ways will be developing the ability to manage the boundaries that separate us as creative dynamics.

I see several layers to this shift. First, there is the importance of recognizing that, as systems, our countries exist in a parallel and thus often competitive relationship. By the nature of things, there will be times when it will be important for each side to say "no," sometimes with a strong voice. At the same time, in moving into the second half of culture as creation, we should find a growing acknowledgement of how we can, and do, benefit each other. This process will take time; there is a lot of past mistrust to overcome. But if we do everything possible to foster this connecting—cultural exchanges, meetings between leaders, any kind of effort that can bring people in contact with people—we should succeed, and the rewards should be immense. Finally, to avoid potentially fatal errors in our policies, it will be important to stay aware of differences between our two countries both in how we make and how we perceive boundaries. The Soviet Union and the United States are not simply two peoples in conflict. We are very specific peoples. By virtue of differences in cultural eneregtic, and to some degree cultural stage, our perceptions about boundaries and the kinds of boundaries we need are not the same. Sensitivity to these various and evolving boundary dynamics will play an important role in keeping our planet a safe place to live.

STAGES IN THE SECOND HALF
OF CREATIVE CYCLE

"Existence is truly a matter of propagation between two infinities ... Midway between the two ... lies a third, which is more than infinite." —D.H. Lawrence

"I sought for help
But no one took me by the hand
I wept, but no one came to my side
I broke into lamentations
But no one harkened unto me."
—Babylonian Penitential Psalm

"I learn less and realize more
I learn in some different more subterranean way.
I am given more and more the gift of immediacy."
—Henry Miller

To talk about stages in the second half of the creative, we must keep a number of variables in mind. They add enough complexity that for most purposes thinking in terms of general themes, as we did in the previous section, is really more useful. But, in certain situations there is value in looking more specifically.

The first of these variables is that not all formative processes progress all the way to late-axis dynamics before integrating. Integration can occur from any stage, either because the needs related to it have been satisfactorily fulfilled, or as a function of the contextual cycle. The number of stages in the second half of cycle can thus vary considerably, and with this, how we experience them.

The second is that the sequence of stages is not invariant. There is a typical progression, but other factors, most specifically the relevant system's primary energetic, can alter it considerably. Integral dynamics characteristically first manifest between the polarities that are most central in a system's functioning.

So while we can talk in general terms of a sequence of stages, in fact what happens is always more complex than this.

The typical order of dynamics makes a mirror image to our familiar formative sequence. In essence, we are turning around and moving back through the stages, only now integrating—manifesting into larger living wholes—rather than differentiating and delineating. Where movement into late-axis reality took us from struggle and doubt into material certainty, as we move into the first stage of integration, we begin to see how doubt, the courage to question what before we had assumed, is precisely the doorway we need to realize a fuller kind of truth. Where movement into middle-axis reality was marked by the separation of good and evil, at the complementary place in integration, we find ourselves standing face to face with what we have made evil, challenged to understand right and wrong in much larger, more relativistic, and personally demanding terms. Where the task with early-axis separation was to let one part in the whole emerge as magic and special, at the parallel point in integration the task is to see how it is all very special ... and at once very ordinary. Briefly, here is how I see the primary dynamics in the four integrative stages:

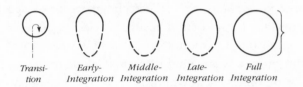

| Transi-
tion | Early-
Integration | Middle-
Integration | Late-
Integration | Full
Integration |

FIG. 10-3. Stages in Creative Integration

The initial stage, early-integration, begins with the first levels of acceptance of the gatekeeper's demands. Here we begin to ask the big questions of value and proportion, to look at the place and purpose of what we are doing in the whole. It is also appropriately time for a certain celebrating, a "thanksgiving" for what has been brought into being.*

In middle-integration, the focus deepens and expands. We engage it at a somewhat more ethical and visceral level. This stage, like the corresponding point in the first half of cycle, is marked by a critical confrontation between the light and the dark. Before, however, darkness was dealt with by rising above it; now the challenge is to meet it head on. Though the words are not always easy to hear, the old face of the enemy now holds mainly wise counsel for us. In challenging ourselves at this new and deeper level, we discover, in whatever the pertinent periodicity, newly

---

* There is often something further happening here as well. Where we are dealing not just with single rhythms but ongoing creative fluctuations, incubation for the next cycle generally first becomes fully engaged around the point of transition.

expanded understandings of truth and right. When the light and dark touch, we get not a loss of light as we might fear, but instead a reality that manifests with all the rich colors of the spectrum.

In late-integration, we meet again the early-axis poles of inspiration and mystery, but in new relationship. We feel the growing wonder of realization. We also come increasingly close to death: the creative cycle is approaching completion. There is a curious juxtaposition of feelings. From one standpoint, we have to face that nothing has really mattered that much; it is all coming to an end, and here we are, not that far from where we started. Yet if we really open to what is here, the feelings are most special. As we look around us, for all that is absurd, at once it all feels quite magical and wondrous. One could say it has always been wondrous, that in fact the journey was a kind of cosmic joke, but that only sees half of it. In truth, things seem wondrous now *because* we have risked the journey.

At full integration, what is simply is, one small bit fuller and more alive as a function of what we have been through.

THE SYMBOLOGY OF INTEGRATION

"We shall not cease from exploration
And the end of all our exploring
Will be to arrive where we started
And know the place for the first time."

—T.S. Eliot

"Heaven and earth determine the direction.
The forces of mountain and lake are united.
Thunder and wind arouse each other.
Water and fire do not combat each other."

—I Ching

"The self is a circle whose center is everywhere and whose
circumference is nowhere."   —C.G. Jung

"When I put on my clown costume, I step through a magic
door and become part of a sacred and powerful tradition."

—Emmett Kelly

How is creative integration represented in the language of the symbolic? This is not as simple to answer as when our focus was polar dynamics. Almost any motif is at least potentially a symbol of integration: whenever we fend off a part of ourselves, in integration it will emerge as a symbol to guide us toward the whole. And it is equally justifiable to say that integration is simply not something that can be depicted symbolically. A symbol is a form, a form of a more germinal nature than material forms, but none the less a form.

And there are symbolic motifs that for various reasons speak with special significance to dynamics of integration. We will take a moment with four of them. Since symbolic language is inherently biased toward the unitary, these motifs each give somewhat more weight to the whole than the parts. But this need not be a problem. It simply asks of us as always that we do a certain translation so that the messages have proper proportion within our present reality.

The first motif is that of the marriage of opposites. Its message has been a central one in these pages: Creation is a dance between polar dynamics; a moment is alive to the degree we can let each voice be present and in its proper balance. As a mythic motif, it can be found manifesting in some way in all early cosmologies. We see it portrayed in the entwined serpents of the Greek caduceus; the lovers of the alchemical marriage; the two sides, power and grace, of the Kabalistic tree of life; the interplaying polarities of yin and yang in Chinese thought; the lingam and yoni in the sexual symbolism of India. Often such motifs include some representation of the fact that these poles are more than just opposites. For example, in the familiar circular representation of the relationship of yin and yang, we see in the light half a small seed of the dark, and in the dark a spot of light.

Another important motif is that for which Carl Jung used the Sanskrit term mandala. A mandala is a radially symmetrical figure that in some way represents both a whole, usually in the form of a circle, and within this, its interwoven parts. We see mandalic forms in such as the rose windows of Gothic cathedrals, the labyrinthian interlocking designs of Celtic and Islamic ritual decoration, and the intersecting axis and transcept of the Christian cross.

No symbol by itself is sufficient to represent integration, but there are a number of motifs that speak with special pertinence to integral dynamics.

ABOVE: *Lovers representing the "perfect solution" in medieval alchemy—a depiction of the marriage of opposites. Germany. 16th century.* BELOW: *"The Holy Grail" symbolizing the "goal" of the creative journey's second half. Detail from* L'Appartion du St. Graal. *France. 15th century.*
OPPOSITE, TOP: *Rembrandt van Rijn.* Faust in His Study. *1652. An example of a mandalic image.*
OPPOSITE, BELOW: *Charlie Chaplin.* Modern Times. *1936. A "wise fool."*

The tree of life can be thought of as a mandalic image that incorporates the fact of our elongate symmetry.

While mandalic images in myth often address most specifically a particular process of integration, they usually, at the same time, address other spheres. In beginning to see the whole of any one creative process, we are connected into the patternings that order reality as a whole. Thus while the Aztec sun wheel was most specifically a depiction of the turning seasons, it was also a map of the cosmos and of the human soul. Similarly, the sand paintings of Navaho healing ritual represent not just health as a recovery of wholeness, but also nature as an ecological whole, and the whole of tribal reality. While the Round Table symbolized the allegiance of a particular group of men, it represented as well the joining of England's warring minor kingdoms into a new order, and the courage of the human heart.

The third motif is different from the first two in that here a single human figure functions to represent the tasks of integration. This requires some subtlety of understanding, as in fact with integration we are past polar depiction, and thus beyond treating reality as something that can be represented with particular personal qualities. Such figures work either by speaking in allegories and paradoxes, or by continually changing form, so as to stay always just beyond our grasp.

The most familiar images are religious personifications that in some way speak from between the Above and the Below, the image of Christ in the West or the Buddha in the East being important examples.* The image of the gatekeeper as I've used it here is another example of this kind of figure.

One of the most fascinating and powerful kinds of integral figures is the wise fool. He wears a face quite different from what most would first associate with integral concerns. We might take a moment to look at him more closely.

---

* Within a stage-specific cosmology, the words of an integral figure will both voice general themes of integration, and communicate codes and beliefs of that particular cultural stage.

Mythically, he is the one figure who can venture anywhere in the pantheon. The fool's task is to undo complacency wherever he finds it, and he wears whatever garb might most quickly bring this about. He is both loved and feared. Because he can be anything, he is just as much nothing. He is the prince of paradox.

We see him in the court jester, whose brazen buffoonery brings both challenge and release to the keepers of royal order. As the Fool of the Tarot, we see him stepping blithely off the precipice of certainty. We see him in public figures such as Mark Twain or Will Rogers, men from whose wit no inflated personage was safe, yet who commanded the esteem even of those who most strongly felt their sting. He is there in the conniving and wily Raven of Tlingit Indian lore, and is an essential aspect of Mercurius, the half divine, half animal prankster of medieval alchemy. He is the Mulla Nasrudin of Islamic tales, naively jumping back in fright at his own shadows so as to teach us about our own.

The wise fool is a teacher, but one as much by nature as intent. Where gods, kings, scientists and priests are the symbolic masters of the Above, and the great goddess and the figures of the underworld the keepers of the Below, the fool is the lord of heart and belly. He throws us into paradox not because he reverses the images of virtue and depravity, but because he holds the two inseparable. The fool demands, with a wink of the timeless, that we let truth, as held form, die. We know this death in our belly's rhythmic applause, and the begrudging but inevitable smile of recognition that captures our lips.

The last motif is one we have already examined at some length: the journey's second half. Sometimes, as with Odysseus' voyage back to Ithaca, or Moses' descent from Mt. Sinai, the theme is one of returning to what one has known, only to discover now that it is very different. In other tales, like that of the Holy Grail, the protagonist seeks for something beyond, only to find instead that it lies in an internal "coming home," in the courage to let truth be simply what it is.

INTEGRATION AND THE
HEALING RELATIONSHIP

*"But what he calls 'demonic' is nothing but the untamed
vitality of the whole."*
—*Karlfried von Dürckheim*

*"The solution to the problem of life is seen in the vanishing of
the problem."*
—*Wittgenstein*

"A sense of humor is a sense of proportion."
—*Kahlil Gibran*

The dynamics of the second half of the creative cycle work at
multiple layers in the therapeutic process. Any time we help a
person find closure on something that has happened in their life—
to grapple with "unfinished business," to deal with things that
before have been repressed—we are dealing with integral dynamics. Issues of integration similarly play a role any time we help a
person make transition between life stages: to leave behind the
safety of childhood to move into adolescence, to say goodbye to the
easy allegiances and veiled dependencies of adolescence to make
passage into young adulthood. They certainly come into play when
our focus is issues of aging. And in an important sense, the dynamics
of integration are always present in the healing relationship: ultimately, our task is to help a person live with power, love and purpose, that is, to have the courage to act from what is right and
timely, to risk the moment as a creative third space.

Frequently in therapy, issues of integration stand forefront as
the pivots around which everything else takes place. This is so
whenever issues of movement into the second half of one's life are
therapy's primary concerns. People most commonly enter therapy of
any duration in their thirties or early forties, during the time when
transitional concerns are most likely to be coming to a head. The
therapeutic relationship becomes a "ritual" vehicle for making

passage into mature adulthood. As this particular transition so often lies at the core of therapy, we might appropriately make it our focus here.

Framed in the ideas of the model, the dynamics of this passage can be thought of as involving four intimately related kinds of transformations. The first two are complementary processes, and one or the other generally leads the way as these changes begin. In the first, we see the person beginning to acknowledge polar parts in themself that before have tended to be disowned. In the second, one begins to be able to do the opposite, to distinguish oneself from polar qualities with which one has tended exclusively to identify. (Ultimately, each of these processes must happen in each direction. Even if our identification is strongly with one pole, there will always be at least some contexts in which that identification will be reversed.) The third transformation requires that the first two have already begun to some extent. In it, one begins to be able to identify with, and act from, the larger whole that contains these things that before were mutually exclusive, and to begin to engage self and others from a more third space perspective. The fourth transformation is the filling-out of the process of integration from one's primary energetic along the various formative stages, so that one comes more and more to be able to appreciate, and to some degree embody, each aspect of the creative whole. Let's take some time with each of these processes.

The engagement of the first may be felt initially in many different ways. We may simply notice that certain parts in us, before set aside, now seem important to develop. For example, a person who has identified with being open and playful may start to recognize the importance of assertiveness; or a person who before has identified with being hard-driving and hard-nosed may begin to see what is missed in not acknowledging and developing a softer side. Or we may begin to recognize that certain qualities that we repeatedly see in others are in fact parts of ourselves. These can be "positive" qualities like strength, creativeness or compassion, or attributes that we find decidedly unpleasant, such as judgementalness, insecurity or a tendency to undermine.

With the second kind of dynamic, we begin to get distance on polar elements that before have been held so close that we could not distinguish them from ourselves. We may begin to recognize that before we have defined ourselves in terms of particular ascendant qualities—say being smart, rich, or powerful—and see that these are not all of who we are, and as well that they are only a small part of what is important. If we have defined ourselves around a more lower pole identity—as a helpless victim of malevolent forces, as someone who is all-giving, or someone who deserves to be taken care of—we may begin to see our stance, and to recognize that fully adult existence requires more. Whatever the new awarenesses, they are not easy to make: they require that we surrender securities that before we took for granted, that we give up beliefs that have served as important mooring lines in our lives.

As these first two processes begin to be engaged, gradually we begin to be able to step back and see a larger picture. This exploring of a "third space" perspective is a paradoxical, often at once exciting and disturbing, experience. Always before, even if we have lived out the halves of our major polarities about equally, it has been possible to see ourselves and our world only from one or the other of these halves at a time. This new vantage gives quite a different view of things. Our first sensing of it can be quite startling; we often quickly discard it. But the more we can risk embodying it, the more we realize this new place is what is true, and that while in some ways the reality it describes is less grand than what we have known, ultimately it is larger. More important, we realize that from here on, it is the only reality that will work. In the second half of things, to be true to ourselves—to love, to be powerful, to be creative —is to be true to this larger reality.

This third dynamic is so centrally important that we should take a few moments to look at its workings from several different directions. Let's start with a clinical example. In this illustration, we see work done with different aspects of the creative whole of the client as "inner characters"—symbolic personages—an approach that provides a very direct window for observing these sorts of shifting inner relationships. (The integration process is happening here from an early, middle-axis primary energetic with

290

some splitting. The upper and outer polarities are embodied most strongly, but the greatest identification is with their less form-defined complements.)

Frank entered therapy at the age of forty one. A major issue for him was his relationship to writing. He had both significant potential as a writer, and a great desire to write, but he had always chosen to do other things rather than risk this that he had most passion for. In the early sessions of our work together he identified two parts of himself that seemed important in understanding what was going on for him: a shorter, somewhat more rotund figure who seemed most concerned with feelings, and a taller figure who was more concerned with ideas. He saw, at least intellectually, how these characters each had important roles to play in the writing process, and equally how each often got in the way, the first by becoming enmired in either sentimentality or self-doubt, the second by being overly critical.

Frank began working in dialogue with these characters, eventually confronting them with his feelings about his inability to write. Shortly thereafter he became seriously ill with pneumonia and was in the hospital for over a month. As a side effect of the antibiotics, he suffered significant disturbance to the functioning of his inner ear, resulting in him being unable to read without becoming dizzy. He became significantly depressed.

On his return, the first month's work revolved around his feelings of grief and anger over his lost capacities. While the prognosis was that given time, most of the loss would likely be compensated for, he felt extremely frustrated by his situation, and I felt most saddened by it. Then in one session, as we again worked with these themes, I realized that while I was feeling deep compassion, I was also feeling some boredom. At first I ignored the feeling, tried to push it away as inappropriate. But the more I listened, the more I sensed there was something important that the feeling was trying to tell me.

Finally I shared what I was experiencing with Frank, and with it a hunch. I told him that I thought it highly likely that the person talking to me wasn't him, but just a part of him. I brought in another chair and had him sit in it so he could look back toward where he had been. The moment he did so his posture changed and he spoke to me as the Frank I remembered from two months previous. It startled both of us. When he looked back, what he saw as image was the stouter of his two previous characters, indeed quite sickly and depressed. But from where he sat he did not feel this. His capacities had not fully returned, but his mood had changed dramatically. He again felt in charge of his life.

The depression did not return and he quite quickly got back to the task of exploring how he was blocking his ability to write, and what he would need now to move on with it. It is not possible to know if the pneumonia itself was related to the work, or whether the lower pole simply came to predominate in response to it. Whatever the case, as the work progressed, he became more and more able to stand back from each of his two characters and to see just how much they had been at war with each other. He became increasingly able to mediate between them, and in this to bring each of their resources creatively into his life. With this he came gradually to feel the excitement of a new kind of identity in himself. He found it more and more possible to live and act from the things he really most cared about, and not just in writing, but in his life as a whole.

Some of the most important aspects of work around passage into mature adulthood often happen directly in the connection between client and therapist, in what Freud called the "transference relationship." For the client, I am not just myself, I also wear the garb of whatever polar elements have tended to be disowned. By the nature of the therapist's role as "authority" in the relationship, there is a bias in this toward rejected upper pole qualities, but any part of the whole can be projected in this way.

The therapist's task here is a subtle one. Framed in the thinking of the model, it is to be in the room in such a way that all poles of the central dualities are a living part of one's presence, to neither fall for the collusion and play out the disowned parts, nor hide them, and cheat the client of what he needs to grapple with. It is never easy, and one always learns much about oneself in the effort, but to the degree the therapist can stay embodied in the whole of whatever that primary dynamic happens to be, the projected polarity will more and more come to stand exposed for the client, like the naked Emperor without his loyal courtiers.

Often in this process of passage the most important role the therapist plays is that of the great and final disappointment. To some degree, everyone enters therapy with the hope that the therapist will give them that long-sought final security and certainty. And, like parents, schools and personal beliefs before, the therapist will fail.

It is often quite a battle. Here the therapist, voluntarily or not, wears the face of the mythic gatekeeper. The battle circles around an uncrackable double bind, one for which the only escape is to give up the search for a final truth. The client needs the therapist to have the "answer," and feels betrayed if it is not forthcoming. Yet, in the polar sort of relationship that defines this need, if the therapist has the answer, then the client must not. If it appears the client might get what he wants, he ends up feeling powerless, exactly the feeling from which he had hoped the answer would save him.

If this confrontation is faced courageously, the client increasingly surrenders polar images of salvation, and begins to embrace a larger, more integral kind of identity. Bit by bit it becomes possible to simply be people together. In *The Brothers Karamazov*, we hear the Grand Inquisitor utter the words: "I tell thee man is tormented by no greater anxiety than to find someone quickly to whom he can hand over the gift of freedom with which the ill-fated creature is born." The challenge we face together is that of accepting the fearsome responsibility and uncertainty of a shared freedom.

Not uncommonly, major parts of this aspect of the work are done in relation to feelings one has towards one's parents. Our parents are our first and most important external experiences of Above and Below, Within and Without. It is in relationship to them that we first develop these dimensions in ourselves. In making passage we begin leaving their images behind, both surrendering our fantasies of them as perfect, and our resentments toward them because they were not. Over time, we increasingly discover the capacity to be imperfect, but ultimately loving, parents to ourselves, and in this to free our own parents, as ourselves, to be simple mortals.

Often some of the first evidence of a more third space kind of identity is the appearance of some kind of integral symbol in one's imagery or dreams. The following example is from therapy with a man who had been working for several months with issues in his life that were intimately tied to questions of adult passage. In the image that came to him we see elements of both the motif of the "pathless path" and the wise fool. (The client has a largely middle-axis personality, with about equal balance between polarities.)

Mark was forty-two when he entered therapy. He was a rugged, square-built man, a therapist himself, and a solid respected member of a small rural community. While he had always been proud of his ability to be in charge, one of his concerns in entering therapy was that now, what had before seemed a strength was getting in his way. He was finding it difficult, both in his work and as a parent, not to always have the "upper hand."

Several months into therapy he began noticing a repeated theme in his dreams, an image of journeying into a dark valley. Within the dream, he had no idea why he was there or where he was going, but somehow he knew it was important to be there.

In our sessions he used waking imagery to explore this motif. Early on, all that could be made out was darkness. The only tangible things were a feeling, that of being out of control—something he didn't like at all—and in the image, a small rabbit that jumped along ahead of him.

He was a bit embarrassed to have a rabbit as an image, but at one point assented to asking it why it was there. In the image, the rabbit replied immediately: "I am your guide." He found this rather absurd, but he could not deny that the image somehow seemed terribly important to him. Later, he asked the rabbit where it was leading him, to which the rabbit replied somewhat fliply, "nowhere at all." Clearly confused and frustrated he asked the rabbit why in the world he needed a guide if they weren't going anywhere, to which the rabbit said simply: "I am leading you nowhere so you won't get lost trying to go somewhere."

When people first begin to engage a more integral sense of self, they often find their connection with it extremely fragile and elusive. In one session it feels very solid, and nothing could be more important. A few weeks later the person barely remembers what it was that was being worked on. Then, at a most unexpected time, it reemerges, filled out in new ways, and with a new intensity.

Sometimes, especially if the therapy process includes active symbolic work, people will come up with personal metaphors to help them keep connected with their new-found integral perspective. I offer a few here to illustrate some of the different ways that people begin to feel third space dynamics.

One client, struggling with the issue of how to be both strong and sensitive in his marriage, had a dream in which he was swimming beneath the surface of a river. Three images presented themselves to him as he swam. The first was a stone, unmoving against the river's force. The second was a leaf, passive in the river's flood. The third image became the guiding image for his new growth. The image was of a fish, swimming amongst the rivers currents, neither struggling inordinately against them, nor giving in to them, but working with the play of the water. The image helped free him to allow room for all his seemingly incompatible qualities, and to find a place within himself from which they could work in increasingly complementary ways.

For a second client, the metaphor was what she called the "erotic thread," an image that had come to her in lovemaking. The intimate edge in her sexuality was very palpable to her. At first, she used the image to help her be in touch with how fully she was risking to be on that edge. She noticed that when submissiveness attempted to masquerade as receptivity, the thread would diminish. Likewise, when she tried too hard to make something happen instead of following the unknown knowing of her arousal, it would fade. With time she saw how what she was learning applied not just to aliveness in intimacy, but to all the threads of potency that made up the fabric of her life. The image helped her find the conviction to live from what was uniquely herself.

For a woman I worked with recently the metaphor was her relationship to death. She was nearing the end of a terminal illness, and we often talked together about her experiences in meeting death. It was a real gift to be with her, because she saw death as something through which to learn about herself and about life. I remember one day her saying with both curiosity and wonder in her voice, "You know Charley, if I deny death, make it my adversary, I'm just somewhere else; I learn and see nothing. Yet if I do the opposite, say, 'O.K., death, I give up, I surrender, take me away,' I am no closer to it. Death is certainly a most wily teacher."

The fourth kind of process seen in integration is defined by a filling out from this growing third space identity. As the opacities that have separated primary polarities begin to fade, the amnesias that have separated creative stages can begin to fade as well. Within any cultural stage, this process happens only within limits—early-, middle- and late-axis dynamics within late-axis culture, for example, are just a slice off the top of creative cycle as a whole—yet the experience is always a profound one.

There are many ways we might first feel it. We might notice a new kind of appreciation for the challenges we faced in earlier parts of our lives. Or we might see a growing awareness of the fact of process, of all things having beginnings, middles and ends, and of how we need to be different in ourselves with these different phases of things. Not infrequently, the place we see it strongest is in a new appreciation for people different from ourselves. In the first half of life, it is extremely hard to understand, or to see much value in, people whose primary energetic is markedly different from our own. As we move through transitional dynamics this changes. Now these same people often seem the most interesting, able to teach us about what we don't yet know, and complement us in the whole.

With the parallel beginning of integral dynamics in the evolution of civilization, this aspect of the creative is today often felt with a new kind of depth. The challenges and rewards of embodying integration at this deeper level came home to me in a very personal way on a recent trip to Ireland, the place of my roots. I share it as an "image" of personal integration that at once embraces aspects of cultural synthesis.

During my stay in Ireland, I spent much of my time exploring

296

the numerous remains from earlier cultural epochs. One of the wonderful things about Ireland is that one can find all the stages of cultural evolution powerfully represented in its archeology—and not in museums, but scattered around the countryside in fields and bogs.

There are petroglyph-etched underground grave passages from six thousand years ago; and Stonehenge-like stone circles and dolmens, ritual sites with huge stones held aloft like children's carefully stacked blocks, from a few thousand years later. There are stone forts from the times of the early Celts, and the remains of monastic dwellings from the early times of Christianity in Ireland. There are towers, forts and castles from the Middle Ages, and, of course, the city buildings of modern times.

As I visited these places, I became fascinated with the fact that if I connected really deeply with these different sorts of dwellings, both with their forms and their history, I experienced those of each epoch in very different ways in my body. I felt at a very personal level how each time lived as a distinct slice in the whole. I became deeply intrigued with seeing just how fully I could engage each of these realities in myself.

Over time, this fascination shifted from trying to feel not just each stage, but how they related to one another. At first, I found this very difficult to do. Immersed in the symbology and lore of one epoch, other periods would seem nearly incomprehensible (and easily, if I wasn't careful, most naive and inferior). Now and then, I would find myself able to connect at some depth with more than one period at a time, and the special richness I felt when I could do this let me know that it was important.

Often, when I woke up in the morning, I would find that I was playing back and forth in myself between these different realities. I could feel that somehow deep within myself I was pushing and tugging at the boundaries between them.

Then, one afternoon near the end of my visit, as I was walking along the ocean and reflecting on my stay, I realized that I was connecting in a way I had been unable to before with aspects of all these realities at once. It took every bit of stretching I could muster, but, just a bit, I was doing it. Tears came to my eyes. I felt an immense awe and gratitude. Somehow at that moment I could think of nothing more important than this: to connect in some small way, not just as idea, but through my flesh, in the whole of the human story.

You might want to play some with your own relationship to these various aspects of integral dynamics. Try these questions:

Where do you feel you are right now in your lifetime as a creative progression? If you are involved with issues of the second half of cycle, how do you experience them most strongly? Where do you feel in relation to the "gate-keeper's" three demands: ultimate aloneness, absence of answers, final responsiblity? What polarities seem most a part of these changes for you? What are the edges—the important challenges—right now in your relationship to, and as, them? How do you feel the relationship between these changes in you personally and changes in the cultural sphere?

Movement past the point of transition in cultural creation changes not just the client's personal experience in therapy, but also much about what the therapist appropriately brings to the thera-peutic context. The beginnings of cultural integration are changing every domain of our lives, and psychology is, as we have seen, no exception. One of the most important aspects in these changes will be the increasing importance of seeing beyond the traditional di-chotomy of health and disease.

Through the course of the book I have been developing one approach to looking at personality differences and questions of health that transcends this dichotomy. As the concepts are im-portant, I'd like here to summarize the main points, and to be more explicit in some areas we have touched on only lightly. For non-therapists, these remarks may provide more detail than is partic-ularly needed or desired—feel free to move on. For those interested in applying these ideas in practice, this should help solidify the concepts in your thinking and give them the delineation they need to be useful tools.

In applying the model psychodiagnostically, there are three overriding themes, each of which interplays with each of the others. First, health is a measure of a system's capacity for alive-ness, with symptoms being ways systems respond when they are challenged with more aliveness than they know how to embody. Second, systems never exist in isolation, but always in intricately evolving relationship with other systems: symptoms are rela-tional dynamics. And third, human differences can be understood in terms of the different parts in the creative whole we preferentially embody; they are a function, first, of the stages we occupy in per-sonal and cultural development, and, second, of our balance within the wholes of those stages—of our primary energetics.

These notions take us beyond customary nosologies in a number of important ways. To begin with, as I have said, they let us leave behind the traditional dichotomy of sickness and health. While people with any particular primary energetic have certain inher-ent partialities in their perceptions and actions, and characteristic patterns of response when the challenges of aliveness are too great, they also have unique richnesses and a place within the creative whole that only they can fulfill.

These ideas go further than customary nosologies in another way as well: they work as a comprehensive system. Most frame-works that address psychological dynamics in any depth describe only a few kinds of personality patterns at all adequately. To think comprehensively one must draw on an array of often contradictory theories.* Here we have a single perspective that seems to quite adequately embrace the whole of our diversity.

---

* In times ahead, we should see the rigid walls that have traditionally separated different approaches to psychotherapy becoming more and more permeable. Certainly one of the most baffling things to a new initiate to the thinking of psychology is how learned and respected people could describe this one organism (the one we should know best) in such strikingly disparate ways. One way of framing differences between schools of therapy is that they reflect perceptions about who we are, made from different primary energetics, and different polarities within these energetics. For example, learning theorists tend to view the person from a largely late-axis, upper pole perspective. From here, the appropriate bottom line is quite reasonably observable behavior. Most traditional analysts also take an upper pole perspective—the primary task

Further, this perspective is not just descriptive of behaviors, but dynamically based. Systems that are at all comprehensive are usually not so much coherent systems as classified collections of clinical syndromes. Because the categories here are not isolated bits, but patterns in relationship, the system itself confers valuable information. For example, through understanding the place of a pattern in the larger creative whole, we can make very good educated guesses both about likely etiologic factors, and what might be most helpful therapeutically.

And finally, because the model's psychodiagnostic notions are based on the core mechanism of our being, they let us understand personality patterns in terms of any and all the different ways that we organize experience. A particular pattern is a statement not just about particular ways of acting, but also about how people order their ideas, their emotional responses, the kinds of symbols that are likely to appear in their dreams, how they live in their bodies, and how they tend to structure and perceive relationships.

Below is a brief survey of the major personality constellations defined by the model. At best, this can be a sketch: each constellation would need a chapter of its own if we wanted to even start to be complete. For each primary energetic past the pre-axial, I've presented first the most common personality characteristics, including both that energetic's particular richnesses and the inherent partialities. Then I have made a few comments about what happens in this energetic when there is significant splitting, either situationally, or as a chronic pattern. I've followed this with a few

---

is seen as understanding—but here there are middle-axis elements as well as late. Analysts are clearest in their thinking around issues such as authority, autonomy, and control of impulses. Jungians and transpersonal therapists are at their best when addressing the issues of people with early-axis personalities—where the magical and the spiritual are important ingredients—and tend to view reality as a whole from a largely early-axis perspective. Humanistic therapists, in counselling us to "get out of our minds and back to our senses" reflect their bias toward late-axis, lower pole dynamics. As we move further into the integral stages of culture, we should find it easier and easier to view from the different parts within the whole of who we are simultaneously, and to appreciate the larger, more living, process that together they describe.

observations about what traits are most likely to appear bodily with this energetic,* and concluded by making brief comparison with more familiar psychodiagnostic categories.

Several important points should be reiterated before beginning. What I will be describing here are polar patterns, extremes. Most peoples' energetics are balances between these extremes. Similarly, while we each inhabit particular axes preferentially, any one person's personality is made up of balances between them all. In addition, it is important to remember that these descriptions are specific in time: they differentiate the whole for an adult person in modern western culture. A similar differentiation for medieval adults, say, or for modern western adolescents, would have important differences.

PRE-AXIAL PATTERNS:

It is really not possible to carry the major part of one's primary energetic in the earliest parts of cycle and function effectively in the context of modern reality. Pre-axial dynamics are primary in present times only when there has been some sort of major disturbance, either an extremely unhealthy childhood environment or a significant biochemical defect. These disturbances act at the most germinal substages to inhibit the person's capacity to move toward form.

As I see it, some variation on this kind of dynamic underlies all the different things we call psychoses. The effect appears to happen earliest in the creative cycle in "organic" psychoses, where the symptoms are a result of direct tissue damage, internal toxicity, or an external pharmacologic agent. In "schizophrenic" patterns, the effect seems to be somewhat later, and in the "affective" psy-

---

* One's primary energetic describes how a person organizes experience in the body, and at once it is a major part of how we shape our bodies. Thus, for each primary energetic we see specific tendencies not just in things like how a person moves, and the parts of the body that a person seems most to inhabit, but as well in things like tissue quality, and to some degree in overall body structure.

choses—severe manias and depressions—somewhat later still.* In the latter, there is some beginning separation, but not yet of sufficient substance to handle major engagements with reality. The response to meeting significant aliveness is severe polarization. The fact that schizophrenic and affective patterns often blend and overlap is easily understandable within this framework.

There are ongoing controversies in psychiatry about whether various psychotic patterns result from biochemical defects, or are a product of aberrant family dynamics. This framework lets us approach the question as more than an either/or. Many things can serve to disrupt the germinal substages of the creative cycle. Environmentally, the cause could be a family matrix in which primary bonding is disrupted, or alternatively, where little if any individual identity is tolerated within the system. Biochemically there could be a genetic defect affecting either the general capacity for rhythmic progression, or the child's specific ability to establish that early bond. I think of the various psychotic patterns not as single things, but as "final common pathways" for a multiplicity of often interwoven etiological processes.

Framing psychosis in this way can help us better understand the symptomatology we see in these patterns. For example, we can think of schizophrenic symptoms in terms of two counterbalancing dynamics. First, they express the pre-axial unformedness of the system. We commonly see such things as hallucinations (the taking of inner reality for external fact), loose associations (a lack of organization in thought), delusions (commonly reflecting a loss of boundary distinction, for example the belief that the person on T.V. is talking directly to you), and withdrawal (from the world of things). At the same time, they express a particular kind of structure, a making of form from what is available within that particular reality. In an important sense, psychosis is not so much a disintegration of the psyche, as an attempt to salvage it. Those loose

---

* There is the additional difference that certain kinds of affective patterns happen episodically in people with otherwise quite diverse personality styles. In the thinking here, something happens to override what is otherwise one's primary energetic. One sees this sometimes in schizophrenic patterns, though here chronic symptoms are more common.

associations make very effective boundaries. Delusions function to create unique identity and, along with hallucinations, provide a safe sense of connection and communication with other than oneself. The common bodily disorganization in chronic patterns—in which the different body parts seem fragmented—reflects each of these complementary mechanisms, being a kind of disruption, and yet, a very effective way to keep the whole from merging into unity.

EARLY-AXIS PATTERNS:

Where upper pole early-axis dynamics predominate in a person's personality, we are likely to be most struck by qualities such as intuitiveness, creativity, spiritual sensitivity, and charisma. Such a person brings major aspects of the magical child into the adult world. Where the outer aspect is strongest these qualities tend to manifest more externally: visual artists, poets and people who are recognized primarily as innovators in most any field, commonly have this energetic as a major part of their personality makeup. Where the more core aspects predominate, concerns are more with inner "artistry." A place we commonly see this dynamic is in people who are drawn to the more ascendant of Eastern spiritual practices, such as Zen Buddhism or yogic disciplines. Where the energetic is strongly ascendant, it can move above the usually symbol-focused reality of early-axis, and more into the world of ideas and things. We see this kind of dynamic in the notorious "mad" professor, and in people who immerse themselves in a kind of magical relationship with things like computers and the intricacies of the physical sciences.

The common shortcomings of people with upper pole, early-axis energetics follow directly from their bias in the creative whole. Such people often have a hard time distinguishing between their dreams and things manifest in reality. With this comes a common difficulty in mobilizing the kinds of sensibilities necessary to carry tasks into realized form. In addition, it is often most difficult for these people to cope with things that involve significant difference. They tend to avoid struggle and frequently have quite fragile boundary structures.

Where there is major splitting, these partialities become amplified. We often see grandiosity, and commonly with this, some degree of paranoia. The person's energetic is like that of the mythic god-king, or the child adored by his parents; if his charisma brings him followers (people to be one with him within a reality he defines), he can be quite magical and charming. But where this is lacking, and certainly most often as an adult it will be, he can feel very frightened and alone. Where the dynamic is weighted toward the outer aspect, narcissistic elements, sometimes accompanied by mania, tend to be most pronounced. Where the balance is more inward, the grandiosity tends to be spiritually rather than personally defined. Psychodiagnostic labels we are likely to see here are such things as schizoid and narcissistic personality disorders, and within Jungian thought the concept of the *puer aeternus*.

Bodily, the tissue quality tends to be soft, like that of a child. Structurally, the body tends to be thin and unusually flexible. These people characteristically look young for their age. They carry the major parts of their aliveness in the inner, "magical" layers of the upper chest, face and eyes. Where there is splitting, the energetic becomes hyper-ascendant and tissues and movements may take on an increasingly brittle quality. As a person moves further and further beyond an age where childlike narcissism is appropriate, this brittleness often becomes the dominant body characteristic. Upper pole, early-axis people tend to be taller than the norm. I have a hunch this is a function of their later than usual onset of puberty, and with this a delay in closing of the skeletal growth plates.

With lower pole, early-axis dynamics, the particularly rich qualities are such things as connection in mystery, a deep capacity to nurture, and spontaneity. Here we are seeing two sorts of things embodied: the playful aspects of the child (as opposed to the numinous and magical), and the child's generative ground. Such people often greatly enjoy working with children, attracted either to selflessly serving the children's "magic," or to a situation where they themselves can live to this degree in the unformed. Where the balance is toward the outer aspect, the qualities that stand out are such things as playfulness, often to the point of a certain pagan wildness, and the ability to improvise. Qualities like caring, and a depth of connection with nature and darkness, predominate when the balance is more inward.

The partialities of people with these kinds of dynamics follow from the fact that here, compared to other energetics, we see the least formedness and the most permeable boundaries. Such people often find it very difficult to manifest in any visible way in the world. Similarly, they have a hard time either allowing much difference and individuality in others, or mobilizing it in themselves. In the face of potential conflict, the person is most apt either to withdraw, or to merge, so that there is in effect no other to have conflict with. The other side of the unique sensitivity to children often seen here is a common difficulty in dealing with their maturation. If such people are not careful, they become suffocating or undermining, acting out their fear of letting new aliveness rise and separate.

Where there is significant splitting, these characteristics become exaggerated. This is where we see some of the strongest tendencies toward depression: the spark of inspiration is simply swallowed before it can appear. Particularly with more internal patterns, strong dependency is also common. Where above we saw the grandiosely self-centered child, here we see the needy child. There is again a magical causality, but rather than being centered in the self, it is centered on an external agent: a charismatic individual, a group (such as a religious cult), or an institution (as with people who develop a dependent relationship with hospitals). With more external patterns, the rudimentary boundary capacity is less apt to be dealt with through this kind of dependent merging, than by an avoidance of social contact. Diagnostic categories commonly given to people with significant splitting include passive-dependent, depressive and avoidant personalities.

We see several kinds of bodily patterns with lower pole, early-axis dynamics. They have in common a tendency toward unboundedness, and embodiment in the early-axis layers, predominantly in the belly and pelvis. With more external dynamics, the body tends to be hyperflexible and often quite animated, not unlike what we see with more ascendant patterns, but with a slightly lower center of balance and generally with somewhat greater body mass. More internally we see two kinds of patterns. In one, the person tends toward being thin and gaunt, a "hungry child." In the second, there is more pudginess, like a child yet to lose its baby fat. There may be significant obesity, with bulk serving as a covert boundary, both keeping distance and obscuring clarity of interface.

MIDDLE-AXIS PATTERNS:

With upper pole, middle-axis dynamics, the positive qualities that stand out are such things as fortitude, courage, and the capacity to lead. With the outer aspect predominant, these qualities manifest most in relationship to external concerns: people who become generals, coaches, union bosses, or "captains" of industry commonly have this energetic as a major part of their personality. Where the inner aspect is stronger, they manifest more in terms of personal and moral issues: upper pole, inner aspect energetics are commonly major parts of the personalities of people like priests, and school principals.

The primary partialities in these patterns have to do with their lack of contact with both earlier and later stages, and their particular relationship to lower pole concerns. Because here we find neither the intuitive sensitivities of early-axis patterns nor the refinement and differentiation of more late-axis sensibilities, the attitudes and beliefs of middle-axis, upper pole people, particularly when the outer aspect is strong, often seem to others quite coarse and simplistic. There is a tendency to view things in narrowly black and white terms. In addition, in such personalities, the need to be in control, to always be on top, (both of others and one's own impulses) can often decidedly limit creative possibilities. From a strongly ascendant middle-axis posture, it is pretty hard to let go and just have a good time.

Where there is significant splitting, this emotional narrowness and need for control is amplified. Increasingly, the person needs to feel struggle and dominance in order to have a sense of identity. In more inner postures this may manifest with others as vicious moralism, or more personally in rigid obsessions and compulsions. With a more external focus, it may manifest interpersonally in sadistic patterns, or socially in racist and dictatorial attitudes and actions.

Aliveness in middle-axis patterns is carried predominantly in the muscles and viscera. In upper pole patterns, it centers largely in the chest, shoulders, arms, jaw and brow. The muscle mass in middle-axis patterns characteristically exceeds what one would expect just from exercise: the isometric posture keeps the musculature in a constant state of exertion. Where the outer aspect predominates, this manifests in the classical "macho" body, with major mass concentrated in the chest, shoulder and neck. Where the inner aspect is stronger, we tend to see a more symmetrical, block-like body.

The primary positive qualities with lower pole middle-axis dynamics are such things as perseverance, amicability and devotion. Where the inner aspect predominates, we see these things in strong commitments to home and family, and in deep religious convictions. With the outer aspect, we see them in a complementary capacity to form strong bonds of allegiance, and in strength and endurance in the workplace. Soldiers and blue collar workers often have significant amounts of this outer aspect in their energetics.

In terms of partialities, lower pole patterns share with their upper pole complements a tendency toward black and white thinking, and emotional concreteness. But, while upper pole patterns need to be on top, here we see the opposite. With lower pole patterns, one doesn't really feel safe unless someone else is in charge. This is no less a need for control, just a different way of manifesting it. Where there is significant splitting, these dynamics become amplified. In more internal patterns, this control through abdication of responsibility manifests in such things as intractable passivity, undermining behavior, and not infrequently, through undermining oneself, in depression. With a more external emphasis, this struggle from below gets acted out more directly in things like chronic contrariness, or when splitting is pronounced, in outright anti-social behavior. Substance addiction and chronic physical illnesses are particularly common with lower pole, middle-axis energetics.

Bodily, it is again the visceral-muscular layers that are most engaged, though here, especially with the inner aspect, the focus shifts more to the visceral side of the picture. Structurally, we find the complement to what we saw with more upper pole patterns. Again there is isometric tension, and with this structural hypertrophy, but here it is engaged from the other side of the either/or. Where there is a preponderance of more outer aspect dynamics, we see again a block-like body, relatively symmetrical but strongly bound. Where the inner aspect predominates, the mass shifts into the belly, hips and thighs.

LATE–AXIS PATTERNS:

With late-axis upper pole patterns the qualities that most stand out are things like clarity of thought, verbal facility, and the ability to deal easily and effectively with things of the material world. Where the emphasis is inner, it is the intellectual aspects of these qualities that get primary emphasis. University professors and scientific researchers commonly have the upper pole, inner aspect of late-axis as the major ingredient in their primary energetics. As we move outward, the focus turns increasingly to more externally material concerns, be it dollars on Wall Street, or the engineer's world of facts and figures.

The partialities in late-axis upper pole patterns again follow quite directly from the nature of the energetic. While people with such patterns tend to be materially successful, they characteristically do less well when it comes to success with finding real closeness in intimacy or depth in their creative concerns. It is not so much that they fear the less formed than that they simply live a long ways from it. The late-axis, upper pole person's great two-edged sword is achievement. Such people do very well at climbing the ladder of success, but have a very hard time ever getting off it. With significant splitting we see a number of kinds of patterns. Probably the most common is the "workaholic," one who uses activity as a way to stay high. Obsessional symptoms are not uncommon. And when life situations challenge the ascendant posture we can see marked anxiety and often suicidal degrees of despair. The recent popularity of concepts like "stress" and "burnout" point to an increasing willingness to examine the partialities of these patterns.

The person with an upper pole, late-axis personality tends to carry their aliveness predominantly at the surface of the body, and vertically in the regions of the face, head and hands. Whereas the either/ors of middle-axis dynamics divide the body in the general region of the diaphragm, late-axis distinction occurs more cervically, giving us the classic separation of mind and body. The musculature tends to be taut and the body lean. Where there is significant splitting, both movements and tissue quality tend toward the rigid.

Common late-axis, lower pole qualities include such things as gregariousness, talent, graciousness and humor. This is the prominent energetic of most people who work in some way as performers. When the outer aspect predominates, we find the strongest focus on such qualities as visibility, pizazz and physicality. Where the balance is more internal, the emphasis is more on emotional nuance.

The partialities here are again a function of the form-defined bias of the energetic. While people in whom this energetic predominates are characteristically quite outgoing and easily expressive of their feelings, their connection, both with themselves and others, is in fact generally only from the more surface layers of the emotional. If there is significant separation, such people often in fact feel very alone, distant both from themselves and from others. One of the traps for people with this kind of energetic is that their identity is often so tied to being visible, being "onstage," that they can't ever take off their smile and admit their aloneness and confusion. A second kind of difficulty for this sort of person relates to the fact that, while they inhabit most strongly the lower pole, they attribute greatest worth to upper pole abilities. Such people are often very fearful of "looking stupid." A common diagnosis given to people with significant separation toward the inner aspect here is that of hysterical neurosis. Where separation is more outer, diagnoses are more varied, but common symptoms we see are such things as obsessive athleticism and over-concern with and perceptual distortions around physical appearance.

Bodily, the charge tends to be distributed fairly evenly over the body surface, with some concentration in the face and genitals. Where there is significant splitting, the charge both becomes more superficial and loses its creative connection between Above and Below. Here the person may become unconsciously seductive, or so obsessed with staying bright and "up" that they feel very little connection with themselves.

Again, this is but a bare outline, but I hope it has helped make the ideas here more explicit and applicable. In trainings I lead, I often choose people for groups so that each of the main patterns are represented. I love watching people coming to realize just how profoundly different other people's reality is from their own, and with this, in time, coming not just to understand these differences, but to know deeply in themselves just how much these differences are gifts.

CHAPTER ELEVEN

LIVING RELATIONSHIP:
LOVE, CO-CREATION,
AND CO-EVOLUTION

"In the beginning is relationship."
—*Martin Buber*

"Love one another, but make not a bond of love.
Fill each others cup, but drink not from one cup ...
Give your hearts, but not into each other's keeping."
—*Kahlil Gibran*

"We now find that the relationships between any two particles
depends on something going beyond what can be described
in terms of these particles alone. Indeed, more generally, this
relationship may depend on the quantum states of ever larger
systems, within which the system in question is contained,
ultimately going on to the universe as a whole."
—*David Bohm*

 I commented at the book's beginning that my first
solid insights about creatively-based thinking came
to me while trying to better understand the living
nature of human interrelationship. To this point in
the model, our focus has been somewhat more on
wholes that define systems—on the reality of individuals, on single
creative acts, on the evolution of isolated cultural groupings—than
on relationships between wholes. Here we shift our attention
slightly to examine more specifically the transformational inter-

connections through which human systems of all types grow and evolve.

With this chapter two important concerns will be forefront: first, looking more thoroughly at what it means to think about human relatedness in four-dimensional terms; second, examining what the model has to say about what likely lies ahead for us as relational beings.

Movement into the second half of culture as a creative process will mean a very significant evolution both in how we think about relationship and in how we live it. This will be the case in all spheres, from the most personal of intimacies, to international relations. A central part of effective living in the future, not just fulfillment in the future, but likely future survival, will be our ability to acknowledge and understand these changes. We will need both to find the places in ourselves from which these new kinds of relating will be possible, and to find ways of thinking about relationship sufficient to the larger realities they are happening within.

What will change in relationship as culture moves through cycle's second half? We shall examine a number of equally important and integrally related things, but what stands out most immediately is this. In moving beyond truth as form, we will more and more leave behind cultural dictates for what constitutes relationship, both codes of appropriate behavior in relationship—from sex roles to consensual codes of diplomacy—and the strictly delineated institutional forms that we have used to define what is and what is not relationship. Not many years ago what we meant by terms like friend, husband, wife, ally, or enemy was pretty straightforward. Today, while we easily long for the simplicity of such times, it is clearly past. What constitutes meaningful relationship in any one situation is becoming an increasingly personal, often complexly multifaceted, and ever-changing question. This newly emerging world of relational dynamics and possibilities is more than just the expression of interesting new options. As with earlier shifts in reality, we will either come to relate within these new, more challenging rules or we will not relate at all. Meaningful existence in times ahead will be predicated on our ability to bring more to the experience of relatedness than has ever before been a human need or capacity.

To function effectively in such an expanded relational reality, we will need new ways to think about what relationships are and what their significance is for us. Creatively-based thinking offers a way to do this. As we might expect, shifting to a four-dimensional perspective for thinking about relationship demands that we be willing to stretch our understanding in some significant ways.

Acknowledging the polar ways we have tended to view intimate relationships helps frame the challenge. From the lower pole of late-axis duality, we approach intimacy through the poetry of romance; we celebrate it's irrationality. Conversely, from the upper pole, we look at relationships more practically, we analyze them, try to demystify their workings. The essential awareness is that for times ahead, neither perspective alone, nor even the two together, will be sufficient to describe, or to help us find, meaningful intimacy. In the future, if ideas about love are to serve us, they must be able in some way to speak from the greater whole of such dualities, from that more transformational place where the rational and the irrational are themselves lovers.

The initial response of each of these poles on encountering a more integral perspective is easily at best ambivalent. From the lower pole there may be distrust and discomfort with the amount of awareness necessary to think about love creatively: "Love's beauty is delicate and sacred—this is too much thinking about what can't be thought about." To this part of us we must respond: "Yes, this concern is warranted—and it is eminently clear that in the future love's beauty will be possible only to the degree we can be sensitively discerning and choiceful in it." The upper pole is equally challenged. From a four-dimensional perspective, it is obvious that as much as we would like to understand it all, the only way in fact to eliminate the mysterious in love is to eliminate love. A creative paradigm offers the possibility of thinking about love, as about life in general, in ways that are highly specific. But to have this, we must be ready to accept love's ultimately unfathomable nature.

Ahead we should see a gradual integration of these polar perspectives. From above we should be able to be increasingly aware in relationship, and not just of the fact of relationship, but of relationships as processes: we should become more conscious both of the creative workings of relationship, and of the unique place and purpose of relationship in our lives as creative processes. In the future it will be necessary to be increasingly skilled "creative managers" in all domains of relationship, both more deeply knowledgeable in the dynamics of human interaction, and newly conscious among the multiplicity of options for interaction. Complementing this new capacity for awareness we should see from below a growing potential for real depth in relatedness. It is the sensibilities of those parts in us we have forgotten that most strongly voice the importance of connection. As we reengage the more germinal aspects of our natures, we should find ourselves not only with a greater capacity for relationship—as for life in general—but with a greater valuing of the place of relationship.

With this chapter, we will begin by looking in somewhat greater depth at how relationship is indeed a transformational dynamic. Then we will examine more closely the creative patternings that order experience in relationship. We will follow this by using the framework of the model to better understand the differences between different kinds of relationships. Throughout, we will be addressing the question of where, today, these patterns are taking us, and what in the future we must bring to these different kinds of relationships if they are to continue to enrichen us.

CO-CREATION

"In the modern concept ... there is no possibility of a detached, self-contained existence."

—Alfred North Whitehead

"All real living is meeting. Meeting is not in space and time, but space and time in meeting."

—Martin Buber

"Love is like everything else. If you don't have it, you can't get it."

—Walt Disney

We have already made a solid start at acknowledging how relationship is ultimately creative. We have looked at how more is needed than balls-on-a-billiard-table models of interaction if we wish to address relationship as something living. We have observed how the realities of all systems, and thus necessarily the relationships they define, are creatively evolutionary. And we have seen how both the reality and the growth of any system are intimately related to each of the systems it is in relationship with: how a king is a king by virtue of a specific kind of creative relationship with a populace, how that which one expresses is always a function of what can be received and vice versa.

An important piece in understanding how relationship is creative is the recognition that thinking of relationship in narrowly causal terms is not a phenomenon just of late-axis reality. Our ideas about human interaction have always been causal and deterministic; it is simply that the causalities evoked by earlier epochs have been of different sorts. We continue to see remnants of these earlier causalities in our attitudes toward relationship. Connecting from that part of us that responds from the unitary sensibilities of the earliest stages, we may get a feeling that two people are "meant for each other," or conversely, to use Shakespeare's wonderful phrase, that a relationship is somehow "starcrossed." Or our words may speak more from the moral imperatives of the middle parts of formativeness, referring to the unsavory outcome of an interaction as someone "getting what they deserve." But most of the time, we think from more material causalities. We speak of doing something *to* someone and having them respond; we say we are with someone *because* we love them. The art with creative thinking is to recognize how each of these isolated causalities describes part of the picture, and how living reality is larger than any of them.

Much of the time, thinking about interaction in isolatedly causal terms doesn't work that badly. However, it falls short if we wish to ask the really fundamental questions of relationship: What makes human interaction into relationship, something more than just mechanical give and take? ... What is the purpose of love? ... What is it that makes different kinds of relationship—friendship, intimacy, love of parents, love of the sacred, love of country—different? It also fails us if we wish to understand relationship in personal, creative terms, the kind of terms we will need to understand it in within the immensely challenging interpersonal realities that lie ahead.

I think of four elements in relationahip that most mark its creative nature. They can help us both in recognizing what we are dealing with in relationship, and in understanding what we must bring to relationship if we are to meet it consciously as a creative process. These are: the integral role of uncertainty, the inseparability of relationship from the fact of change, the creative nature of determination in relationship, and the critical place of rhythm. Let's take a moment with each.

First, nothing lies closer to the kernel of relationship than the essential fact that it involves uncertainty. The password for the doorway of caring is always some variation on the word vulnerability. When we risk feeling in relation to another, whether those feelings are tender or hostile, we never know ahead of time exactly what they will bring. The best we can do is to create rich potential spaces for what we think we want, and to step courageously into them. There is the possibility for living connection in a moment precisely to the degree we can let that moment be something that has not been before.

Equally as important, to the degree that relationship is alive, it involves change. The interpersonal as a living dynamic has no real meaning in static terms. In our fears of the unknown we may try to keep our relationships from changing, but even if we are successful, they don't stay the same; instead they become constricted and confined. In time they simply die. Real relationship is an ever-evolving, shared creative journey.

The third element concerns what ultimately is the referent in relationship. While we commonly think of where relationships go either in terms of the interaction of wills, or destiny, clearly more than either of these are at work. A creatively-based systems perspective lets us see a larger picture. When we call something relationship, what we are saying is that the systems involved, to some small or large degree, comprise a third system. And any creative system, while connected to all others, is also distinctly generative, a self-organizing whole. This third creative whole not only defines the existence of relationship, it is the functional "intelligence" of the relationship. Relationship works to the degree that we can risk to honor what this creative whole needs in order to be alive.

In working with couples, I often have them arrive together at an image that somehow represents the interactional space between them. It can be anything: an old wooden bridge that they meet upon, a dwelling that together they are creating, a teeter-totter in a park that together they are riding. I then ask them how they feel about the image, how they might like it to grow, and what they would need to risk from their side in order for it to grow. I am continually struck by how, when the attention is shifted from the either/or of "what I want" and "how I want you to change" to this third focus, the feelings in the room change. I am also struck by how frequently, when two people can risk to experience in relation to this third reality, they find agreement as to what needs to be done. It may be scary to admit this truth, risking it may increase vulnerability, but the truth is there if they wish to act on it.

I find the following exercise useful for making palpable the relationship between uncertainty, change, and creative determination in interactions. You might find another person and try it.

Sit facing your partner, close enough so that your knees are almost, but not quite, touching. Take a few moments before starting to just connect into yourself. Then, when it feels right, reach out your right index fingers so you are touching finger to finger. Then one of you begin to move your finger, making a simple dance in the air. The other person's task is just to follow, to mirror these movements. After several minutes, switch roles.

Do this long enough to exchange several times, then begin to switch roles at shorter intervals, then unexpectedly, and finally simply let go of roles entirely. See if you can find a place where the movement seems to come almost from itself, where each person may seem more expressive or receptive at different moments, but where the referent is increasingly the dance itself. Notice what kinds of things enhance this creative connection for you, and what things disturb it. Notice your particular responses to the potency, uncertainty, and intimacy of the process. Finally, let an image form for the particular dance that is happening with that person.

You might want to try this with a different person, or try using different parts of your body, words, or your whole body. You might also use this as a metaphor to think about the different relationships that are presently important in your life. If each were such a dance, what would it look like? What kind of image might best represent it? And what are its "edges:" the things these movements and images seem to be asking of you?

Because of the improvisational nature of this exercise, it emphasizes the less form-defined aspects of relationship, the connection more than individual intent, the moment rather than experience over time. But it makes useful illustration, as these are the aspects of the creative reality of relationship that we tend to be least in touch with, and the parts where the relationship between uncertainty, change, and living choice is most intimate. Relationship grows and evolves as an expression of the unique generativity that exists, and can be risked, between its participants. This generativity is both what makes connection relationship, and what directs the movements of it as relationship.

The fourth theme in understanding relationship as creative is its inherently rhythmic nature. We have addressed some of the larger rhythms in relationship already in beginning to look at stages in relationship, and in examining how what defines relationship changes through cultural time. The fact that relationship is a creatively rhythmic phenomenon manifests as well within much shorter time frames. In the exercise, if you mapped the movements that felt creatively right, you would see interweaving cyclic patterns: a small tentative movement, then a big thrusting movement, then a moment of more inward collecting.

There are few things more critical to the life of relationship than honoring its rhythmic nature. Relationship organizes as an infinite interweaving of great and small creatively rhythmic processes. The following quote from Anne Morrow Lindberg sits outside my office door:

"When you love someone you do not love them all the time
in exactly the same way ... it is an impossibility.
It is even a lie to pretend to.
And yet this is exactly what most of us demand.
We have so little faith in the ebb and flow of life,
of love, of relationships.
We leap at the flow of the tide
and resist in terror at its ebb.
We are afraid it will never return.
We insist on permanency, or duration, or continuity, when
the only continuity possible in life as in love is in growth,
in fluidity—in freedom in the sense that dancers are free,
often hardly touching when they pass,
yet partners ultimately in the same pattern."

The small rhythms of relationship are myriad. Times to be close, times to be apart, times to feel, times to think, times to assert, times to allow. Living relationship breathes. When relationship is right, its rhythm is as primary as a heartbeat. When relationships get stuck, this rhythmicity is lost. We take up a safe middle ground, unable either to get really close, or to be really separate.

The rhythmic nature of living relationship points up an essential awareness about love. We usually equate love with closeness, in creative terms, with the esthetic of oneness. In fact, love, like life, is a statement about balance, about meeting and separation in timely relationship. One could well claim that it is this honoring of rhythm that really defines whether something is love—this more than frequency of contact or intensity of feelings. My exchanges with the woman at the grocery store and the man at the gas station are infrequent, and rarely consist of more than a few sentences of small talk. But they are exactly right. The fullness I feel in my body when we connect tells me those exchanges are no less love than words spoken with my closest friends.

This critical importance of honoring rhythm pertains not just to the moment to moment ebbs and flows of relationship, but as well to the dynamics of larger periodicities. For example: to feel love in its connection with parents, the young infant needs unity to be nearly complete; if there is much distinction at all, feelings of fear quickly override those of love. In contrast, an adolescent or young adult

319

would quite appropriately experience anything even close to that degree of parental closeness as the antithesis of love.

To understand relationship as something alive, we have no choice but to step beyond our usual form-defined thinking. Relationship is creative; indeed it is the fundamental crucible of our natures as creation.

CREATIVE STAGES IN RELATIONSHIP

> "... Today the stormy sea
> lifted us in a kiss
> so high that we trembled
> in a lightning flash
> and, tied, we went down
> to sink without untwining ...
> Between you and me
> a new door opened
> and someone, still formless,
> was waiting for us there."
>
> —Pablo Neruda

> "It is always difficult to give oneself up.
> Few people anywhere ever succeed in doing so,
> and even fewer transcend the possessive stage
> to know love for what it actually is:
> A perpetual discovery, an emergence in the
>   waters of reality,
> and an unending re-creation."
>
> —Octavio Paz

Let's take a few minutes with some of the larger creative periodicities that play a role in relationship. Certainly a major one is the developmental sequence of our lives as a whole. The kinds of bonds available to an infant, a child, an adolescent, a young adult, a mature adult and an elder are different in every sphere of relationship. In the interest of brevity, I will simply include occasional reference to this aspect of change as we go along, trusting that enough has been said in earlier chapters to make the big pieces in this picture relatively self-evident. Equally significant in questions of relationship are changes that occur as a function of our place in cultural evolution. In a moment, we will look at some important aspects of this that we have not yet touched on.

If we wish to be consciously creative in relationship, the aspect of rhythm, besides the small ebbs and flows, that will most reward our sensitivity is the developmental sequence through which relationship comes to be. In relating, we are commonly so immersed in the moment that we have little sense of that moment's significance in time. In the past, this wasn't particularly a problem. But with the solid hand-holds of cultural convention dissolving more and more, it will be increasingly important to be able, not just to enjoy our feelings, but to understand them with some degree of perspective.

In first introducing the concept of creative stages, I briefly outlined the common developmental progression in relationship. There is value in looking at this sequence in somewhat more detail. Let's make one last trip through the creative stages, focusing primarily on how these realities manifest in the development of an intimate relationship. Because of its emotional charge, intimacy lets us see the stages inherent to all kinds of relationship in highest relief.

The pre-axial stage in relationship is a time of internal preparation—for the integration of earlier experiences of relationship, for deepening in one's relationship with oneself—for doing the internal growings that will let this new relationship be something that is in fact new.

Early-axis dynamics commence with the first recognition of new attraction. Feelings may at first be barely recognizable, or they can be quite overwhelming, eclipsing more structured parts of who we are and throwing us as a whole into the uncharted beginnings of things. We feel the unformed lower pole in "falling head over heels," the magical upper pole in becoming a bit "starry eyed." This stage is at once profound and easily a bit crazy. It is a time of risking a most vulnerable thing; and it is a time when it is easy to confuse the excitement of possibility with more realized relationship. Even when the feelings seem quite immense, the actual shared aliveness at this stage is yet quite small. But even our illusions have their place; they compel us to take the next fearsome steps toward really personal closeness, something we might not find the courage to do if we knew the distance that truly remained between fact and fancy.

If this new bond is happening within childhood, this may be the only stage we see. By virtue of the permeability of child reality, such bonds can be quite close. Or they can be primarily fantasy, offering most intense feelings when the actual contact has been but a few shared words, or even just gazing from afar. In later life, relationship can end here too, either because there is not enough substance for it to go further, or from fear of dealing with the issues of the next stage. Sometimes development in a relationship stops at this point, but the people remain together. If this happens, the relationship becomes ordered around habitual patterns of fantasy.

With the next stage, the "honeymoon" draws to a close and we begin dealing with the difference between possibility and manifest reality. It is not unusual for us to usher in this stage by asking our partner to don the complementary nightmare garb to our original golden image. The fact that there are discrepancies between the original dream and reality is often felt at first as a quite personal violation. In time all of this settles into a period of sorting out: working out who takes charge when, risking to express the resentments along with the joys. It is here that we ascertain if the relationship is worth working for, and begin the task of distinguishing the sharings and boundaries that will allow greatest fulfillment. Feelings during this the most emotion-focused period are often intense and widely vacillating. Issues of control are central, and feelings toward the other can flip from intense love to loathing and back again with disorienting rapidity.

Relationships in adolescence tend to end their development in this stage. Later in life they can stop here either because it becomes clear that there is no reason to go on, or out of fear of moving into the more committed reality of the next stage. Relationships that fixate at this stage tend to be either highly controlled or chronically struggled.

By entry into late-axis dynamics there is a general mutual acceptance that the relationship is important and worth working for. The major groundwork has been established, and one focuses on the kinds of details that allow for on-going effective partnership:

learning the other's wants and needs, noticing what is most fun to do together, defining what each person is for the other. The roller coaster feelings of the earlier stages stabilize as complementary roles and routines are found.

This stage becomes available in late adolescence and early adulthood, allowing love to move beyond the dreams and vacillating passions of earlier periods to take greater solidity as form. Each person becomes increasingly defined for the other. Again this can serve as a stopping point in the growth of a relationship, either from good judgement or fear. When it does, and people continue together, relationship tends to become dry, habitual, and objectified. The partners come more and more to "take each other for granted." More than connection as form is needed for enduring love.

As relationship moves past this stage, one begins to confront issues of transition. As with this point in other creative rhythms, initial feelings may be anything but bright. Transition, as always, demands that we surrender what before seemed most important. Here it is the romantic dream: the hope, acknowledged or not, that this other person might be the answer, that just being with them would make us forever safe and happy. The specter of this loss can seem like the final demise of love. But if we persist, we find that while the reality beyond this sacrifice is more ordinary than our dazzling dream, it is in truth a much greater prize. In surrendering our polar identities as great answer and great disappointment (and the energy-consuming dramas necessary to maintain them), we discover a growing ability to love each other, and ourselves, as simply who we are.

In the second half of love, like the second half of any creative process, the best expressions of truth are paradoxes. Here love increasingly demands that we acknowledge our separateness, but in this reveals in ever new ways how we are one. It forever reminds us that we cannot choose its destination, but in the vulnerability that this awareness demands, it increasingly teaches us the real meaning of choice. It continually confronts us with the fact that the secret to love lies in being selfless, all the while revealing that real selflessness lies in the courage to honor oneself. And while demanding that we face the knowledge that there is no security in love, it demonstrates in infinite ways how love is the only security.

How encompassing these integral changes are is a function of the defining cultural stage. As I have outlined, before now, these integral dynamics in relationship have always taken place within the roles and forms of a defined cultural truth. In the future, these changes will increasingly be happening within a similarly transforming cultural reality.

RELATIONSHIP AND CULTURE

"I never met my husband till the day I married him, but it was a love match till the day he died. And why shouldn't it be for he was a fine big man."

—Pieg Sayers
An Old Woman's Reflections
(From her life on the Blasket Islands off Ireland's West Coast)

"We owe to the Middle Ages the two worst inventions of humanity—romantic love and gunpowder."

—Andre Maurois

"The most characteristic aspect of marriage in the future will be precisely the array of options available to different people who want different things from their relationships with one another."

—Jessie Bernard

While we may disagree with Andre Maurois' sentiments about romantic love, his comment reflects an important, often overlooked, reality about the experience of relationship. We tend to think of love's vicissitudes as, for better or worse, constants in the human condition. In truth, our experience in each sphere of human interaction is profoundly relative in cultural time.

If we had a whole book to devote to questions of relationship, we could look at how each of the different kinds of relationships—friendship, intimacy, relationships to family, community and culture—have evolved through the epochs. We will limit our focus here to one specific theme in the cultural evolution of relationship, one relevant to all these relational forms. It adds an important new variable to our previous considerations about how reality has evolved, one that is both significant in its own right, and particularly pertinent to questions of what relationships will be like in the future.

Each stage in the evolution of culture not only redefines the organizing esthetics of interaction, as well it reorders the boundaries that determine what can become relationship. Two kinds of social boundaries define our experience of identity within cultural reality. Each has evolved in specific ways over the course of cultural time. And the evolution of each has been a major part of the story of who we have been as relational beings.

The first of these boundaries defines what I call the *sphere of cultural identification*. The sphere of cultural identity is the largest interpersonal whole in which we feel a sense of belonging. Through the course of history, this perimeter has gone through successive expansions: from our origins in the tribe; to clan, village, city-state, and region; eventually to the nation-state; and now increasingly to the globe, to social identification with the whole of humanity.

The second boundary defines what I call the *sphere of personal identification*. This is the perimeter I was referring to earlier in suggesting that the determining "body" in tribal reality is more the tribe itself than the individuals who make up the tribe. The sphere of personal identity is the smallest social unit with a significant degree of autonomous existence in the cultural whole. Another way of saying it is that it is the smallest human grouping that effectively embraces the creative entirety, that includes in it all the pertinent parts and polarities of the available creative reality. This periphery has similarly progressed through a specific evolutionary sequence, but here the direction of movement has been opposite to that for the cultural whole. With each stage in culture, as we shall explore, fewer people have been needed to establish this periphery.

Each of these directions of change reflects an aspect of the increasing capacitance that has manifested with each cultural

325

stage. Expansions in the sphere of cultural identity have asked us to embody an ever-growing world of experience and an ever-expanding complexity of differences. Contractions in the sphere of personal identity have challenged us to embody the creative whole within smaller and smaller systems.

Let's move briefly through the interpersonal realities of the different cultural stages emphasizing the evolution of these primary organizing spheres. We can use the question of how marriage partnerships are determined as a simple measure of the personal periphery.

In early tribal societies, our two spheres are, for all intents and purposes, synonymous. The tribe, or at most the tribe along with nearby, blood-related tribal groupings, defines the outer boundary of social identification. Anyone outside this boundary is most explicitly "other," a demarcation enforced not only by differences in belief and attire, but usually as well by barriers of language. At the same time, the tribe here functions to define the sphere of personal identity. Individuality is as yet an embryonic notion. Looking to our matrimonial measure, we see that, in keeping with this, marriages are not uncommonly decided upon by the tribe before birth, or arranged sight-unseen between members of related tribal groupings to reinforce bonds of intergroup identity.

As we move into early-axis times in culture, we see the sphere of cultural identity expand significantly. With the gradual shift from hunter-gatherer to agrarian economies, the social perimeter extends to include clan, village, and even regional identifications. Concomitantly, the sphere of personal identity becomes distinct and shrinks somewhat. Major decisions are now appropriately made by subgroups within the cultural whole. Decisions such as who will marry whom and with what people friendships are appropriate are now the province of multi-generational extended families (though made always within the codes of the social whole).

With middle-culture, the cultural whole expands further, clans and regions drawing together to create kingdoms, spheres large enough to embrace major differences in tradition. To find someone who is "other" in an absolute sense, one must travel ever-increasing distances.

At the same time, the personal sphere continues to contract, though the family unit is still multigenerational and extended. Decisions of any import require, if not the instigation of parents, grandparents, and other important family members, at least their blessing. While in the realm of courtship we hear, in the troubadors' idealizing of romantic love, first hints of a role for individual choice, by all evidence such was much more the stuff of poetry than practice, and even when realized something very different from romance as we think of it. The bard's words idealized unconsummated love; to act on one's passions was regarded as violating the purity of attraction. Marriage bonds were arranged by families, often with the help of someone especially knowledgeable in such things, a village "matchmaker."

In late-axis reality, with both the possibility of greater structure and definition in governance and expanded capacities in transportation and commerce, we see the periphery of social identity extend to the borders of the nation-state. In the later parts of this stage, this sphere expands somewhat further to include alliances between nations.

At the same time, the borders of the sphere of personal determination continue to shrink: first to the more limited extended family, and then by the conclusion of this stage, all the way to the nuclear family, to a single woman, a single man, and their children. While the myth in this stage is that the individual is now primary social determiner, in fact, for social decisions of any major import, the determining whole is still the family system. The personal decisions of children are made from within the system of the family of origin. Marriage characteristically occurs immediately upon leaving this system, providing a new family system, and a new identity in it as mate and parent. Again, how marriage choices are made nicely delineates where the determining power resides. Late-axis reality takes us a further step toward the realization of individual choice in marriage: the poetry of unrequited love is replaced by the notion that somewhere there exists a "perfect other," one who we only need find to live "happily forever after." But even though now the task of finding one's partner is increasingly that of the future betrothed, marriage doesn't happen without parental approval. One must ask for the bride's hand. In the marriage ceremony parents "give the bride away" (and less overtly the groom), publicly both affirming where the fundamental power lies, and conferring this power to the new whole.

While for the most part we have moved beyond this late-axis reality, in our conventional thinking we still tend to view its forms, the nuclear family in the context of the nation-state, as what is right and true. But there is no reason for social evolution to stop here, and by all evidence it has not. Movement into transitional times has brought, and is continuing to bring, significant further changes. And in keeping with other dynamics at the midpoint of creative cycle, these changes express at once simply a next quantal step in development, and needs and challenges fully new to the human species.

As we move toward the transitional apex, we see the sphere of cultural identity making further expansion, extending more and more toward the globe as a whole. In today's world, the bonds of national identity are clearly in perturbation. In all fields of concern—economics, government, art, religion—it is becoming increasingly clear that future reality will be a global reality. If there is any doubt that our culture is now the planet, we need only note that news from half way around the world today gets to us faster than mail from a neighboring town.

The further shift in the sphere of personal identity is less immediately obvious, but is at least as significant. We are seeing an evolution of the basic creative unit from the family and couple, to the individual. We are shifting from a reality in which two adults as halves have defined the primary whole, toward one in which each person has the potential to manifest as a multi-potential entirety.

We see evidence for this new evolution all around us: marriage now in actual practice a matter of personal choice; a growing acceptance of single life as a valid option; dramatic changes in our past knee-jerk reproof of such things as sex before marriage, single parent families, and children born out of wedlock. Along with such changes in our views about the relational unit, we see radical revisions of our past ideas about what it means to be a man or to be a woman. We see women gaining parallel roles in the marketplace, and men taking on tasks and roles traditionally the province of women. We see court-ship roles, in the past strictly gender-defined, becoming increas-ingly diffuse. And we see things such as clothing and hairstyles, be-fore used to signal and exaggerate differences between men and wo-men, growing increasingly interchangeable. Whereas in our past, gender defined two distinct polar domains of choice, more and more we see a reality of interplaying continua of roles and attitudes.

The model suggests that the kind of polar bonding we have been accustomed to living out in relationships will be shifting from the interpersonal to the intrapsychic. The completeness, the realiza-tion of the archetypal whole that before has come through bonding with the opposite sex, will increasingly be found, and indeed only be findable, in a new kind of intimacy with oneself.

These kinds of changes easily bring quite charged responses. They are denounced as undermining the sanctity of the family and the whole foundation of human morality. At once, because they offer that we might leave behind the constraints of sexual stereo-types, they are hailed as a final liberation for relationship. A creative perspective suggests that the reality is larger than that seen from either of these polar views. These changes represent nei-ther relational Armageddon nor relational salvation. They offer the possibility of a new kind of completeness in relationship ... and, to realize it will require that we face some major new challenges.

Transition, as always, confronts us with disturbing ironies. The realization of each of our new relational peripheries is a profound achievement, one that greatly expands freedom and possibility. Yet, these achievements each have a hidden side, a shadow real-ity of sufficient proportion that it seems at first it might negate the whole purpose of this realization. In these ironies lie important keys to understanding what lies ahead.

The hidden side in the personal sphere can perhaps be seen most clearly in intimate relationships. It concerns the question of just what will be the basis for love in the future. In the past the "glue" in the bond of intimacy has been precisely the "two-halves-makes-a-whole" dynamic that we seem to be leaving behind. This has been the central force in both the pragmatics and passions of

Dramatic shifts are taking place both in how we perceive
relationships and what we must bring to them if they
are to give us fulfillment.

ABOVE: *Henry Moore.* Family Group. *1948-1949.* OPPOSITE,
TOP: *Auguste Rodin.* The Kiss. *1901-1904.* OPPOSITE, BELOW:
Pieter Bruegel the Elder. Peasant Wedding. *1565.*

love. Our ability to reliably add to each other's lives has been based on the inherent complementarity of interlocking sex roles, and the experience we most associate with love—the magnetism of romance—has been a direct function of our polar halves and the electricity that inextricably links them.

Will men and women in the future really have enough to offer each other to justify what must be put into love, or the commitment necessary for healthy child rearing? If men can embody deeply the feminine, and women the masculine, and if each is able to perform most of the tasks that used to be the other's province, will there be sufficient motivation for intimate bonding? Clearly there is still sex. But for the tasks of enduring relationship our erotic touchings are rarely enough. On first glance it seems that just as we are coming to the place of greatest potential for fully personal love, we are losing any reason to risk it.

Our new image of a "planetary family" similarly has a hidden, disturbing side. While a single world community could offer immense new freedoms and the possibility of leaving behind many of the divisive passions that before have led to suffering, it seems, at least at first glance, that two things, each in our past essential to human meaning, would be lost. First, with regional differences at this scale of things little more than statistics, the rich textures of cultural diversity would quickly be lost to the faceless homogeneity of mass culture. Second, with the individual now fully preeminent, the past glue of philial relationships would be absent. It seems it might be the case that just as it is becoming possible for us to love all of humankind, and not just in the abstract but in practice, we may be losing the necessary foundations for the experience of such love.

To understand the positive potential in these new peripheries, we need to see them in the context of the larger evolutionary processes of which they are parts. The essential recognition is that while in terms of form they represent evolutionary endpoints—it is hard to imagine a sphere smaller than the individual or larger than humanity and life as whole—in the story of relationship as creation they are anything but final destinations. The realization of the individual as an autonomous choice-making unit is at best a midpoint in the developmental story of determination: there are essential processes of inner connecting and expansion of capacitance yet to come with cycle's second half. And the processes have immensely important implications for intimacy and relationships of all sorts. Similarly, our acknowledgement of a global reality is just a first step in the process of cultural integration necessary for us to live and love as planetary citizens.

If there will still be love in times ahead, what will be its basis? If the old polar affinities and ready complementarities will no longer be there, how will love work? As with all questions past creation's midpoint, more than a simple one line answer is required. The model suggests the new picture has a number of equally important, integrally related parts. They point toward ever more exciting possibilities in love—not easy possibilities; they are ones that will demand a great deal of us—but possibilities that will well reward our efforts.

Focusing again on intimate love, it is clear that while we will be leaving much behind that before made love possible, we will also have ever more to bring to the experience of love. Each step in our cultural development makes us capable of embodying more aliveness, of being creative in ever fuller ways with each other. While the old kinds of polar magnetisms will be gone, we will be more capable of giving to the affinities we do feel the risk and commitment necessary to have them blossom as meaningful love. In addition, because our reconnectings will more deeply ground us in the parts of our being that are fed by relationship, we should find ourselves giving relationship greater priority.

A second essential piece concerns the multiplicity of forms that intimate relationships will most likely take in the future. If all that was to be possible was love as love has been—a form-defined, all or nothing, proposition: either you love someone or you don't, and here is what it looks like if you do—love would be doomed. Love in this sense requires absolute complementarities. New options in relationship, combined with a growing ability to recognize love as a process, should let us approach love, as we must, as an ever-evolving exploration of the particular ways of being together that, for two particular people, at a particular time, are creatively right.

A third piece relates to how in the future we are most likely to experience gender. If social evolution stopped at the peak of transition, gender would, in times ahead, be less and less a factor in the bonds of relationship. Ours would be an increasingly unisex reality, one in which gender complementarities would play ever-diminishing roles. But transition is not the end point, and what we know about the dynamics of integration suggest a significantly more interesting picture.

Unisex is a description of gender identity at the apex of patriarchy, at that point in the creative cycle when we are most distant from the primal levels in ourselves. Integration offers a larger reconnecting into the flesh and the archetypal. A primary characteristic of these more elemental levels in our being is that they are inextricably permeated by the essential gift of gender.

From a four-dimensional perspective, we can see that while creation takes men and women equally toward wholeness, wholeness in a woman and wholeness in a man are not the same thing. Wholeness in a woman results in a whole woman, in a man it results in a whole man. In the future we should find ourselves leaving behind sexual stereotypes and more and more appreciating just how great individual differences can be. But at the same time, we should find ourselves increasingly moved by the particular sorts of beauty and power to which being embodied as a man or a woman can offer special access. The implications for complementarity in intimacy in the future are significant.

The key to the planetary village being more than barren monoculture is this same remembering, only here in the "cultural body." The more ascendant parts of ourselves are attracted to large social peripheries: from Above we like to see just as far as we can see. But parts more intimate to ground feel real satisfaction only if there is some significant degree of personal contact. In the future, relationships should be ever more valued parts of our lives. And along with our new planetary perspective, we should see a renewal of identification with spheres of social reality small enough to give our hard won individual and global identities more immediate and personal meaning. In years ahead we should find statements like Rene Dubos' counsel to "think globally and act locally" an increasingly appealing kind of wisdom.

TYPES OF RELATIONSHIP

"Love is the basic ontological datum."

—*Marcel*

*"The seat of the soul is where the inner world and the outer
world meet, and where they overlap. It is in every point of the
overlap."*

—*Novalis*

*"The man who, being really on the way, falls upon hard
times in the world, will not, as a consequence, turn to that
friend who offers him a refuge and comfort and encourages
his old self to survive. Rather he will search out someone
who will faithfully and inexorably help him to risk himself."*

—*Karlfried von Dürckheim*

If we wish to think about the creative workings of relationship
in any detail, we need to be able to distinguish between different
types of relationship. We generally assume that what distin-
guishes different kinds of love and relationship is simply that we
are directing our feelings toward different objects. In fact, different
kinds of human interconnection organize energetically in quite specific ways. The model gives us a way to understand the dynamics of
these differences.

As preparation for exploring these ideas, try the following exercise:

Imagine yourself in each of the following situations,
being particularly sensitive both to the quality of feelings
that arise and where you feel them in your body. First,
imagine being with a close friend. Then with someone you
don't particularly like. Then remember back to being a
child and connect with the kinds of feelings you had toward your parents. If you yourself are a parent, explore
how you feel your connection with your children. Next
take some time with the various feelings that are a part
of intimate bonding—romantic feelings, sexual attraction,
respect, conflict. If you are a man, get in touch with the

particular kinds of connecting you feel being with a group of "the guys;" if you are a woman, with the bond you feel with a close group of women. Then explore any other kinds of "love" that are important to you—love of country, love of God, love of nature.

In introducing horizontal dynamics in chapter eight, I spoke of there being three basic kinds of patterns in interrelational dynamics: parallel patterns, polar patterns, and patterns where one system serves as the generative context for another. We might take some time now to fill out these notions—to examine more closely how these different patternings work, and to see how an understanding of them can help us more fully understand the creative workings of relationship. As I described earlier, a particular relationship may involve just one of these patterns, or may include aspects of all three.

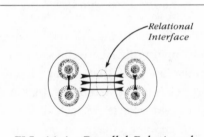

Relational Interface

FIG. 11-1. *Parallel Relational Dynamics*

Parallel dynamics are the simplest to think about. Here the creative connection is happening between analogous systems—two friends, two businesses, two countries—and the basic dynamic is a simple, horizontal creative give and take. This "philial" kind of connecting can organize from almost anywhere in our bodies depending on what is being connected about, and where, from core to periphery, it most touches us. In groups, we feel this kind of bonding in a number of different ways. We use words like brotherhood or comradeship to refer to the more upper and outer aspect of these bonds, feeling them most in the chest, shoulders, and arms. The complementary, more archetypally feminine dimension of group bonding organizes more inwardly and from the lower chest, belly, and pelvis.

How we experience such parallel connectings are a function of all the pertinent organizing rhythms. Contextual rhythms affect not just the kinds of connectings we are likely to make and the quality and distance of boundary in these connectings, but also who it is possible to make these kinds of connectings with. Positive philial feelings are reserved for people who are within the relevant defining sphere of group identity—the same team, the same ethnic group, the same country. Depending on where we are developmentally, those perceived as being on the other side of the moat of distinction may be experienced variously as non-existent, strange, evil, as competitors, or, past the point of transition, different but potentially enriching to us. If boundaries shift, our feelings toward the same person or group can change with remarkable rapidity and totalness, a good example being changing sentiments between nations as lines of allegiance move about from decade to decade.

Integration within culture as creation should have a profound effect on how we live these parallel sorts of bonds. As individuals increasingly become creative wholes, and social identity expands to a global periphery, we should find ourselves less and less needing to base philial bonds on such things as absolute loyalty and agreement—on the other being "on our side." We should find an ever greater tolerance and appreciation for difference in all spheres, and a growing recognition that the "friends" with the most to give us are those who are equally willing to applaud our courage and challenge our partialities.

Polar relationships are similar to parallel ones, except that here the systems embody to some significant degree energetically complementary parts in the relational whole. The systems can be

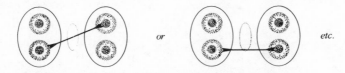

FIG. 11-2. Polar Relational Dynamics

individuals or groups; the polarities can be vertical, horizontal or a combination; and the creative connectings can be happening within any relational sphere. Within culture as a system, we see polar relationships between, for example, the left and the right, between artists and scientists, and between the upper class and the lower class. In smaller groupings we see them in such relationships as those between management and labor, and between an expert consultant and a client. We see them as well between the various roles taken in family systems.

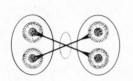

FIG. 11-3. Cross-Polar Relational Dynamics

Frequently, polar relationships are to some degree "cross polar," that is, in them each part in the system takes an aspect of each pole. The bonding of intimate love is a good example. Here we each become at once Above and Below to each other: we "fall in love," and at once elevate and idealize our mates, making them "one in a million." The particular balance of this cross polarization will depend on the relative energetics of the two people involved.

Again, the developmental stages of all the pertinent periodicities play a role in defining what these relationships will look like. How we see our own polar identity, how we see poles opposite, and who we will choose to have polar relationships with are all profoundly relativistic dynamics. And once again the changes inherent to integration in culture will have profound effects. In all spheres, we should see our tendency to take isolated polar stances evolving such that we can both more fully embody the whole of the

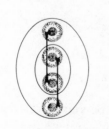

FIG. 11-4. Dynamics Where One System is the Creative Context for Another

relevant process, and more fully appreciate the parts we and others most play in it.

In the third kind of relational dynamic, one creative whole serves as the generative context for another—the culture as context for the family, the family as context for the individual, the individual as context for the inner relationships of a particular creative task. Here the relating poles are within systems of different magnitude, and one system, at least in the early stages, fully encircles the other. Parents are at once an Above above the child's upper pole and a Below below its lower; a Without beyond its outer pole, and a Within within its inner.

Both the reality of the contextual system, and the developmental stage of the generative process, as we have seen, profoundly effect how this kind of relationship will be felt. With this, the dynamics of integration have particular pertinence. Transition marks the point where the newly generated system individuates from its context, becoming whole in and of itself. Once this point is past, contextually-based dynamics between the systems are gradually replaced with various permutations of parallel and simply polar relationships.

Movement past transition in cultural development should effect such generatively patterned relationships at a number of levels. Within the cultural sphere we should see it manifest in an evolution beyond the perception of cultural figures as symbolic parents. Increasingly we are finding ourselves able to regard authorities—teachers, doctors, ministers, political figures—less as mythic personages and more as simply people. In addition, this shift should alter relationships within smaller spheres of generativity. Parenting makes a good example. While the relationship between parents and children will always be contextually polar, in the future, this polarization should be less absolute. These changes are already in progress. Today, children are beginning to experience and state their uniqueness in a way that is really quite new: in addition to classical rebelliousness, we see a growing capacity for real individual identity. And a commensurate kind of growing is happening on the other side of the equation. Both men and women are realizing that it simply no longer works to give over the entire child half of reality to children. To be as creatively vital as we must be in today's changing world, the "child" must be an ongoing, living part of each of us.

CO-CREATION, CO-EVOLUTION, AND THE HEALING RELATIONSHIP

"What is happening with you, with us,
what's happening to us?
Ah our love is a harsh cord
that binds us wounding us and if we want
to leave our wound, to separate
it makes a new knot for us
and condemns us to drain our blood
and burn together."

—Pablo Neruda
"Love"

"When men and women are in love, they share the mistaken
belief that they live in the same world; when they 'love' one
another, they acknowledge that they live in different worlds,
but are prepared once in a while to cross the chasm between
them." —Thomas Szasz

"In the heaven of Indra there is said to be a network of pearls
so arranged that if you look at one you see all the others
reflected in it. In the same way, each object in the world is
not merely itself, but involves every other object and in fact is
in every other object."

—The Yoga Sutras of Patanjali
(trans. C. Johnston)

Our changing relational realities have immense implications for psychology. We have already touched on some of this relevance with regard to the healing relationship itself: allowing the relationship between therapist and client to be more fully co-creative, less a simply polar dynamic; making more readily available the germinal depths of our being, and with this opening the potential for ever more complete kinds of potency. The therapeutic alliance is a kind of relationship that could only be conceived with some beginnings into integral understanding. In its fullest manifestation it is a beautiful and powerful expression of creative love, a love that neither tries to protect the other person from what might cause discomfort, nor asks them to be something they are not. It is a love that comes from a place from which an honest relationship to what *is*, though what is can never be completely known or controlled, is embraced as the one thing that can be trusted.

One of the major contributions that psychology can make in today's world is to help people creatively meet the changing realities of relationship. I work a lot with couples and families. More and more frequently I encounter situations where it is clear that the pain and confusion a family feels is much less a function of failings on anyone's part, than the simple fact that the rules of relationship are changing. We are being confronted with profound new kinds of uncertainty in relationships, and often have no way of understanding the perturbations we feel except to conclude that something must be wrong.

Everyone we work with in therapy is having to deal in some way with changing relational realities. Adolescents are having to cope both with kinds of freedom well beyond what their parents knew, and equally new dangers. Old people are having to recognize that their reality is now a more independent one, that the kind of total care they gave their parents in their old age may not now be an appropriate expectation. Religious people are having to deal with internal questioning about spiritual absolutes that they once took for granted, as are deeply patriotic people having to grapple with the loss of the nation as a symbol of unswerving right and virtue. One of the most significant things therapists can do in these times is to help people develop the awarenesses, skills, and sensitivities necessary to deal with these changes.

How can we most help? Often the greatest gift we can give is simply perspective. People can deal with immense uncertainty if they can understand why things are uncertain. A few simple guideposts can often turn what before seemed a nightmare into an adventure. For example, in working with a couple, the simple notion that we are moving from a "two halves makes a whole" intimate reality toward one where we can relate more as whole people, can make many previously contradictory feelings suddenly make sense, and significantly alter how a couple perceives and deals with conflict.

An important part of offering cultural perspective is acknowledging something of the magnitude and significance of the shifts that are taking place. It is easy to make the new opportunities into new demands: "I should be whole and so should you." I often share with people that while I see us at a most exciting time in the story of relationship, it is also a most difficult and awkward, in-between time. I emphasize that we are but infants in the changes that are happening, and that even at our deaths we will likely still be but children in them.

Past perspective, we can offer people skills that will help them more effectively honor relationship as something creative: the ability to use the shared aliveness of the relationship as its ongoing referent; the ability to be sensitive to moment to moment rhythms of relationship; the ability to honor the different developmental realities of relationship, and to see the larger processes of which they are parts.

These ideas about relationship let us add one last important piece to the model's ideas about psychological health and dis-ease. As should be clear, all the diagnostic notions developed thus far apply directly to issues of relationship. Our capacity for aliveness is our capacity to relate. The stages we occupy in the various aspects of our development are specific relational realities. And our primary energetic is a statement not just about how we connect in ourselves, but equally about how we connect with others.

The further awareness here is that frequently symptoms are more than just things we do in relation to others: quite often they are things we do *with* others. They are collaborative dynamics.

I refer to shared symptom patterns as *co-dependent* dynamics. In co-dependent patterns we make tacit collusion (co-illusion) with another against challenges to our capacitance. The unacknowledged bargain is this: "I will protect you from your fears, if you will protect me from mine."

Like symptoms in general, co-dependent dynamics may manifest only in particularly stressful situations, or may be ongoing. Three variables define what we will see. The first two are familiar: the capacitances and primary energetics of the individuals or

groups involved. The third variable is the particular polar relationship within which the collusion organizes. In any specific co-
dependent dynamic, the collusion may be principally between analogous energetics (both ascendant, both descendent, both inner,
both outer) or between opposites (one ascendant, one descendent; one
inner, one outer). Using the control oriented polarities of middle-
axis dynamics to illustrate, in the first kind of situation we might
see two friends colluding variously to feel powerful, or to feel
powerless. In the second, one person would play victim to the other.

Usually both vertical and horizontal dynamics in some way
play a part. Where they are both involved, the collusion can manifest in any of the possible permutations. In that victim/oppressor
dyad, we might see paired a loud, demanding oppressor (upper pole,
outer aspect) and a timid, withdrawn victim (lower pole, inner aspect), or conversely a stern, taciturn oppressor (upper pole, inner
aspect) and a rebellious, acting-out victim (lower pole, outer aspect). Equally, we could see the taciturn oppressor and the timid
victim paired, or the demanding oppressor and the rebellious
victim.

Again we are dealing with a topic that could fill many volumes
if addressed in any detail. Let it suffice here to outline some of the
characteristics that co-dependent patterns have in common, and to
offer a few clinical examples.

How are co-dependent patterns alike? And what can we understand from these similarities about how co-dependent patterns function to protect systems from challenges to new aliveness? I think of
four common characteristics.

First, as with symptoms in general, co-dependent responses involve an exaggeration of the usual separation between polarities,
and with this an increased tendency in each system to identify exclusively with one pole. The effect of the collusion may be either to
provide a convenient opposite to the pole identified with, or to affirm and reinforce a projection of that opposite onto other figures in
one's environment. Either way, the result is a diminishing of the
creative interaction between the polarities.

Second, we see a characteristic dampening of the normal ebbs
and flows of relationship. We see interpersonally the same stat-

ically held juxtaposition that is happening intrapsychically. By blocking rhythm, the "respiration" of relationship, we reduce potential aliveness. We are protected both from the further intimacy with the other that might come with moving closer, and the further intimacy with ourselves that might come with moving away.

The third dynamic relates to what happens to awareness during co-dependent moments. Our attention becomes split, at the same time fixated on the other, and held protectively within. We become at once self-centered, and outer directed. This split guarantees that interaction, rather than be creative, will be reactive, a reflex either/or. In effect, the interactional space, the moment as a third space dynamic, disappears.

Finally, most co-dependent patterns involve the creation of pseudo-aliveness. Along with mechanisms to diminish contact with oneself, the other, and the vulnerabilities of one's world, we see dynamics that function to create the illusion of often extreme amounts of contact and aliveness.

Like symptoms in general, co-dependent patterns can be thought of equally well as patterns of pathology or successful mechanism of adaptation. They are at once ways we distort reality, and ways we filter it so that we get just the amount and type we can creatively handle.

The following example illustrates a chronic co-dependent dynamic between parallel systems. (The primary energetic of each person centers about midway between middle- and late-axis, with the outer aspect of the upper pole predominant.)

> Gino and Fred had been friends for many years. Each was in his late sixties, and the president of a small manufacturing company in the same part of town. As long as either could remember, they had been getting together for lunch and sharing a few drinks to celebrate the victories and commiserate over the frustrations of their work. Not having any family or other friends, they were each the other's most important source of support and encouragement.
>
> When I first saw Gino, he was in the hospital recovering from a heart attack. He was a proud, determined and

very individualistic man who, with few resources but his wits and the sweat of his brow, had in his youth started his own business in a field that had not existed before. His business had been his life. He ran it now as he always had like the supreme patriarch of a large Italian family.

In talking, Gino revealed that he had been anxious and depressed much of the previous year. The source of the depression was evident: his business was collapsing. Gino's solitary, iron-handed style of leadership had worked well when it was fired by his youthful vigor and the business was small. But the plant had gotten bigger, the technology more intricate, and though he was unwilling to admit it, Gino's mind was just not as quick as it had been. The predicament was complicated by his stubborn independence. It was very hard for him to ever ask for help, and he had never allowed anyone the information or training they would need either to assist him with decisions, or to take over after he was gone.

His inseparable friendship with Fred contributed further to the problem. Fred was as fearful of sharing power in his business as Gino. In their noon times together, they had created elaborate fantasies of conspiracies among the people under them. Their relationship had become a collusion to keep their fears of loss and inadequacy from being unearthed.

In our talking together, Gino was gradually able to admit to himself that the business was in trouble. He came to see that if he didn't begin grappling with his fears of shared leadership and the denial of his aging, he would lose the one thing that mattered to him. The most important piece in this was finding the courage to look at his relationship with Fred, to own the collusion and confront Fred with what he saw happening. Because of the longevity and depth of their caring, the relationship survived the confrontation, and in time helped to provide the strength they each needed to make the needed decisions.

The next example illustrates a co-dependent pattern in which the two participants play opposite roles. (The dynamics are about equally vertical and horizontal and involve dynamics centered about midway between early- and middle-axis.)

Paul and Jill had been married for six years and had two small children. They had lived throughout their marriage in a small northwestern town. Paul worked as a pipe fitter. Jill, along with mothering, worked part time in a local antique store.

They described their reasons for seeking counselling as continual arguments and a seeming inability to be really close. They shared that in fact they deeply loved each other, pointing out that they would call each other frequently when they were apart, and were quick to jealousy if there was interest in other people.

As we talked, the co-dependent nature of the arguments became quickly apparent. They tended to happen at one of two times: when Paul and Jill were beginning to feel more intimate, or when they were going to be apart for some reason. The effect was to keep the relationship at a safe middle distance. They could not get close because of the buffer of antagonism, but neither could they really separate: when they parted they were always angry, and because of this were always thinking about each other. Along with this, the sparks from their exchanges provided a safe and predictable source of drama, and helped them know that the other still cared. After an argument, they would make love, and the lovemaking would be particularly passionate.

Paul and Jill had complementary styles for starting and maintaining an argument. Paul's was to be critical. Paul's boss at work put him down; at home he put Jill down. Small things could be quickly turned into catastrophes. Jill played her less visible part well. She knew what things would push Paul's buttons, and in plays of confused innocence, could use them with flawless timing. And when the predictable flurry arrived, she was there to take it. Her stance was to admit enough transgression to keep Paul's involvement, yet to keep things sufficiently muddy that there was never a real sense of resolution. (Characteristically, with the children, she joined Paul in the upper pole, and the children very competently played out the lower.)

In our work together, Paul and Jill gradually learned to be aware of this reflexive pattern and to distinguish it from connecting that was more vulnerable and alive. They learned signals to give each other when they felt they were getting stuck, and little by little ways to extricate themselves. Increasingly the difference between the predictability of their melodrama and the vulnerability of their real passions became clear to them, and they became more able to simply be together as two separate caring people.

Movement beyond a co-dependent pattern is signaled by the appearance of those characteristics that we identified at the beginning of the chapter as evidence that relationship is creative. We see increasing room for uncertainty and change. We see the referent in relating becoming something more than just one person's will set against another's. And we see more and more room for the living rhythms of relationship.

Albert Camus, in his essay "The Myth of Sysiphus," makes the statement: "If man found that the universe could love he would be reconciled." With movement culturally into the second half of the creative cycle, and the reconnectings that are inherently a part of integration, the future should more and more reveal the ways in which the universe indeed "loves." It will be a different sort of love than our fears commonly lead us to long for, neither the womb-like love of eternal oneness, nor the love of guarantees. But from the place of our species adulthood, we will find it is .quite enough, indeed that there is no way it could be more.

CHAPTER TWELVE

THE PLANETARY IMPERATIVE

*"[We are] in the midst of a great transformation comparable to
the one that confronted medievalism and shook its institutions to the ground ... The old ideas and assumptions that
made our institutions legitimate are being eroded. They are
slipping away in the face of a changing reality, being replaced
by different ideas, as yet ill-formed, contradictory,
unsettling."*

—George Cabot Lodge

*"The idea of brotherhood is not new, but what is special to our
times is that brotherhood has become the precondition for
survival."*

—Leon Eisenberg

"There is no easy formula for this renewal."

—Lewis Mumford

 With this final chapter we turn our attention specifically to questions of cultural change. How can the
model help us understand our often bewildering present, and plan for what is an unquestionably challenging future?

In putting forward the basic contours of the model, I have applied it in one domain, the field of psychology and psychiatry, in
some detail. Here we turn to other arenas—government, religion,
business, science, the arts, education. We will look both at how the
model can be used to understand present changes in these realms and
how it can be used to reframe thinking in a way more in keeping
with a living reality. Our treatment here will necessarily be brief.
But having some major guideposts in different domains should help

to stimulate thinking in these areas and to provide a deeper understanding of the larger pattern of change.

Our pressing cultural quandaries are sufficiently unsettling that we often do our best to keep our distance from them. This is understandable: the challenges are difficult to grasp, and the problems they relate to are so all-pervasive that we easily feel impotent to have any significant effect. We often act unconsciously to keep the culturally critical questions at arm's length, using whatever is our customary style for fending off new aliveness. We may move inside them, focusing on more personal concerns, and leave what is happening in the world to others. Or we may push outside them, reacting to signals for change by putting on blinders and working harder and harder at things which are less and less effective. We may drop below them and become terminally cynical. Or we may hop above them and become advocates of some reassuringly simple answer (our choice reflecting the part of the creative whole that for us offers the most easy refuge): an ultimate technological fix, a new fundamentalism—a return to the comfortable surety of absolute right and wrong, a "New Age" of magical solutions.

But it is increasingly clear that avoidance, no matter what our particular style, will less and less be an option. In the language of the model, we are making passage into cultural adulthood: responsibility for the welfare of species and planet is now explicitly ours. It is essential that we be aware and proactive in the changes that are upon us.

The model offers a framework for being conscious, comprehending, and empowered in these changes. It is a framework that specifically demands that we leave simple answers behind us, but, at the same time it gives us a highly differentiated approach to dealing with truth beyond such simple answers.

The basis for the model's ideas about cultural change should now be very familiar. Within the model are two major new ideas about culture and how it evolves. First, culture is a creative process, and as such, organizes according to a predictable sequence of formative configurations. Second, our present reality corresponds to a specific point in that sequence, one with identifiable tasks. Assuming the accuracy of these notions, we should expect the model to be a powerful tool for defining the challenges that lie ahead for us in any sphere. It should, as well, be able to tell us what we must bring to these challenges if we are to successfully turn the page into the next chapter of our ever more amazing human story.

IN PREPARATION

"Never doubt that a small group of thoughtful, committed citizens can change the world; indeed, it's the only thing that ever has."
—*Margaret Mead*

We have examined in detail how the model can be used to differentiate individual experience. Before looking at questions of social change, we should do some further differentiating in the cultural sphere. This will both give us a deeper understanding of culture as a creative dynamic, and provide information needed for addressing some key questions about present change processes.

After the basic notion that culture can be divided into creative stages, what more is important to see?

First, it is essential to recognize that each stage in culture is also a creative process, and by virtue of this itself goes through the available creative stages. For example, within the Age of Reason as a whole, we can see quite distinct early-, middle-, and late-axis substages. First came a period of initial inspiration and discovery. This was the time of Galileo, Newton and Descartes, and the first emergence of the scientific paradigm; of Michelangelo, Da Vinci, and Raphael, and the beginnings of Europe's artistic renaissance; of Columbus, Cortez and Magellan, and the birth of a new age of exploration; and of Martin Luther, and the first images of a new kind of relationship with the divine. Following this came a period with a decidedly more middle-axis flavor, the Age of Empire. We saw here struggles between the great European powers for dominance in the new world, open conflict between social classes, and the first establishment of the structures of industrialization. The last two hundred years, what we might call the Age of Technology and Individualism, has been most definitively late-axis, with the estab-

351

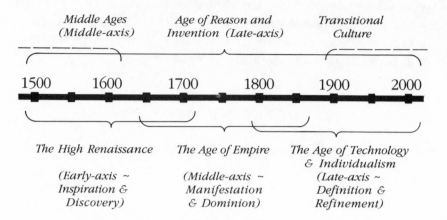

FIG. 12-1. MAJOR SUBRHYTHMS IN LATE-AXIS CULTURE

lishment of institutional government, a new elevation of the individual in the writings of people like Thomas Paine and Jean Jacques Rousseau, the realization of universal education, and the full flowering of scientific preeminence.

Further, we can see that within any substage there are even smaller creative fluctuations. The last twenty years in the United States illustrates this well. Within the encompassing issues of transitional dynamics, we can see much smaller cycles that imbued this esthetic with qualities from each of the earlier stages. In the sixties and early seventies we saw primitive and early-axis sensibilities: the magic youth of the "flower child," strong advocacy of matriarchal values such as earth and peace, neo-pagan sexual norms, and fascination spiritually with both Eastern and Western mystical thought. The mid-seventies and early eighties were marked by a growing middle-axis emphasis: fundamentalism in religion and mounting conservatism in politics, a new moralism in religion, in music the sudden popularity of previously ignored middle-axis forms like country western. With the mid-eighties, we have moved into a kind of "new materialism." Increasingly "yuppie" values have come to predominate. The carriers of the "answers" in the sixties and early seventies were pacifists, gurus and hip psychologists. In the late seventies and early eighties they were fundamentalist preachers and the new right. With the mid-eighties, we see our culture turning to business leaders, management consultants and economists to find out how things "really" work. As a general rule of thumb, if we look back thirty years, what we see will seem startlingly familiar.

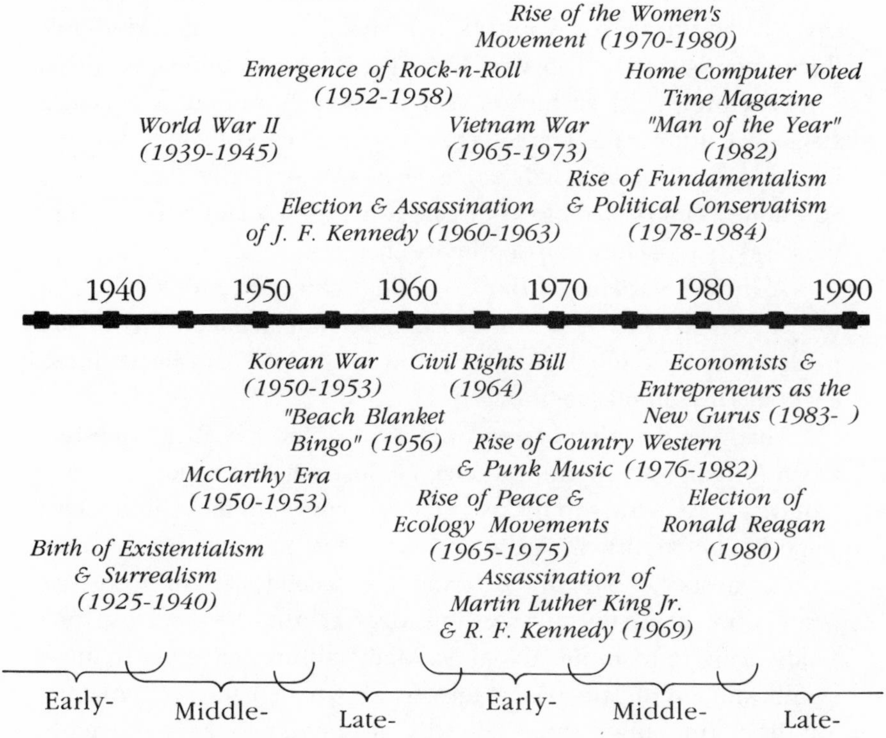

Rise of the Women's
Movement (1970-1980)

Emergence of Rock-n-Roll
(1952-1958)

Home Computer Voted
Time Magazine

World War II
(1939-1945)

Vietnam War
(1965-1973)

"Man of the Year"
(1982)

Rise of Fundamentalism

Election & Assassination
of J. F. Kennedy (1960-1963)

& Political Conservatism
(1978-1984)

| 1940 | 1950 | 1960 | 1970 | 1980 | 1990 |

Korean War
(1950-1953)

Civil Rights Bill
(1964)

Economists &
Entrepreneurs as the
New Gurus (1983-)

"Beach Blanket
Bingo" (1956)

Rise of Country Western
& Punk Music (1976-1982)

McCarthy Era
(1950-1953)

Rise of Peace &
Ecology Movements
(1965-1975)

Election of
Ronald Reagan
(1980)

Birth of Existentialism
& Surrealism
(1925-1940)

Assassination of
Martin Luther King Jr.
& R. F. Kennedy (1969)

Early-   Middle-   Late-   Early-   Middle-   Late-

FIG. 12-2. RHYTHMIC FLUCTUATIONS IN THE LAST HALF CENTURY

Besides understanding the rhythms that define the edge of cultural growth, there is another variable to take into account: cultural bodies, like individuals, have primary energetics. Nations and ethnic groups differ not just in their place in development, but also in the parts of the creative whole they most value and inhabit. For example: England, Germany and France are at very similar points in culture as a creative process, yet they clearly have very different "personalities." The Britisher, with his "stiff upper lip" displays a decided bias toward the inner aspect of the upper pole of late-axis; the German's more stolid pose is decidedly

more middle-axis in flavor; and the Frenchman, with his more romantic tastes, has a clear predilection for the esthetics of the lower
pole of late-axis.

In looking at stage related qualities, then, we must make several important discriminations. First we must discern what kind of
rhythm they relate to. A middle-axis dynamic in a small rhythmic
fluctuation is different in very basic ways from middle-axis within
a subrhythm, which in turn is very different from middle-axis as a
stage in culture as a whole. The dynamics are different, and the
implications for what will come next are markedly different. In
addition, we must be able to distinguish these dynamics from those
we see as a simple function of primary energetic.

A further variable in thinking about cultural energetics relates
to the obvious fact that cultures are not homogeneous. They are
made up of individuals, and different individuals can be at different points in cultural evolution.

This fact has important implications for a critical question
when thinking about cultural change: just what in a population is
required for a culture to make a quantal change, to move into a next
stage in its evolution? An attentive reader, hearing my assertion
that as a species we are entering the second half of formative
process, might easily question my ideas about where we can presently claim to be in this dynamic. Many cultures have yet to move
significantly into late-axis reality. And where late-axis dynamics
are the norm, only a small minority of individuals have moved to
any significant degree into integral understanding.

Three variables define our place in cultural dynamics: first,
the mean—the average embodiment in the population; second, the
spectrum—the number of stages spanned; and third, the cultural
edge—where the substantive innovation is taking place. (Figure
12–3 depicts the mean, spectrum, and edge for major world regions
and for a number of smaller regions that are unique in their
predominance of early stage dynamics.) The important awareness
here is that the most significant of these variables at times of
qualitative change is that creative edge. An amazingly small
number of people can create the critical mass necessary to bring
about a significant shift in reality. We need only look to our last

FIG. 12-3. CREATIVE DISTRIBUTION OF THE ADULT POPULATION IN VARIOUS WORLD REGIONS

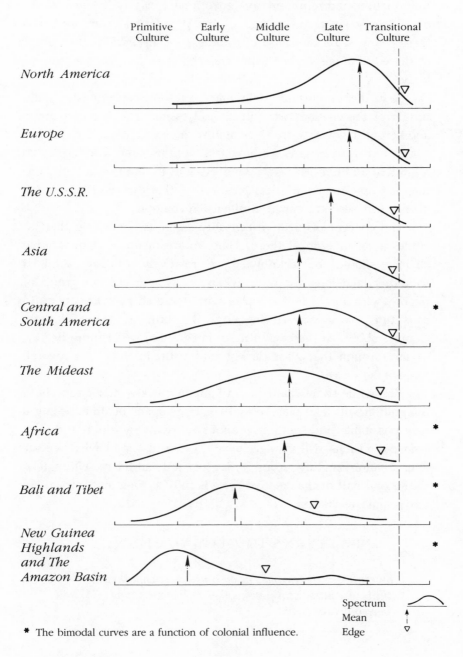

*   The bimodal curves are a function of colonial influence.

major shift in paradigm to see this dramatically illustrated. The leap in understanding that gave birth to the scientific age, the Reformation, and representative government was understandable to only a very small percentage of the population, even well into these changes. As the sense of rightness for an individual is found at the edge of his or her experience, so it is also for the cultural body.

A further important preliminary question concerns the likely timing of the changes we will be addressing. The question offers another nice window into the nature of creative change. Within conventional paradigms we have two options: they will happen as a gradual additive process, taking place over centuries and millennia; or from a more mystical perspective, that they will happen all at once, in a "second coming," a millenial revolution.

The concept of creative causality suggests something that includes a bit of each of these. That we are in times of qualitative change should be acknowledged relatively quickly. And it shouldn't take long for there to amass a large enough group of people, with a sufficient grasp of what these changes are about, to constitute a working "cutting edge" for bringing many of these changes about. At the beginning of integration, we begin to be able to see through that glass darkly, and with this to get an overall sense of the whole.

Yet, while some changes can happen quickly, major aspects of integration will take place only over large spans of time. Seeing a new possibility and bringing it about are two very different things. And our visions will change; what we see first, and what we see later in more mature visions, may be quite different. Ultimately, the second half of the creative cycle is fully as long and intricate in its dynamics as the first.

PATTERNS IN GLOBAL CHANGE

"[our future will] demand a whole range of accomplishments capable of contradicting one another and yet remaining coherently co-present ..."

—*Paolo Soleri*

"There are no passengers on Spaceship Earth. Everybody's
crew." —*Marshall McLuhan*

What should we see as key themes in the future if the cultural thesis of the model is accurate? In approaching any domain, I think in terms of four primary change variables, variables that are relevant to change in any sphere regardless of that sphere's particular focus or content.

Each of the variables has been an important theme throughout the model. In times ahead we should see in all spheres: 1) the realization of post-material understanding, 2) the creative integration of traditional polarities, 3) the achievement of personal and global identity, and 4) the creative integration of previous stage-specific realities.

In using the model to examine a particular domain, I start by asking myself several key questions. I ask first what, in essence, that domain is about: In creative terms, what are its functions in the whole? I then ask myself what the really central issues are in that domain. I am not interested in short term problems, but in the defining quandaries, the issues that will shape the future in that domain. Then I take the four parameters and examine how each might apply within that specific domain. I am particularly interested in what they seem to say in regard to those major, pivotal quandaries.

Let's take a moment with each parameter:

I. THE REALIZATION OF POST-MATERIAL UNDERSTANDING

This variable has two parts. The first is familiar: the elucidation of post-material, post-mechanistic referents for understanding. In all domains we should find form-defined measures of truth increasingly inadequate—education measured as the accumulation of information, wealth as the accumulation of goods, or defense as the accumulation of armaments. The new measures will have an important common characteristic: they will, each in their own way, be measures of life. This reframing not only changes how

357

we think about truth, it redefines the domain: education becomes anything which increases our capacity to effectively engage life, wealth anything which increases the quality of our lives, and defense anything that protects the possibility of timely living relationships between peoples.

The second part of this variable shifts our attention from ideas to institutions. The ability to conceive in more living, creative terms relates to the structures in which we do the conceiving as much as the conceiving itself.

Within material reality we commonly equate function with institutional structure. Thus it is very hard for most people to separate such notions as governance and government, healing and health care, education and schooling, religion and the institution of the church, or love and the institution of marriage. In times ahead we should find ourselves more able to understand institutional structure itself not as truth, but as a context for creative process. The result will be increasing multiplicity in available structures, and ever greater sophistication in understanding the times and situations where different kinds of structures are most appropriate. In other words, we should find people increasingly adapting structures to fit their purposes, rather than tailoring their lives to fit structures.

Actually, this greater freedom in choice of structures should be just a first step. Increasingly we should find ourselves able to reconceptualize our accustomed Newtonian notions of institution in creative, "post-structural" terms. This is not just an interesting option, but ultimately an imperative to effective functioning in all spheres.

A striking example comes from the domain of governance. It seems certain that in the future it will be important to have some sort of global governance—but what sort of form should it have? With our democratic heritage, the most immediate image for us is of some sort of world congress with representatives and rule by majority.

But closer examination reveals some real problems with this sort of structure on a global scale. National government is already impossibly unwieldy; on a global scale it would be far more so. And majority rule, besides wiping out diversity, would be terribly inefficient. In our increasingly complex world, it would be impossible to find consensus for anything but the most trivial of concerns. In decision-making on a global scale, we are all minorities.

Using traditional paradigms, if this late-axis model does not work, the only option is to regress to an earlier form. Many learned people have proposed that the only real alternative to world chaos is a global totalitarian state.

But if we can step beyond thinking of government in mechanistic, form-defined terms—as an overriding structure—we discover that other options do indeed exist. And in them lie the potential for whole new dimensions of responsiveness and efficiency. In the new and larger view, government becomes an ongoing interplay between multiple spheres and levels of social decision-making—local, national and global. With the shift to viewing government in terms of multiple systems and patterns of creative organization, governmental "structure" becomes as much process as form—an evolving organic "body" of interrelated choice-making systems.

It may at first be unsettling to notice that with institutions of this sort, there would be no one who was once-and-for-all in charge. But if we look at history from a creative perspective, we realize that in truth this has always been the case. The "thing" in charge has always been the whole of the process of creation. Kings dictate and senators orate, but their proclamations have always been but the voices of one pole of larger co-determining dynamics. In the youth of our species we have needed the security of feeling there was someone or something in final control. But the only control we have ever had has been our courage to honor the emerging edge of reality. As we move into our species maturity, we should find ourselves more able to consciously accept this inherent creative insecurity. In doing so we will be able to "determine" our way in an ever more direct and consciously co-creative manner.

Post-material ways of thinking about organization will be essential in all domains. Form-defined institutions work well only so long as truth is relatively stable. There is no more obvious fact about the information age than the rapidity with which facts are changing. Whether in government, business, education or religion, it will be increasingly important that the forms in which we work reflect the one thing that is stable: our natures as creative process.

II. THE CREATIVE INTEGRATION OF TRADITIONAL POLARITIES

As we have seen, the first half of a formative cycle is marked by the separation of reality into an evolving sequence of polar truths. In the second half, these polarities reconnect, revealing the larger processes of which they are parts.

My next questions when examining a domain concern these polarities. I want to know what the primary defining dualities in that realm have been. And I want to see if I can find a way to conceptualize that lets me understand them as complementary creative elements in a larger time-relative process.

Two points are important to emphasize if we want to get really practical results. First, it is essential not to confuse integration with simply defining truth in terms of oneness. The fundamental duality is unity versus distinction; saying truth is really unity does not resolve it.

Failure to understand this is a common source of well-intentioned but naive and ineffective thinking. For example, the contention in new physics that there is no final objectivity is often translated to mean everything is subjective, equally unknowable. In the name of integral thought, we are hearing a victory cry for the spiritual in the battle of science and religion. Similarly the duality of mind and body is often "resolved" by simply treating them as the same thing. The real challenge is to find large enough ways of thinking that we can understand the obvious fact that mind and body or objective and subjective are often very different, discern the different relationships that exist between them at different times, and delineate the functions these various patternings of reality serve in the creative whole.

A second common trap is to see a bigger picture, but to miss its relativity in time. For example, business people are coming to recognize that traditional top-down management styles are often not the most creatively effective. The first type of error would be to conclude the opposite, that consensus forms of decision making are in truth the best. The second, more subtle trap would have one realize the importance of a balance between directive and communication-oriented styles in management, but then take the balance seen as right in one situation and assume it is right for all. To keep a living perspective, we must not lose sight of the evolutionary nature of living process. A fully integral model of management would delineate the different balances of hierarchical and consensual modes appropriate to different times and situations—to different stages in the growth of a business, for businesses of different types and sizes, at different stages in the development of a new product, and for people with different personality styles and roles within the business.

III. THE ACHIEVEMENT OF PERSONAL AND GLOBAL IDENTITY

As discussed in the last chapter, our times are marked by dramatic evolutionary steps in what we identify as ourselves. For the first time, people as individuals are beginning to embody the creative whole, and at the same time we are extending our cultural periphery to include all of humanity. In examining a particular domain, much can be learned by exploring how these changes will affect it.

The gradual realization of our new sphere of personal identity will have three primary kinds of effects. First, it should result in a growing willingness and capacity for individuals to take responsibility in both their personal and cultural lives. People will find it less and less satisfying to give their power to polar symbols of authority: physicians, teachers, theologians, politicians. In a consciously creative reality, these people become resources rather than answers. The rewards for being cultural children will continually diminish. The Age of Reason proclaimed full authority for the individual; individual empowerment in fact requires this further essential step.

Second, this realization should result in role stereotypes increasingly giving way to a deepening capacity to see others as unique beings. Roles are a function of form-defined complementarities: men and women, employees and employers, teachers and students. As individuals embody more of the whole, they become better able to view others as wholes.

Third, we should find that all of our contexts for living—the workplace, home and family, places of learning, places of worship—are challenged to become more creatively dynamic and personally responsive. Whole people need creatively whole environments. For example, it used to be enough that the workplace provided income and some degree of security. Increasingly we should find businesses able to keep the best people only if in these environments a person can meet other quite different sorts of needs as well—for a sense of personal and social purpose, for community, for ongoing creative growth.

The expansion of the social whole to a planetary scale has equally profound implications. In every sphere we will discover just how small the world is. We will see how our every action ripples around the globe and how choices in the most far away places affect our own. With the proliferation of nuclear might, we will be ever more challenged to face the fact of our species' mortality, and in this to recognize that we have but one future—we are in it together. We should find ourselves less and less able to generate the polar animosities necessary to perpetrate war and justify oppression, and less and less willing to do harm to the planet for short term profit. Those first few photographs sent by the Apollo astronauts from the moon's surface—images of the earth as a small, delicate living orb—powerfully symbolize these changes. They are like mandalas for this emerging planetary consciousness.

I see these changing peripheries of identification not as supplanting earlier boundaries, but simply marking the end of the first half of a developmental journey. In times ahead we should find ourselves increasingly able to utilize all sorts of different social peripheries as they are most appropriate. In government, we see smaller peripheries being reengaged in movements for regional autonomy, and in attempts to revitalize and empower neighborhoods. Similarly in business, along with new global interdependency, we see a growing recognition of the value of decentralization. From the technical side we are recognizing that sky-

We are being challenged by two new major spheres of identity: The individual is coming to embody the creative whole, and cultural identity is expanding to embrace the whole of the planet. [The earth as seen from the Apollo 16 spacecraft.]

rocketing transportation costs combined with new communications technology means that much which was done before at a centralized setting is now better done locally. With this, there is the increasing realization that one of the easiest ways to make a work environment creatively rich is to keep working units small enough that ongoing contact and personal initiative happen naturally.

IV. THE CREATIVE INTEGRATION OF PREVIOUS REALITIES

A final perspective, one that can offer rich insight, follows directly from the nature of the second half of creative cycle. We can understand the future in any domain as a gradually emerging larger synthesis of that domain's previous stage-specific realities. In examining a domain, I go through its history asking myself what the defining truths in that domain have been during each of its major epochs. I then ask how I might understand each as a part in a larger creative process. I also ask myself what each stage uniquely contributes in that process. In theory, each stage should both bring an essential element to the greater whole of understanding, and reveal itself, when standing alone, as decidedly partial.

The domain of education makes good example. There is clearly something intuitively right about the emerging concept of "whole person" education, the notion that in the future, education will need to be not just of the mind, but of the body and spirit as well. But using our late-axis frame of reference, that truth is hard to get at. Does this mean that the critical tasks of education are to put prayer in schools and expand athletic programs? By thinking in terms of how these modes have been lived through history, we can better delineate the vision. Spirituality includes contemporary religion, but equally the primitive's reality of nature as spirit, the magic of myth and symbol, and the spirit of the scientist mapping life's mysteries. I think of spirituality, in the big picture, as the study and experience of how things are connected—a most appropriate educational cornerstone. Similarly, while the body needs to keep fit, it is also the vehicle for feeling, and, even more basically, it is a fundamental kind of knowing. The body as the greater whole of these things, the body as something we are as well as have, certainly has a rightful place at the core of education.

In the next section I will be applying these four parameters to the future of some of the major domains of human endeavor. I will be painting with necessarily very broad brushstrokes, trusting the reader to look beyond limitations in specifics to the larger picture I am trying to convey. Some of the changes I will refer to have yet to manifest in any clear way; others are already well in progress. Few of these ideas about future change will be fully original; my contribution is the integrating framework, a way to understand what on the surface may seem to be disconnected processes as aspects of a single critical change dynamic.

EDUCATION

"We are rejecting the old assumption that most learning happens in classrooms and is supervised by institutions. Learning—self-directed, independent, experiential—is integral to modern life."

—*Barry Heerman*

"We have the inalienable right to be educated by everyone and everything in the community."

—*Theodore Roszak*

As education is fundamental in all realms of understanding, it seems an appropriate place to begin. From a creative perspective we could define education generically as anything which gives us new skills and understandings for creatively engaging life.

Education had a dramatic and central place in the Age of Reason. The realization of universal education and the proliferation of institutions of higher learning constituted some of its greatest achievements. And these successes played important roles in what would be possible in other domains. They made possible both the literacy necessary for representative government, and the transmission of skills critical to the tasks of industrialization.

But essential changes are now clearly needed in education. The forms that worked so well for fueling the democratic and industrial revolutions are increasingly coming into question, and frequently simply ceasing to work. The institution of education, regarded as almost holy until very recently, is rapidly losing its favored position. The status of teachers is deteriorating, students are less and less satisfied, and even by education's own chosen yardstick—performance on standardized tests—something is clearly amiss.

The model suggests we are coming to need both new kinds of structures for learning, and new definitions and perspectives regarding just what education is about. Education is ceasing to be vital because our forms and definitions have moved beyond their time appropriateness.

I. THE REALIZATION OF POST-MATERIAL UNDERSTANDING

A Post-material Referent—For the tasks of literacy, simple material referents—the learning of facts, the acquisition of certain skills—were quite adequate, both for defining a curriculum and measuring success. With the rapid turnover of information and the new, more personal kinds of challenges in today's world, we clearly need a much more dynamic vision of what education is about. Learning how to learn is becoming as, or more, important than specific content learned—not just for a leisured elite, but for everyone. Things like self-knowledge, the ability to ask questions of purpose, and the capacity to deal creatively with new situations, should become "basic curriculum." Facts and skills should continue to have a central place, but always in terms of whether their acquisition really increases personal and social aliveness.

Post-material Structure—Our late-axis equating of learning with schooling, and schooling with an image of classroom, blackboard, thirty young students, and chairs in rows, should become radically expanded. We should come to think about education as a lifelong process, and one utilizing of a multitude of resources: relatively traditional classrooms, where appropriate; computer hookups; apprenticeships in the community; travel; peer learning; personal growth experiences; and the hands-on experience of trying out ideas in the world. Where education takes place in an institutional setting, it should be more and more common for participation in decision-making within that institution to be regarded as part of the educational process.

366

II. THE CREATIVE INTEGRATION OF TRADITIONAL POLARITIES

Teacher and Student—Our conventional image is polar and largely unidirectional—teacher as pitcher, student as cup. With time we should see the emergence of a great variety of learning relationships. For strictly fact-oriented learning, the traditional image may often be most efficient, with some modification in posture to better acknowledge shared worth. In many situations, most obviously in peer learning, a co-exploratory relationship offers greater riches. Where the focus is more on personal growth, the most rewarding posture for the teacher is often very different yet, more that of facilitator with the referent for truth clearly in the learner. Whatever the posture, we should find teachers increasingly acknowledging that teaching is most alive when in some way they are learning as much as they are teaching.

School and Community—We should see the walls of the school becoming more permeable. This should happen in both directions: community resource people becoming active participants in the schools, and students engaging in outside learning. It should be increasingly common to see schools conceived as community resource centers, where people of all ages can go to access information, and where projects benefiting the community are seeded and supported.

Student and Student—Conventional education is defined competitively: for one student to excel another must fail. A competitive paradigm is sometimes relevant, but when used exclusively it shortchanges us of one of our most potent learning resources—our fellow students. We should see more and more research into the many powerful applications of cooperative learning strategies.

Intellect and Feelings/Body/Intuition/Spirit—We will see an increasing recognition of the importance of engaging all parts of the person. Addressing more germinal and personal parts of who we are deepens the comprehension of ideas. And it is essential if we wish to engender students' capacities for thinking innovatively, and their ability to grapple with issues of meaning. Teacher education should come to stress the sensitive use of experiential methods.

Right Answer and Wrong Answer—The rewards in the conventional educational paradigm are for getting right answers—for not making mistakes. With our new models, we will find ourselves able to grasp the critical place of not knowing in really creative learning, and fostering approaches that engender appropriate courage for making mistakes. We will come to recognize just how much we have to learn about the power of curiosity, wonder and improvisation; and how much we have to gain from that learning.

III. PERSONAL AND GLOBAL IDENTIFICATION

At the heart of all these changes stands the shift toward the embodiment of the whole. It points toward learners becoming increasingly self-directed, and increasingly demanding environments that are creatively vital. It should also give us more teachers who are capable of bringing all of themselves—head and heart, teacher and learner—to the process of teaching, and who will take initiative in shaping environments that are embracing of the entirety of the person.

Future education will clearly be global education. New communications technology can bring the world's news into the classroom as it happens. Some of our greatest rewards will likely come from what we can learn about other peoples, and from our growing capacity to learn and experience in relation to the planet as something whole and alive. All peripheries, from self, to relationship, to region, to planet and cosmos will have important places in future education.

IV. THE CREATIVE INTEGRATION OF PREVIOUS REALITIES

These directions for change are nicely synthesized by looking at them in relation to past educational realities. With each stage we have seen a particular mode of understanding given greatest emphasis—from kinesthetic knowing in tribal times, to "I think, therefore I am." We also see characteristic kinds of learning relationships emphasized.

We can hear pre-axial sensibilities in a number of likely important ingredients in future education: learning by doing, an increased use of ecological and systems perspectives in both the content and process of learning, more frequent use of cooperative learning methods, and a recognition of the importance of the body in learning. Aspects of early-axis reality are echoed in the recognition of the importance of room for improvisation and uncertainty in education, and with this new value given to experiential approaches that tap into the imaginal, intuitive, symbolic layers of knowing. Education in middle culture was of two sorts: moral education in the church, and craft-oriented learning in apprenticeships. We should see these concerns reflected in a growing willingness to give ethical and emotional issues a central place in the learning process, and in a growing utilization of learning resources in the community. And we should see late-axis sensibilities expanding—through ever more sophisticated educational technology, through a growing ability to realize the ideal of maximum accessibility to learning resources, and through a new kind of respect for refining the intellect, not just for its role in learning, but for the sake of thinking.

BUSINESS AND ECONOMICS

"Without work, all life goes rotten, but when work is soulless, life stifles and dies."
—*Albert Camus*

"We have not inherited the earth from our fathers, we are borrowing it from our children."
—*Lester Brown*

"I am wealthy in my friends."
—*Shakespeare*

Our most recent age has been a time of monumental growth in the marketplace. We have seen new inventions, products that both save labor and expand human capacity, brought forth at a prodigious rate. We have seen business come to rival government and surpass religion as a social force. And we have seen the realization of a standard of living for the masses beyond anything known before.

While our everyday view of the health of business counterchanges with the dance of the bulls and the bears, beneath the surface there are clear indications that qualitative changes in our understanding of economics are both needed and beginning to take place. The forms and values that have defined business and economics in the industrial age are moving past their time of relevance.

If the model is accurate, we will see transformations not just in how we do business, but in our core ideas of what business is about. Our four parameters help rough out the territory. At its most basic, I think of business as how we exchange things of value within social systems.

I. THE REALIZATION OF POST-MATERIAL UNDERSTANDING

A Post-Material Referent—In business as we customarily think of it, the referent is material accumulation—the dollar. This measure, used abstractly, is really very new. A desire for money as such, not too many centuries back, would have been called greed and listed among the seven deadly sins. The material has always been part of the equation, but in the past, other factors have always been more important in defining the bottom line: honor, craftsmanship, relationship to the sacred, cooperative bonds in tribe and community.

The isolated and universal material referent in economy, like the concept of objectivity in science or democratic choice in governance, has been a vital voice in the delineation of the individual and culture as form. Its role has been most directly felt in the important task of dissolving class structure and moving beyond power by privilege. It has been the "great leveler," offering, at least in theory, an arbiter equally available to all.

And, too, it is clearly moving beyond its timeliness. Unmodified, it would lead us more and more toward the personally isolating specter of mass culture, toward an increasingly estranged and impersonal workplace, and toward a disastrous insensitivity to our planet's long term human and environmental needs.

Individually, in the future, we should find ourselves less and less inclined to define status in terms of a person's "net worth." Other sorts of measures—the quality of one's friendships, one's social contribution, a sense of meaning and integrity in one's work, one's health, the beauty of where one lives—should find ever greater emphasis.

At a corporate level, we should find the public increasingly demanding that businesses be socially responsible, and workers more and more requiring a creatively meaningful work environment—one that allows for a sense of pride and purpose in what is produced. We should see these changes happening in two steps: first, in a recognition that social responsiveness and more enlightened management practices are in fact profitable, and, later, in a shift to a posture that takes financial assets as an important but clearly not sufficient measure of business success.

With our identity tightly tied to the dollar as deity, such changes, likely at first motivated as much by economic limitations as enlightened thought, may easily feel like sacrifice. In the larger picture, they will be anything but. While in the first half of the creative cycle a more and more abstracted materiality appropriately defined value, as we move into the second, less and less energy is needed to fulfill the symbolic needs of separation. A whole new kind of efficiency becomes possible in our relationship to the material. As we leave behind the material as the primary definer of identity, we realize the ability to utilize it more and more effectively as a tool. Too much materiality becomes as undesirable as too little; it becomes excess baggage, the owned in effect owning the owner. In the big picture, the adoption of a post-material referent is anything but a rejection of the profit motive. Rather it is the realization of a more inclusive and more living definition of profit. Seen four-dimensionally, the "American dream" of materially-defined happiness and ultimate security reveals itself as youthful fantasy, a dream that could never come true, and one which is in fact far from anything we would ever want to come true.

Post-Material Structure—One of the most fascinating areas of change in business involves new concepts in management. Traditionally, business has used top-down decision-making. In times ahead, we should find general agreement that some significant degree of mutual participation in decision-making is not only necessary for morale, but essential for making decisions that work. We will see the appearance and advocacy of "heterarchical" management models, perspectives that attempt to find the marriage of directive and participatory modes appropriate to different contexts.

II. THE CREATIVE INTEGRATION OF TRADITIONAL POLARITIES

Management and Workers—The empowerment of workers in decision-making is central to making the workplace a place of purpose. Business should increasingly recognize that the hands-on experience of the work force is one of a company's greatest creative resources. From the other side, we should find managers more and more recognizing the importance of personal contact and involvement in good business leadership.

Business Ethic and Human Ethic—The current tendency to regard issues such as personal ties, esthetic sensibilities, and long-term good as secondary concerns in doing effective business should change dramatically. Isolated material ethics like *caveat emptor* will be replaced by codes that make companies accountable for the social effects of their products. Businesses that prevail and prosper will be ones that not only produce goods, but benefit the greater good in doing so.

Business and Not-Business—Our traditional notions of economy measure acts that directly produce dollars, while ignoring the larger "invisible economy" of work done in the home, volunteerism, and cooperative exchange. Increasingly we should find the status of these later kinds of activities rising and their value taken solidly into account in efforts to promote "the economy."

Business and Community—The model implies changes both between business and the larger community, and within businesses as communities. To be seen as successful, businesses in the future will have to function as much more than just a source of jobs. The successful businesses will be those that become valued, long-term contributors to all aspects of community well-being. In addition, with a growing desire for community in times ahead and more people choosing not to have families or to spend a greater proportion of time outside the home, we should find a growing trend toward opportunities for community within the workplace—company lounges and recreation facilities where everyone can meet on an equal footing, office sports teams, outings and shared personal and professional growth experiences.

Logic and Intuition—Good business leadership is traditionally regarded as a result of hard-headed adherence to cold, hard facts. Research is now showing that really successful managers are adept as well at tapping the more germinal parts of understanding: they take their hunches seriously and refine the art of seat of the pants piloting. With ever more rapid information turnover and an increasingly four-dimensional work reality, the ability to work in ways that access all parts of a person should be highly valued and consciously cultivated. In the past, business has rewarded methodicalness, and feared creativity as a force which "rocks the boat." In the new model, the businesses that prevail will be the ones that can attract the most creative people.

Work and Play—When work and play become split as an either/or, life as meaning easily disappears as a conscious element in our choice-making: we work to earn money and we play to escape from our work. As we more fully embrace the whole of our creative natures, we should find it essential that we experience our work not just as labor, but to the best of our abilities, as manifestation. From the other side, we should find it ever more important to have our "leisure time" activities be not just diversion, but in the fullest sense, "re-creation."

III. THE ACHIEVEMENT OF PERSONAL AND GLOBAL IDENTITY

The influence of the personal embodiment of the creative whole can be felt in all of these observations. Put simply, in the future, people will become more self-actualizing. And we will create and search out environments that are nurturing and stimulating to this growing sense of wholeness. The successful businesses will be ones that succeed internally in becoming such environments, and externally in fostering such qualities in the larger world.

On a planetary scale, we should see both a growing sophistication in understanding global economic interactions, and a growing capacity to see these interactions in larger than "us and them" terms. A solely adversarial posture in international trade, in which trade and war are equivalent pursuits, should be increasingly seen as outmoded. Along with this will come a growing unwillingness to make short term profits at the expense of long term planetary well-being.

Simultaneous with this expansion of periphery, we should see smaller peripheries come to have a greater importance in business. In the year 1900, it was a pretty good rule of thumb that greater centralization meant greater efficiency. This formula no longer necessarily holds. With today's sophisticated communications systems, it is now possible to engage in a board meeting from one's living room, or to "sit down" with one's editor 2,000 miles away to revise a manuscript. And with new technologies, much manufacture is as easily done on a small scale as a large one. These, combined with the fact that smaller working units allow for a greater sense of participation and pride in workmanship, should mean that in the future, smaller scale will often mean larger "profit." We should see this reflected in trends toward regional autonomy within the structure of large corporations; more independent entrepreneurship (the small, flexible, locally-knowledgeable business will in many situations have the advantage); and, within the workplace, the growing use of small, self-managing work groups.

IV. THE CREATIVE INTEGRATION OF PREVIOUS REALITIES

Economics as we commonly think of it, the science of the exchange of capital, is a function specifically of late-axis reality. Earlier stages don't have a lot to say as long as we stay within that narrow definition. But they can help us greatly in defining a more living economic standard, a "unit" of measure for wealth larger than just the ledger sheet, and in addressing the health of business as more than just a short-term consideration.

As we have seen, in pre-axial reality value lay in connection with tribe and nature. The hunter paid homage to his kill, the builder to the tree cut to make the tribal longhouse. Objects had value to the degree they could enhance this linkage with nature and with the tribal whole. The ability to give things away was often more important than having them, for the exchange of gifts engenders relationship. One quality of the new economic arbiter should be that the more of it we have, the more we feel a sense of living connection—to ourselves, to other people, and to the simple fact of being alive.

The ultimate determiner of value in early-axis times was how fully an act was an expression of divine magic and artistic inspiration. In times ahead, the degree to which something enhances the possibility of innovation and personal connection in creative purpose should have a very important place in our thinking about what constitutes riches.

In middle-axis culture, the bottom line in questions of personal worth was honor; in made objects it was integrity of craftsmanship. Increasingly we should find ourselves demanding honesty, quality, and responsibility in the marketplace, and demanding in our own lives that we can truly take pride in our work.

And as in late-axis reality, our new measures should include the emancipation from privilege that comes with an arbiter abstracted from ties of blood, and a valuing of technologies that can increase the quality of life.

THE ARTS

"A world of made is not a world of born."
—*ee cummings*

"Let us give a human meaning to the super-human struggle."
—*Nikos Kazantzakis*

"Art teaches nothing but the significance of life."
—*Henry Miller*

Art differs from the domains we have explored thus far in that, at any stage, art takes its primary significance from the more germinal aspects of that stage's reality. Thus, during our most recent epoch, while business and institutional education became both more elaborated and more powerful, the arts, though finding a new grandeur and sophistication, at the same time moved gradually to a more peripheral role.

With the Age of Reason, we witnessed a wondrous evolution and refinement in the form-defined aspects of artistic creation. The high art of late-axis times—symphony, opera, ballet, the great masters—was a monumental paean to creative realization. Yet, simultaneously, we saw the arts moving further away from the central influence they held in more primitive times. Along with its new richness and visibility, we saw a gradual relegation of art to the status of decoration and entertainment. Art was the prime voice of the subjective in a reality of the objective: a woman adored and admired for her decorative charms, but asked to leave the room when it came time for the real decisions to be made.

We are clearly at a time when important changes for the arts wait off-stage for their cues. In recent decades, art has lost both direction and much of its remaining potency; in approaching transitional times, the germinal pole, art's well-spring, grows more and more faint. At stage right we see the forms of classicism, once profound, but now often simply encrusted symbols of privilege. At center stage we see the glittering consumerism of the entertainment industry, sometimes with a human statement, but as often just escape. At stage left stands the avant garde, alternating moments of real innovation with parades of difference for its own sake.

What does the concept of integration suggest for art in times ahead? As for other domains, it points toward changes not just in content, but at the most fundamental levels: in how we define art and its place and purpose in culture. If the model is accurate, times ahead for the arts should be rich ones. Integration connects us into our germinal voices and returns to them a forgotten respect.

And as with other domains, for the arts there will be necessary sacrifices. The central one is the surrender of art as something distinct—distinct from the ordinary person, distinct from other realms of endeavor: the surrender of art as Art.

Our four parameters again help delineate these changes. I think of art as the act of timely expression from the germinal aspects of our being.

I. THE REALIZATION OF POST-MATERIAL UNDERSTANDING

A Post-Material Referent—In the Age of Reason, the contexts of artistic expression became more and more materially defined. Music and dance came to focus on performance, the audience distinct and the work a finished and repeatable "piece." Visual creation came to be signed, framed, and hung in galleries, with the artist for the first time viewed as a specialist, an esthetic professional. Fame and visibility became of increasing importance. And art for the first time became fully treatable as a commodity, something to exchange in the marketplace.

This shift occurred not just in how we handled art, but equally in its esthetic, in what was felt to be beautiful. The esthetic came increasingly to voice the finishing and polishing aspects of creation. Music moved toward increasing technical intricacy and formal clarity, away from the pulses of rhythm and the more mysterious tonalities of earlier times. Painting focused on more secular themes, and became increasingly occupied with masterful depiction. Dance movement became more anatomically precise and specifically choreographed.

In times ahead we should see changes in both of these aspects of artistic expression. Art should more and more come to be regarded as not just a province for professionals, and not simply in terms of object and performance, but as part of daily life. And we should see the gradual emergence of esthetics that embrace ever more fully all levels and stages in our creative natures. The possible forms in this development are endless; the measure of achievement here becomes the living fullness of the expressive act, the degree to which it somehow speaks to the creative whole.

Post-Material Structure—Within late-axis esthetic, "real" art happens within highly defined disciplines and is given expression in specific institutional settings—art galleries, concert halls. As the cycle advances, the boundaries between artistic disciplines and between art and other aspects of living should become ever more creatively permeable.

II. THE CREATIVE INTEGRATION OF TRADITIONAL POLARITIES

Artist and Non-Artist—With the creative whole increasingly available to the individual, we should be better able to appreciate the ways in which we are all artists, and at once to value more deeply those with particular artistic gifts. Movement toward integration will make it possible for languages like movement, image, poetics and sound—the vocabulary of the artist—to be not just the province of certain isolated figures, but available and valued aspects of each person's identity. This will allow us to see more clearly how much that we do which we would never call art can none the less be deeply creative.

Artist and Audience—We should see an expanding variety of accepted roles and postures for artists, from the accustomed one of object and performance creation, to styles with a much more participatory relationship with an audience, to ways of working that have the artist being more of a creative facilitator—one who is skilled at helping others explore their creative depths.

One Discipline and Another—There should be ever greater

intermedia collaboration—dancers and visual artists, musicians and poets. In addition we should see growing interest in doing joint projects that extend well outside the usual bounds of art—a musician exploring forms with an architect, a poet working with a politician to find words for new kinds of understanding, a sculptor collaborating with an ecologist and a city planner to brainstorm more organic ways for thinking about urban environments.

Art and Psychology—We have tended to hold questions of art quite separate from those of well-being. That a person might make beautiful art and live an unhappy life has not been thought incongruous; indeed, in keeping with the marginal role of the arts, it has been almost expected. This should change dramatically. We should see a new emphasis among artists on awareness and personal exploration. And we should come to regard "good" art as that which in some way honors the healthy living whole.

From the other side of the polarity, we should find ourselves thinking of psychological health, as we have here, in a way that recognizes its integral relationship with things creative. Ultimately, well-being is a statement about the integrity with which we live our lives as works of art.

Art and Politics—We should see a similar healing of the split between art and the political. In traditional formulations, art and politics don't mix; at best, we get artful propaganda. But, when the individual feels a deep sense of connection to, and responsibility in, one's cultural reality, it becomes impossible to make esthetic statements that are not social statements. We should find art leaving behind its role as cultural decoration, and remembering its voice as mythic trickster, oracle, and devil's advocate at the edge of social truth.

Art and Science—When thinking is grounded in a larger paradigm, art and science reveal themselves as simply the left and right hands of a single process of creative discovery. Significantly, today we find art coming to utilize the stuff of technology, and science using the language of poetry.

379

III. THE ACHIEVEMENT OF PERSONAL AND GLOBAL IDENTITY

The increasing ability of the individual to embody the whole can be felt in all of these changes. It opens the door to the average person discovering his or her artistic nature. And it offers to the artist the possibility of a complementary integration—and a way past the common feeling of being a stranger in one's own land, past needing to be and act as something separate.

Our global consciousness will give us ever greater access to artistic endeavors from all over the world, from New York to New Guinea. The cultural cross-fertilization inherent in this should be a powerful stimulus toward discovering esthetics that respect and give voice to the creative whole.

Smaller peripheries should similarly take on new roles. In early times, art was a way of dancing, singing and imaging the life and bonds of community. As our focus shifts away from the artist's role as expert, we should find renewed interest in creative efforts that speak from the unique resources and sensibilities of our own locales.

IV. THE CREATIVE INTEGRATION OF PREVIOUS REALITIES

The realities of earlier stages give evocative hints about the place and purpose of art in times ahead. As we have seen, in earliest times, there was really nothing which was not art; each object—from ritual adornments to cooking utensils—was seen as having animistic potency and was created and treated accordingly. A central theme in times ahead should be a growing permeability between art and daily life. Early-axis art was a celebration of magic and mystery in ritual. Effective art in times ahead should have the capacity to reach into the deep chthonic levels of our sensibilities, and make no effort to hide the fact that art's essential purpose is transformation. The art of middle-axis culture resided in two relatively distinct domains: the formal art of religious devotion above, and the "folk art" of community sharing below. Expanded engagement with both spiritual and social relationships should be important threads in art's future message. In late-axis culture, the classical arts resided above, while art as entertainment inhabited the below. In the approaching expansion of sensibility, both functions should be conserved and find new evolution. We should find both a deep respect for expertise and refinement of form, and a strong appreciation for the place of personality, individuality and frivolity in "serious" art.

These past realities can help us not just with framing the future purpose of art, but as well for understanding what will strike us in times ahead as artistically beautiful and significant. The esthetic preferences of an age—the rhythmic structures, tonal patterns, uses of color and line, the shapes, and patterns of language that most move people—are direct statements about the organizational processes underlying the reality of that age. We should find a growing tendency toward major esthetics being creatively integrative of our earlier sensibilities.

I often do workshops in which I present music from different cultural epochs and discuss the common characteristics found in the music of all cultures at particular stages. We look at how these characteristics evoke very specific kinds of bodily experience and specific conceptual realities. We then play with what music might sound like if it included elements from all the stages.

The emergence of a new, more integral esthetics has already begun in music, and can be found by anyone alerted to it, and able to see past some common misunderstandings that can confuse the picture. First, we need to avoid confusing integral sensibilities with what one anthropologist has called the "aloha amigo syndrome," a mish-mash esthetic—homogenization. We also need to avoid falling into the trap of thinking that there is only one type of integral music. Integration can occur with relation to any stage, and any polar dynamic within that stage. For example, in the classical sphere we see integrative expansion in such things as experiments with the use of folk culture melodic patterns and improvisation. We see it from a different direction in the use of more complex rhythmic sensibilities in rock and jazz. It is there as well in the work of traditional musicians who are utilizing late culture elements in their music in ways that don't just modernize and water down the traditional esthetic, but expand and deepen it.

HEALTH CARE

*"To develop the health of a man, it is necessary to understand
not only the development of cells and organs, but also the
development of the individual and the species. And if the
health of a man is to become fully manifest, it must prevail
not only in the individual, but in mankind as well."*

—*Jonas Salk, M.D.*

"Illness is a creative opportunity ..."

—*Kenneth Pelletier, M.D.*

Modern medicine is appropriately seen as a preeminent accomplishment of the Age of Reason. The past 150 years especially have been times of miraculous advances: the immense saving of lives that followed the discovery of microbes and the initiation of sterile technique, the development of vaccines and the subsequent near elimination of many major infectious diseases, the antibiotic revolution, and the new generation of inventions—transplants, ever more sophisticated diagnostic technology, genetic engineering.

Yet, medicine today is clearly in a time of crisis. Popular confidence in the medical profession has ebbed dramatically. Health care costs are skyrocketing. And social/ethical questions simply not addressable within medicine's historical paradigm are becoming increasingly impossible to ignore: euthanasia, abortion, complex issues of malpractice and social responsibility. If the model is accurate, changes are in process that will not just alter how health care is delivered, but change some of our most fundamental ideas concerning what health care is about.

We can frame many of the most fascinating changes ahead in terms of one of the central themes at the midpoint of any creative cycle: the recognition of the fact of mortality. Medicine is having to face squarely the specter of death, both as a symbol—the fact of limitation, death as the surrender of a godly image—and death in a very literal sense—the fact that death is a part of life.

Conventional medicine is based on a heroic mythology. Illness and death are the enemies and our task as physicians has been to defeat them, in the individual and the world, at all costs. From all sides, the cultural reality that has supported that mythology is changing.

A major part of this is a direct function of medicine's success. With new advances we can keep a person "alive" almost indefinitely. For the first time, we are having to face that saving a life is not always consistent with quality of life. We are having to acknowledge that often, in the big picture, death is not our enemy, but our friend.

And this is only a first piece. In the future we will increasingly be confronted with situations where we must "choose" death even when it is still possible to prolong life in a meaningful way. Early advances in medicine, like better sanitation and antibiotics, were relatively cheap. Most more recent ones have been colossally expensive. We will find that the creed of prolonging life and eradicating disease at any cost is simply not an economic option. There is no escape from this challenge, and the profound maturity it will demand of us.

A further piece in this meeting of mortality involves not a limitation in resources, but, as I see it, one fundamental in reality. We will have to face that disease, as much as we would like, cannot be eliminated; past a certain point, we will find that neither new advances, nor more money will significantly alter statistics. Ultimately, we will come to understand that disease, in the big picture, is, like death, not just an enemy to be defeated, one half of an either/or, but something of much more profound significance.

In its day, medicine's heroic image of victory over darkness brought immensely rich rewards. Initially, giving up this image may feel like a major sacrifice. But a larger vision of medicine, while certainly demanding more of us, will ultimately be both more fulfilling and more health-giving.

Our four parameters can help us delineate some of what likely lies ahead:

I. THE REALIZATION OF POST-MATERIAL UNDERSTANDING

A Post-Material Referent—Within late-axis culture, it has been our practice to define health and healing almost exclusively in material terms: health as the absence of disease; body separate from mind; a purely material, causal relationship between healer and healed; and treatment as repair done on broken tissues. In time, we should find ourselves thinking and measuring in much broader and more personal ways: from a creatively causal perspective, and in terms more akin to the concept here of aliveness.

Post-Material Structure—Institutional medicine has for most people been synonymous with health care. Our standard image has been of the doctor as expert and active agent in change and the hospital as the context for healing. This should evolve into a more multifaceted and personally empowering picture. We are now seeing people taking greater responsibility for their own health, and utilizing a variety of health care resources. This trend should continue. We should find ourselves better able to utilize the institution of medicine in its proper place, as one tool rather than absolute truth.

And the institution itself will undergo significant changes. We should see increasing pressure toward making care equally accessible to all. Along with this will come new patterns of shared responsibility in decision-making, both in the care itself—between doctors, nurses, and other members of the health care team—and in the administration of that care—between care providers, hospital managers, and the communities served.

II. THE CREATIVE INTEGRATION OF TRADITIONAL POLARITIES

Healer and Healed—We should find ourselves gradually accepting that we are, each of us, the final "expert" and vehicle of our individual well-being. As this view comes to prevail, we should find health professionals increasingly desiring to step down from their past position as the knowers and doers of healing, to assume the less grand, but ultimately more powerful and fulfilling role of person and knowledgeable healing resource.

Mind and Body—As we understand more of the biochemical concomitants of psyche and the the psychology of soma, we will be more and more able to approach healing as an integrally creative process.

Medicine and Not-Medicine—We should see a broadening of accepted kinds of healing resources—along with the tools of traditional allopathy, such things as biofeedback, nutrition, meditation and prayer, approaches from the medicine of other cultures such as acupuncture, and techniques for delving into the psychological aspects of illness. Rather than pitting one form against another as rival panaceas, we should become increasingly sophisticated at understanding when, and for whom, different approaches are most effective.

Personal Health and Environmental Health—We will become ever more cognizant of the relationship between the health of our world and our personal health. We will increasingly find ourselves regarding all the factors that go into creating a healthy environment as "health care" priorities: clean air and water, parks, meaningful employment, schooling, adequate housing, safe neighborhoods.

Psyche and Techne—We should increasingly recognize the importance of having the personal and technical aspects of medicine working together as a single whole. Along with new medicines and techniques, we should see a growing emphasis on the human side of medicine: on the healing relationship, on the health of the healer, and on the importance of treating the person rather than just symptoms.

Life and Death—We should become more and more comfortable with death as a part of life, and increasingly sensitive to the importance of the death experience for patient, family, and healer.

III. THE ACHIEVEMENT OF PERSONAL AND GLOBAL IDENTITY

Our emerging capacity to be aware in the whole of our health reshapes the reality both of the healer and the healed. For each, it both empowers in new ways, and reveals the limits of power.

Our growing global identity should result in an ever greater availability of health care information and technologies worldwide. Complementing this, we should see a new kind of appreciation for the place and importance of indigenous healing practices.

IV. THE CREATIVE INTEGRATION OF PREVIOUS REALITIES

Each previous health care reality can be seen as contributing to this larger picture. In tribal times, health was a function of one's degree of harmony within the body of tribe and nature. Increasingly, we should recognize how health in the broadest sense is a statement about the quality of our connectedness—with ourselves, with our friends, and with our world.

Early- and middle-axis cultures have overlapping spiritual, physical, and emotional explanations for illness and systems for treatment. The beginnings of a reconnection into these kinds of sensibilities can be seen in the present interest in such things as the "placebo effect" and the role of stress in illness. Increasingly we should find value in addressing the roles we play in our own health—something we should get increasingly adept at doing without regressing to the blame and guilt common with earlier realities. We should more and more come to regard health as being as much a function of internal listening as of external intervention.

And along with these rememberings into the more internal aspects of health, we should see a growing refinement of the more technical aspects of physical medicine, and a growing sensitivity to how best to apply them in the whole.

GOVERNANCE

"I know no safe depository of the ultimate powers of society but the people themselves."

—Thomas Jefferson

"An ecologist has to consider the parts—each in its place and as related to, rather than as subsidiary to the whole. It would undoubtedly be good if political leaders ... would get to know that method."   *—Biologist Edward Ricketts*

"If after the political, economic, and financial experiences of recent years, we still think that states, however proud and independent that they may feel, can go it alone in these matters, ignoring each other's interests and above all the interests of the impoverished and backward states, then we are beyond redemption. Before long in our affluent, industrial, computerized jet society, we shall feel the wrath of the wretched people of the world. There will be no peace."   *—Former Canadian Prime Minister Lester Pearson*

Within the framework of the model, governance is the choice-making and boundary setting function in the social whole. Today we hear critical rumblings of change in this most important of spheres: growing impatience with the inefficiency of bureaucracies, diminishing faith in the judgement of elected officials, a growing reluctance to support the fervencies of nationalism. Limited to our usual perspectives, it is difficult to make sense out of the changes that are occurring. The model can help.

Human history, as we have seen, tells the story of a gradual evolution of social determination toward the capacity for individual choice. We have moved from nature and fate as the all-embracing determiners in pre-history—to, in early-axis culture, the establishment of a first, more conscious counterbalance in a single ascendant figure of "choice," the leader as divine channel—to, in middle-axis culture, the realization of a privileged class and in the figure of a king or dictator, a more human symbol of determination—to, in late-axis culture, with representative government, an image of the community of the common person as the ascendant determiner.

The key to understanding present change is the recognition that while the image in late-axis culture has been one of the individual as choicemaker, the reality has been yet a good distance from actual government "by the people." Governance has been government by institution, the upper pole in social determination embodied in the edifices of bureaucratic structure. The basic dynamics have continued to be polar. While elected officials have not been gods, neither have they been just mortals, something most obvious with strongly mythologized figures like George Washington or John Kennedy, but in fact always a significant dynamic. During these times we have elected people to be our leaders, then given our ascendant power to them and the structures they inhabit.

With present times we see further movement in this progression, increasingly beyond government by institution and political "machine," into a new "information age" in politics. The media is playing an ever greater role in the decision making process. There are new freedoms here, but as always with transitional dynamics also major new, and easily unexpected, challenges. Again, while the myth is otherwise, we are still a good distance from functioning popular governance. If we went no further, what we would have for our efforts would be an ever more soulless mass media culture, and governance in which one person/one vote was increasingly in fact one dollar/one vote.

Ahead we should see governance in all spheres taking on new forms and new definitions. With this we should find ourselves understanding leadership in new ways: less as something separate, and more as simply one human function in the whole. And we should find ourselves, both individually and collectively, taking increasingly ongoing and participatory roles in social determination.

I. THE REALIZATION OF POST-MATERIAL UNDERSTANDING

A Post-Material Referent—The traditional referent in politics is power, competitive advantage. While political rhetoric often waxes eloquent about the common good, politics in practice has been an adversarial undertaking, one in which "truth" is determined by victory or, at best, compromise. Ahead, we should find ourselves increasingly able and willing to have our referent be in fact what is best for all. The meaning of authority should gradually shift from the ability to wield advantage, to the capacity to be in touch with what in truth would be most advantageous.

Post-Material Structure—All aspects and modes of governmental structure should become more heterarchical and multicentric. As I have emphasized, there is a loss of a certain image of security in this shift—no one once and for all in charge, and no longer the ability to define decision-making in terms of simple branching diagrams of authority—but when it is timely, it is in such more organic governmental mechanisms that the greatest security, efficiency and security ultimately lies.

II. THE CREATIVE INTEGRATION OF TRADITIONAL POLARITIES

Government and Governed—We should come to view governance not just as representative, but as participatory. Our involvement in decision-making will increasingly extend beyond the ballot box. Besides altering governmental structures, this should lead us to search out new kinds of qualities in people who have leadership positions—the capacity to be facilitators as much as directors, the ability not just to represent the people but to be one of them.

With this, we should find ourselves more and more viewing governmental structure as just one aspect of governance, just the upper pole in a larger organism of determination. This change should alter not just how decisions are made, but also what decisions are made. Dwight D. Eisenhower once said: "I'd like to believe that the people in the long run are going to do more to promote peace than the governments. Indeed, I think that people want peace so much that one of these days governments had better get out of their way and let them have it." The bridge-building necessary for world peace will likely happen as much or more through individual initiative and contact than through government negotiations—the voice of the lower pole of a new more integral conception of governance.

Us and Them—In all spheres, we should become better able to recognize that our perceived polarities—capitalist and communist, Republican and Democrat, this ethnic group and that—are less a function of irreconcilable differences than of an increasingly vestigial need to loathe others in order to love ourselves.

389

Left and Right—Politicians, in the new model, will increasingly be taking political postures that don't conform to party lines. The new stances should be not so much "middle of the road" as able to encompass the whole road. For example, we should more and more recognize that hawks and doves hold equally partial postures: belief in authority by brute force or a view that hides from the need for boundaries and their protection are equally naive and dangerous. People will be taking stands that before would have seemed politically contradictory: advocating both local control and spending for social programs, being conservative economically but conciliatory in international relations.

Centralization and Local Control—We should see an increasing shift away from our late-axis assumption of efficiency in centralization. It will be replaced with a new emphasis on finding the most appropriate scale for each process of determination, from individual, to neighborhood, to special interest group, to region, to nation, to planet. From a creative perspective, the more a decision lies in the hands of those who are in truth affected, the greater the larger efficiency.

IV. THE ACHIEVEMENT OF PERSONAL AND GLOBAL IDENTITY

The growing ability to embody the creative whole is central in this shift toward more participatory and organically structured governance. With it, government ceases to exist in a polar relation to the governed, becoming instead a vehicle for individual empowerment.

Our new global identity should manifest both in new global modes of decision-making, where this is the appropriate scale, and in a growing ability to experience and live from our common humanity.

As these extremes are reached, we should find ourselves making use of the whole expanse of available spheres of determination. Interestingly, while in "developing" countries we see growing solidification of national identity, in the post-industrial world we find emerging bonds of identity with very different peripheries—bonds defined by such things as linguistic heritage, cultural roots, climate and topography, and shared traditions of liveli-hood. With this, our global identity should become much more than just a recognition that we are all one. It should include a growing capacity to treasure the fact of differences. In the future, we should see a growing appreciation for diversity, an increasing recognition of what would be lost if the many colored threads of the fabric of humanity were bleached to a single hue. We should see inter-group antagonisms, long a reflex response to difference, gradually re-placed by a deeply felt cooperative protectiveness.

IV. THE CREATIVE INTEGRATION OF PREVIOUS REALITIES

Each stage contributes an emphasis on a particular periphery of determination, from tribe (neighborhood, work group) to globe, and certain values and priorities to be included in the processes of determination. From pre-axial time we get the recognition that governance is not just about people, but about the welfare of animals and plants and the globe as a living body. Early-axis sensibilities contribute spiritual, artistic, and philosophical values, and play a central role in our ability to think about governance in creative terms. From middle-axis ideas about choice we get the importance of integrity and morally just behavior, sensibilities that, when ex-panded to a global scale, should play an important role in our ability to move beyond an isolatedly competitive model for dealing with intergroup issues. From late-axis reality we should harvest the high value put on individual rights and individual choice, now expanded both to more fully appreciate our interconnectedness and to understand the nature of personal power in much more vital and participatory terms.

SCIENCE AND TECHNOLOGY

"Our current struggle with [advanced physics] may thus be only a foretaste of a completely new form of human intel-lectual endeavor ..."

—*Physicist Geoffrey Chew*

*"Man is that being in whom the earth becomes conscious of
itself."*
—*Thomas Berry*

"I want to know God's thoughts, the rest are details."
—*Albert Einstein*

The future should offer us both a rich new proliferation in the
wonders of science and technology, and a new capacity to understand the appropriate place of such wonders in the larger picture.
In the Age of Reason, science and technology have been deities, and
that view we will leave behind. But, with that surrender of privilege, science and technology should become ever more useful and
effective tools for increasing our capacity to live.

A hundred years from now, looking back at our present period,
we might find ourselves viewing it variously as the end of the
scientific age, or that time when the scientific perspective blos-
somed into its full maturity. If we think of science as the belief
structure that challenged and superseded the priestly dominion of
truth of the Middle Ages, then we must accept that we are witnessing the passing of an era. Whether our focus is ecologically-based
biology, the chemistry of Prigogine, the mathematics of Gödel, or
the quarks and quasars of the new physics, the message is the same.
The past criteria defining scientific truth—fully objective and
repeatable observation—and the traditional underpinnings of
scientific thought—determinism and mechanistic causality—
apply only within certain limited parts of reality as a whole.

Shifting our focus from already formed ideas to the spirit of
inquiry, however, reveals science at a new dawn. Science has always called for courage in observation and an incorruptible
adherence to the evidence, even in the face of conflicting beliefs.
Science, conceived within a larger paradigm, carries on this proud
tradition: its theories have expanded observation beyond anything
we have known and shaken accepted reality to its foundations. It
should continue to do so.

Technology will in a similar way contribute greatly to the
reality ahead, and yet undergo some significant changes in how it
is seen and used. We will certainly have to surrender our image of

technology as the great and final answer, as what in the end will save us from all toil and discomfort (and even, eventually, from our mortality). We will have to accept that this is a dangerous illusion, one that keeps us from facing the real substance of the issues that challenge us.

At the same time, we should find technology playing a most important and respected role in the transformations ahead. New inventions will continue to expand human capability and multiply the efficiency of our actions. Our ever more amazing capacities for miniaturization should help us greatly in the task of conserving precious resources and realizing the goal of a sustainable planet. New information technology, by making knowledge more accessible to the common person, may be one of the most important ingredients in increasing personal empowerment. And by making it possible to accomplish the repetitive "machine" tasks of society more efficiently, new technology should more and more free us to devote our energies to the interpersonal and creative functions that are our unique heritages as humans.

Again, we can use our four parameters to delineate these changes. Within the model, I think of science and technology as the study and invention of the material in reality.

I. THE REALIZATION OF POST-MATERIAL UNDERSTANDING

A Post-Material Referent—The new science expands our old material definitions for truth in a number of key ways: by looking at the world in terms of interlocking, evolving systems; by recognizing that what we can see, even with the best of equipment, is far from all there is to see; by accepting that knowledge is never totally separate from the knower and the mode of knowing; and by acknowledging that uncertainty is always a part of truth. In the future we should see a growing family of new, more living perspectives in scientific thought.

Post-Material Structure—The institution of science should change significantly. We should see the bounds of appropriate inquiry becoming increasingly permeable. Along with this we should see a growing willingness to examine and question the ethical appropriateness and economic value of scientific endeavors.

II. THE CREATIVE INTEGRATION OF TRADITIONAL POLARITIES

Cause and Effect—New models should come increasingly to be framed within some kind of creative systems perspective.

Subjective and Objective—While science and technology will keep their major focus where these approaches are most useful—in the reality of the formed—there will be an increasing acknowledgement of the place of the germinal and the personal in any full understanding of reality.

Science and Religion/Art—The other face of the new expansion of possibility in science is that science must give up its claim to exclusive understanding. Biologists and poets, physicists and philosophers, should more and more recognize that it is one and the same world they are describing, and that what the other understands may be the missing piece to their own understanding.

Science, Technology and Society—Science and technology will be challenged to give up their immunity to questions of social responsibility. The populace will demand that we look closely to see what endeavors are in fact likely to benefit us, which are perhaps interesting but not of sufficient social value to justify their expense, and which are likely to lead to harm.

Science, Technology and Nature—The task is shifting from deciphering and mastering nature, to purpose and participation in nature.

III. THE ACHIEVEMENT OF PERSONAL AND GLOBAL IDENTITY

The ability to move beyond a reality defined solely by "the light of reason" is a direct function of our new capacity to embrace at once the mysterious and the manifest in ourselves.

Science, as that part of inquiry that has pushed furthest into the formed, has had the capacity to view from a global perspective for quite some time. What will be added with integration will be the ability to be touched by lower as well as upper pole aspects of this understanding: to recognize the kinds of connections that underlie interactions in the materially manifest, to feel and embody as well as understand, our living planetary wholeness.

IV. THE CREATIVE INTEGRATION OF PREVIOUS REALITIES

From pre-axial times we get the recognition of ultimate connectedness; from early-axis, our new understanding of the place and power of the germinal dimensions in reality; from middle-axis, the essential recognition that science is not separate from personal and moral questions; and from late-axis reality, integrity in observation and a capacity for and valuing of precision.

SPIRITUALITY

"And so, this is the inheritance—this is the wavelength
which connects us
with the dead man and the dawn
of new beings not yet come to light."

—*Pablo Neruda*

"No more second hand god."

—*Buckminster Fuller*

"Every man is more than just himself; he also represents the
unique, the very special and always significant and
remarkable point at which the world's phenomena intersect,
only once in this way and never again."

—*Herman Hesse*

With late-axis reality, the story of religion, like that of art, has been one of at once a growing refinement and sophistication, and a gradual relegation to a secondary role. These two domains both take their primary power from the more unity-defined poles within any cultural stage—dynamics that diminish in relative potency with each advancing stage in the first half of cycle.

With the Age of Reason came a major evolution in our relationship to, and as, the sacred. For the first time that relationship had the potential to be direct. Before, there were always intermediaries—priests, the early-axis divine leader, a tribal shaman—always external final interpreters of divine will. In the Age of Reason, spiritual truth shifted from the realm of decree to that of individual belief.

But along with this new freedom, came a further step in the diminishing of connection in soul and mystery that is the foundation of spiritual experience. In journeying from animism to pantheism to fundamentalist monotheism to liberal monotheism, we have moved increasingly toward a place where the sacred is little more than a topic for philosophical conjecture. With transitional times we see a vacillation between near complete forgetting of the spiritual dimension, and absolutist belief that becomes amplified in its fervency by the superficiality of actual spiritual connection.

What will be the place and appearance of religion in the stages of culture ahead? Again, changes will likely be of a dual sort. On one hand we should see an important new awakening of the spiritual dimension. With movement into the second half of cycle, we begin the anamnesis, the un-forgetting of our connection in source; we can begin to understand in deeper and deeper ways how truth is not just the many, but also the one. Post-material reality offers the possibility of a profound spiritual renewal, not just a return to what we have known, but a greatly expanded vision. For the first time, there is the potential to realize the sacred from the full maturity of our being.

Yet, one could as easily frame these changes as the final demise of religion. In this realm as in all others, transition demands of us a major sacrifice. Here it is that we surrender our image of the divine as an all-protecting parent, our image of god with a capital G. In individual development, passage into mature adulthood requires that we surrender once and for all the pictures we have held of our parents as all-knowing protectors. Similarly, to make that passage as a species we must leave behind those secure epochs when God was an all-knowing and all-loving overlord, and we his special children.

If it is no longer sufficient to think in terms of an ascendant creator causally working the strings of life's dramas, who then is running the show? From a fully four-dimensional perspective, the question becomes its own answer: What seems the case is that the show itself is running the show—a notion which is no answer at all, and yet, if understood in a fully creative sense, perhaps an ultimate kind of revelation.

The past quarter century has been a time of rich rumblings in the realm of the spirit. There has been a significant movement away from religion as institution. But at the same time, we have seen a growing recognition of the importance of the spiritual and its relevance to the issues of purpose that now confront us. We have seen fascinating shifts and perturbations: in rapid succession the birth of the ecumenical movement, a sudden interest in Eastern thought and spiritual practice, and a new call to Christian tradition. While there have been regressive currents, in the large picture, the trend has been toward expanding the vision and scope of our spiritual sensibilities.

The model's four parameters of change can again help in envisioning this future more specifically. In the model's terms, the spiritual is the study and experience of how things connect and come into being.

I. THE REALIZATION OF POST-MATERIAL UNDERSTANDING

A Post-Material Referent—In times ahead, value in the sacred should become increasingly personal and time-relative, moving from such external, form-defined measures as the avoidance of specific sinful acts and thoughts, or the accumulation of good deeds, to something more akin to the concept here of aliveness. From this larger place, connection in spirit becomes our ability to sense the core of living truth, to feel its interconnections, and to act as its timely expression.

Post-Material Structure—We should be increasingly able to

separate the experience of the spiritual from the structure of the church, both as institution and as doctrine. This will free us both to use all manner of structures and experiences as parts of our spiritual lives, and to creatively modify traditional structures and teachings so that they can serve us most richly as realities change.

II. THE CREATIVE INTEGRATION OF TRADITIONAL POLARITIES

God and the Person—With the process of integration, we see a double, simultaneous movement: the divine coming more "down to earth," and the individual accepting new, more godly responsibilities. Spiritual truth from a creative perspective is no longer absolute, but "meta"-determinate—profoundly interrelated, often mysterious, and certainly awe-inspiring, but no longer omnipotent, omniscient and omnipresent. From this larger place, the ability to live and act, not just in spite of, but inspired by, the fact of such creative uncertainty, becomes the ultimate expression of the sacred.

Good and Evil—Moral truth should become at once an increasingly important concern, and recognized as profoundly time and context relative. Integration will bring with it an ever growing recognition of the importance of grappling with ethical questions, both personally and culturally. And at the same time it will bring whole new ways of thinking about these issues, ones that ask that we step beyond dogma and condemnation, to confront each moment's relationship to life.

Us and Them—Inherent to theologies that make an absolute separation of Above from Below—God from person, good from evil—is some notion of the "chosen" and "not chosen." When we have "God on our side," by the nature of things, there is always some "other" that we denigrate and dehumanize. Ahead, we should find ourselves less able to generate these kinds of polar sentiments, and less willing to tolerate them around us. More and more we should recognize that to *be* is to be chosen.

Sacred and Secular—Within a creatively-perceived reality, form and spirit dance hand in hand. We should find our theologies increasingly becoming religions of daily life, theologies of "ordinariness" in that ultimate sense of wonder simply at what is. From here, notions of the divine as something separate from life should more and more reveal themselves as standing in the way of the godliness of that life.

Body and Spirit—Increasingly we should recognize that spirit in its fullest sense is an expression of our ability to connect deeply in all of who we are.

III. THE ACHIEVEMENT OF PERSONAL AND GLOBAL IDENTITY

That the creative whole can be embodied in the individual is a pivotal part of these changes. It is the basis both for the possibility of our accepting new levels of personal responsibility, and for new potentials in experiencing really personal and intimate connection in the sacred. The new notion is not that somehow the individual is now God (though our perceptions at the peak of transition can be essentially this), rather, simply, that the sacred is an on-going, evolving and integral part of who we are as living wholes.

With the realization of our global identity, we should increasingly find ourselves experiencing the sacred as something universal in humankind. Balancing this new universality, we should see at once a new fascination with roots and traditions. We should find ourselves feeling the fact of our different religious beliefs not so much as a threat, but now as a rich source for learning. We should more and more be able to appreciate how the one comes alive through the many.

IV. THE CREATIVE INTEGRATION OF PREVIOUS REALITIES

Again, we can think of emergent forms as expressing a larger integration of earlier sensibilities. As with the pan-spirituality of primitive times, we should find ourselves thinking of the spiritual not as something distinct, but simply as attunement with life. As with the mystical spirituality of early-axis culture, we should find ourselves embracing archetype and ritual, but doing so in a new sense, sometimes in collective enactment, but as often in the simple treasuring of those spontaneous playful and serious moments when somehow we touch what is most elemental and intimate in ourselves. As in middle-culture religion, spirituality in the future should include a deep concern with questions of ethics and right choice, but framed now in the language of timeliness and integrity. As with the more philosophical theologies of late-axis, the individual mind should have a central place, its potency now multiplied through an ever deeper embodiment in personal and collective mystery.

THE CHALLANGE OF PASSAGE

"A period of chaos seems inevitable ... Accurate interpretation of this disorder is crucial. The form—and success—of society's policies and actions will depend a great deal on whether the disruptions are seen as necessary steps in the change toward a more workable system or are perceived as capricious and essentially destructive."

—Willis W. Harman

*"After the final no there comes a yes,
And on that yes the future of the
world depends."*

—Wallace Stevens

One might easily respond that my interpretation of the model's implications suggests quite an optimistic view of the future. In one sense it does. Inherent in the model is the idea that capacitance increases throughout the course of a creative process. The dynamics of integration require qualitative changes, but they ultimately take us into a more richly rewarding reality.

But, these ideas also suggest that times ahead will be dramatically challenging. The transitional stage in the creative cycle is a profound and easily very frightening period—fully a time of passage.

I am acutely aware of a parallel between our present times and a common dynamic in suicide. A person is presented with a challenge that demands a major and uncertain transition. While the new possibilities may seem rich and worth the risk to outsiders, the individual may see only the fearsome face of loss and uncertainty. Not infrequently, people choose the "safe" darkness of physical death over an encounter with the more unknowable dark figure of transformation that must be met if the journey is to continue. The midlife transition, that point in the lifetime rhythm where we must make the step beyond form-defined truth, is one of the most common times for suicide.

I see the critical tasks of leadership in today's world as very similar to those of a therapist with such a client. The only difference is that here we are both client and healer. The challenge is to sense enough of the possibilities that we can understand the fears we must face as a vital part of the process of change. If we can do this, we will find that within the immense uncertainties ahead lie rich rewards, and the potential for a profound new maturity in our being.

INDEX

CREDITS

Grateful acknowledgement is made to the following for permission to reprint previously published material:

Wesleyan University Press: For excerpts from *The Branch Will Not Break*, by James Wright. Copyright 1961 by James Wright.

University of New Mexico Press: For excerpts from *The Way to Rainy Mountain* by M. Scott Momaday. Copyright 1969 by the University of New Mexico Press.

Oxford University Press: For excerpts from *Primitive Art and Society* (the Gola master), by Warren L. d'Azevedo. Copyright 1973 by Oxford University Press.

New Directions Publishing Corporation: For excerpts from *The Captains Versus*, by Pablo Neruda. Copyright 1972 by Pablo Neruda and Donald D. Walsh.

Randomhouse, Inc: For excerpts from *Gifts from the Sea*, by Anne Marrow Lindberg. Copyright 1955 by Pantheon Books, a division of Randomhouse, Inc.

Illustration Credits:

Chap. 1: (Da Vinci) Museé du Louvre, Paris.Photo - des Musees Nationauex. Paris.

Chap. 2: (Graham) From "Letter to the World," 1940. Photo—Barbara Morgan; (Animal Dance) Australian Information Service. Photo—Don Edwards; (Rousseau) The Museum of Modern Art. Gift of Mrs. Simon Guggenheim. Oil on canvas, 51" x 79"; (Mask) The Fine Arts Museum of SanFrancisco. Gift of Mrs. Edwin R. Dimond.

Chap. 3: (Amma) From *Le Renard Pâle* by Marcel Griaule and Germaine Dieterlen. Copyright 1965 by the Institute d'Ethnologie, Paris; (Ptah) From *Studies in Egyptian Mythology*, by E. A. Budge. Copyright 1904 by Thames and Hudson, London. (Michelangelo) Vatican Museum, Rome.

Chap. 4: (Shell) From *Collecting Seashells* by Kathleen Yerger Johnstone. Pen and ink drawings by Harry Inge Johnstone. (Parker) From *Bird: The Legend of Charlie Parker*, by Robert George Reisher. Copyright 1975 by Lyle Stuart, Inc., Seacaucus, New Jersey; (Swing) Copyright Kosti Ruohomaa, Black Star.

Chap. 5: (Child) Copyright Gerry Cranham, Photo Researchers; (Arunta) From *The Arunta* by Sir W. B. Spencer and F. J. Gillen. The British Library, 1927, London. (Tree) Bayerische Staatsbibliothek, Munchen, Federal Republic of Germany. (Kekayan) Reproduced by courtesy of the Trustees of the British Museum; (Snakes) Ajit Mookerjee, New Delhi. Photo—Jeff Teasdale; (Black Elk) from *Black Elk Speaks*, by John G. Neihardt. Copyright John G. Neihardt. Published by Simon and Schuster and the University of Nebraska Press.

Chap. 6: (Picasso) The Art Institute of Chicago, Paul Rosenberg and Dr. G. F. Reber, Lausanne Collection. Oil on canvas, 56" x 64". (Willendorf) Naturhistorisches Museum, Vienna, Austria. (Pole) From *Artcanada*, "Stones, Bones and Skin: Ritual and Shamanistic Art," December 1973. Photo—Eberhard Otto; (Shrinmo) Reproduced by courtesy of the Trustees of the British Museum.

Chap. 7: (Roualt) Museum of Art, Carnegie Institute, Pittsburgh. Patrons Art Fund. Oil on canvas, 30 1/4" x 21 1/4"; (Shuttle) National Geographic Society. Photo - Jon Schneeberger; (Akhenaten) Egyptian National museum, Cairo; (God) From *Bible Moraliseé*. Archives of the Osterreichischen Nationalbibliothek, Vienna, Austria.

Chap. 8: (Curie) By permission of Mrs. Henry Richardson Labouisse; (Arthur) From *King Arthur and His Knights*, by Howard Pyle. Drawing by Howard Pyle. Copyright 1910 by Charles Scribner's Sons (Warrior) Reproduced by courtesy of the Trustees of the British Museum; (Krishna) Reproduced by permission of the India Office Library and Records (British Library).

Chap. 9: (Coco de mer) Durham University Oriental Museum, Durham, England. (Muse) Photo—Sonia Halliday, Buckinghamshire, England; (Schwind) Kunsthalle Rostock, German Democratic Republic. (Renoir) Art Institute of Chicago, bequest of Kate L. Brewster. 43 3/4" x 30 1/2".

Chap. 10: (Lovers) Kantonsbibliothek Vadiana, St. Gallen, Federal Republic of Germany; (Grail) Bibliotheque Nationale, Paris; (Rembrandt) The Spencer Museum of Art, University of Kansas. Gift of Sen. August W. Lauterbach. (Chaplin) United Artists.

Chap. 11: (Moore) The Museum of Modern Art, New York. (Rodin) The Tate Gallery, London; (Bruegel) Kunsthistorisches Museum, Vienna, Austria.

Chap. 12: (Earth) National Aeronautics and Space Administration.